*Trust in the Lord with
all your heart, and lean not
on your own understanding;
In all your ways acknowledge
Him, and He shall
direct your paths.*

—

Proverbs 3:5–6 NKJV

YOUR
BEST
YOU
EVER

YOUR
BEST
YOU
EVER

Daily Motivation to Achieve Your Dreams

INTRODUCTION

The shelves are filled with self-improvement books. But, if you're a Christian, you probably already own at least one copy—and more likely several copies—of the world's foremost guide to spiritual, physical, and emotional well-being. That book is the Holy Bible. The Bible is the irreplaceable guidebook for people—like you—who seek God's wisdom and His truth.

God has a plan for every aspect of your life, including your spiritual growth and your physical health. But God will not force His plans upon you; to the contrary, He has given you the ability to make choices. The consequences of those choices help determine the quality and direction of your life. This book is intended to help you make wise choices—choices that will lead you to a better place—by encouraging you to rely heavily upon the promises of God's Holy Word.

During the next 12 months, try this experiment: Read a chapter each day—and while you're at it, try spending at least a few minutes thinking things through and talking things over with your Creator. When you do, He will fill your heart, He will direct your thoughts, and He will guide your steps.

Would you like to have a life that's above and beyond the ordinary? Talk to God about it. Do you have questions that you can't answer? God has answers. Are you seeking to improve some aspect of your life? The Bible is the greatest self-improvement book of all time. Do you want to be a better person and a better Christian? If so, ask for God's help and ask for it many times each day . . . starting with a regular, heartfelt morning devotional. When you do, you might just change your day . . . and your life.

YOUR BEST YOU EVER

Then He who sat on the throne said, "Behold, I make all things new."
Revelation 21:5 NKJV

Because you've picked up a book entitled *Your Best You Ever*, it's likely that you're about to make some important changes in your life. If so, congratulations! You've graduated from something (or somewhere) to something else (or someplace else), and you're about to embark upon your next Big Adventure.

As you think about ways to build a brighter future—and as you consider the countless opportunities that will be woven into the fabric of the days ahead—be sure to include God in your plans. When you do, He will guide your steps and light your path.

Perhaps you desire to change the direction of your life, or perhaps you're determined to make major modifications in the way you live or the way you think. If so, you and God, working together, can do it. But don't expect change to be easy or instant. God expects you to do your fair share of the work—and that's as it should be. Nonetheless, if you trust the Father completely, and if you don't give up, you're destined to become your best you ever.

The amazing thing about Jesus is that He doesn't just patch up our lives, He gives us a brand new sheet, a clean slate to start over, all new.

Gloria Gaither

BUILDING A BETTER YOU

If you're graduating into a new phase of life, be sure to make God your partner. If you do, He'll guide your steps, He'll help carry your burdens, and He'll help you focus on the things that really matter.

SPEND TIME WITH GOD TODAY AND EVERY DAY

You shall have no other gods before Me.
Exodus 20:3 NKJV

One of the best ways to improve the quality of your day is to start it with God. So, if you're wise, you'll form the habit of spending time each morning with your Creator. When you do, it will change your life.

When you begin each day with your head bowed and your heart lifted, you remind yourself of God's love, His protection, and His commandments. And if you are wise, you will use your morning prayer time to align your priorities for the coming day with the teachings and commandments of God's Holy Word.

Each day has 1,440 minutes—can you give God a few of them? Of course you can . . . and of course you should. So if you've acquired the unfortunate habit of trying to "squeeze" God into the corners of your life, it's time to reshuffle the items on your to-do list by placing God first. And if you haven't already done so, form the habit of spending quality time each morning with your Creator. He deserves it . . . and so, for that matter, do you.

I suggest you discipline yourself to spend time daily in a systematic reading of God's Word. Make this "quiet time" a priority that nobody can change.

Warren Wiersbe

BUILDING A BETTER YOU

Your habits will determine, to a surprising extent, the quality and tone of your day. In fact, daily life can be viewed as an intricate pattern woven together by the threads of habit. And no habit is more important to your spiritual health than the discipline of daily prayer and worship.

WALKING WITH CHRIST EVERY DAY

*He that loveth his life shall lose it; and he that hateth his life
in this world shall keep it unto life eternal. If any man serve me,
let him follow me; and where I am, there shall also my servant be:
if any man serve me, him will my Father honor.*
John 12:25–26 KJV

As you begin the next stage of your life's journey, whom will you walk with? Will you walk with people who worship the ways of the world? Or will you walk with the Son of God? Jesus walks with you. Are you walking with Him? Hopefully, you will choose to walk with Him today and every day of your life. God's Word promises that when you follow in Christ's footsteps, you will learn how to live freely and lightly (Matthew 11:28-30).

Are you worried about the day ahead? Be confident in God's power. He will never desert you. Are you concerned about the future? Be courageous and call upon God. He will protect you. Are you confused? Listen to the quiet voice of your Heavenly Father. He is not a God of confusion. So talk with God; listen to Him; and walk with His Son—starting now.

A disciple is a follower of Christ. That means you take on His priorities as your own. His agenda becomes your agenda. His mission becomes your mission.

Charles Stanley

A LESSON FOR THE HEART AND SOUL

If you want to be a little more like Christ . . . learn about His teachings, follow in His footsteps, and obey His commandments.

FAITH AND FITNESS

Cast your burden on the Lord, and He shall sustain you;
He shall never permit the righteous to be moved.
Psalm 55:22 NKJV

Faith and fitness. These two words may seem disconnected, but they are not. If you're about to begin a regimen of vigorous physical exercise, then you will find it helpful to begin a regimen of vigorous spiritual exercise, too. Why? Because the physical, emotional, and spiritual aspects of your life are interconnected. In other words, you cannot "compartmentalize" physical fitness in one category of your being and spiritual fitness in another—every facet of your life has an impact on the person you are today and the person you will become tomorrow. That's why your body is so important to God—your body is, quite literally, the "temple" that houses "the Spirit of God" that dwells within you (1 Corinthians 3:16).

God's Word contains powerful lessons about every aspect of your life, including your health. So, if you're concerned about your spiritual, physical, or emotional health, the first place to turn is that timeless source of comfort and assurance, the Holy Bible. When you open your Bible and begin reading, you'll quickly be reminded of this fact: when you face concerns of any sort—including health-related challenges—God is with you. And His healing touch, like His love, endures forever.

Only by walking with God can we hope to find the path that leads to life.

John Eldredge

BUILDING A BETTER YOU

Before you begin a new exercise program, see your doctor: As the old saying goes, it's better to be safe than sorry.

CHOICES, CHOICES, CHOICES

Therefore, whether we are at home or away,
we make it our aim to be pleasing to Him.
2 Corinthians 5:9 HCSB

Your life is a series of choices. If you want to build a better you, you'll need to make better choices.

From the instant you wake up in the morning until the moment you nod off to sleep at night, you make lots of decisions: decisions about the things you do, decisions about the words you speak, and decisions about the thoughts you choose to think. Simply put, the quality of those decisions determines the quality of your life.

So, if you sincerely want to lead a life that is pleasing to God, you must make choices that are pleasing to Him. He deserves no less . . . and neither, for that matter, do you.

Many jokes are made about the devil, but the devil is no joke. He is called a deceiver. In order to accomplish his purpose, the devil blinds people to their need for Christ. Two forces are at work in our world—the forces of Christ and the forces of the devil—and you are asked to choose.

Billy Graham

BUILDING A BETTER YOU

First you make choices . . . and pretty soon those choices begin to shape your life. That's why you must make smart choices . . . or face the consequences of making dumb ones.

CHANGING FOR THE BETTER

I will give you a new heart and put a new spirit in you....
Ezekiel 36:26 NIV

If we sincerely want to change ourselves for the better, we must start on the inside and work our way out from there. Lasting change doesn't occur "out there"; it occurs "in here." It occurs, not in the shifting sands of our own particular circumstances, but in the quiet depths of our own hearts.

Are you in search of a new beginning or, for that matter, a new you? If so, don't expect changing circumstances to miraculously transform you into the person you want to become. Transformation starts with God, and it starts in the silent center of a humble human heart—like yours.

No matter how badly we have failed, we can always get up and begin again. Our God is the God of new beginnings.

Warren Wiersbe

More often than not, when something looks like it's the absolute end, it is really the beginning.

Charles Swindoll

BUILDING A BETTER YOU

Your journey with God unfolds day by day, and that's precisely how your journey to an improved state of emotional or physical fitness must also unfold: moment by moment, day by day, year by year.

IN FOCUS

Look straight ahead, and fix your eyes on what lies before you.
Proverbs 4:25 NLT

What is your focus today? Are you willing to focus your thoughts and energies on God's blessings and upon His will for your life? Or will you turn your thoughts to other things? This day—and every day hereafter—is a chance to celebrate the life that God has given you. It's also a chance to give thanks to the One who has offered you more blessings than you can possibly count.

Today, why not focus your thoughts on the joy that is rightfully yours in Christ? Why not take time to celebrate God's glorious creation? Why not trust your hopes instead of your fears? When you do, you will think optimistically about yourself and your world . . . and you can then share your optimism with others. They'll be better for it, and so will you. But not necessarily in that order.

Whatever we focus on determines what we become.

E. Stanley Jones

Jesus challenges you and me to keep our focus daily on the cross of His will if we want to be His disciples.

Anne Graham Lotz

BUILDING A BETTER YOU

First focus on God . . . and then everything else will come into focus.

FAITH THAT MOVES MOUNTAINS

I tell you the truth, you can say to this mountain,
"Go, fall into the sea." And if you have no doubts in your mind and
believe that what you say will happen, God will do it for you.
Mark 11:23 NCV

Because we live in a demanding world, all of us have mountains to climb and mountains to move. Moving those mountains requires faith.

Are you a mountain mover whose faith is evident for all to see? Hopefully so. God needs more men and women who are willing to move mountains for His glory and for His kingdom.

God walks with you, ready and willing to strengthen you. Accept His strength today. And remember—Jesus taught His disciples that if they had faith, they could move mountains. You can, too . . . so with no further ado, let the mountain-moving begin.

Faith is the gaze of a soul upon a saving God . . . a continuous gaze of the heart at the Triune God.

A. W. Tozer

Only God can move mountains, but faith and prayer can move God.

E. M. Bounds

A LESSON FOR THE HEART AND SOUL

Feelings come and feelings go, but God never changes. So when you have a choice between trusting your feelings or trusting God, trust God.

GOD'S TIMETABLE

Therefore humble yourselves under the mighty hand of God,
that He may exalt you in due time.
1 Peter 5:6 NKJV

Self-improvement takes time. But sometimes, the hardest thing to do is to wait. This is especially true when we're in a hurry and when we want things to happen now, if not sooner! But God's plan does not always happen in the way that we would like or at the time of our own choosing. Our task—as believing Christians who trust in a benevolent, all knowing Father—is to wait patiently for God to reveal Himself.

We human beings are, by nature, impatient. We know what we want, and we know exactly when we want it: RIGHT NOW! But, God knows better. He has created a world that unfolds according to His own timetable, not ours . . . thank goodness!

Will not the Lord's time be better than your time?

C. H. Spurgeon

He has the right to interrupt your life. He is Lord. When you accepted Him as Lord, you gave Him the right to help Himself to your life anytime He wants.

Henry Blackaby

BUILDING A BETTER YOU

You don't know precisely what you need—or when you need it—but God does. So trust His timing.

ABANDONING BAD HABITS

Do not be deceived: "Evil company corrupts good habits."
1 Corinthians 15:33 NKJV

It's an old saying and a true one: First, you make your habits, and then your habits make you. Some habits will inevitably bring you closer to God; other habits will lead you away from the path He has chosen for you. If you sincerely desire to improve your spiritual, physical, or emotional health, you must honestly examine the habits that make up the fabric of your day. And you must abandon those habits that are displeasing to God.

If you trust God, and if you keep asking for His help, He can transform your life. If you sincerely ask Him to help you, the same God who created the universe will help you defeat the harmful habits that have heretofore defeated you. So, if at first you don't succeed, keep praying. God is listening, and He's ready to help you become a better person if you ask Him . . . so ask today.

You will never change your life until you change something you do daily.

John Maxwell

You can build up a set of good habits so that you habitually take the Christian way without thought.

E. Stanley Jones

BUILDING A BETTER YOU

Choose your habits carefully. Habits are easier to make than they are to break, so be careful!

BE STRONG, HAVE FAITH

Watch, stand fast in the faith, be brave, be strong.
1 Corinthians 16:13 NKJV

As you take the next few steps in your life's journey, your faith will be tested many times. Every life—including yours—is a series of successes and failures, celebrations and disappointments, joys and sorrows. Every step of the way, through every triumph and tragedy, God will stand by your side and strengthen you . . . if you have faith in Him.

If you place your faith, your trust, indeed your life in the hands of Christ Jesus, you'll be amazed at the marvelous things He can do with you and through you. Faith is a willingness to believe in things that are unseeable and to trust in things that are unknowable.

Today and every day, strengthen your faith through praise, through worship, through Bible study, and through prayer. God has big plans for you, so trust His plans and strengthen your faith in Him. With God, all things are possible, and He stands ready to help you accomplish miraculous things with your life . . . if you have faith.

Faith reposes on the character of God, and if we believe that God is perfect, we must conclude that his ways are perfect also.

A. W. Tozer

A LESSON FOR THE HEART AND SOUL

You cannot see the future, but God can . . . and you must have faith in His eternal plan for you.

USING YOUR GIFTS

God has given gifts to each of you from his great variety of
spiritual gifts. Manage them well so that
God's generosity can flow through you.
1 Peter 4:10 NLT

All people possess special gifts—bestowed from the Father above—and you are no exception. But, your gift is no guarantee of success; it must be cultivated and nurtured. Otherwise, it will go unused . . . and God's gift to you will be squandered.

Today, make a promise to yourself that you will earnestly seek to discover the talents that God has given you. Then, nourish those talents and make them grow. Finally, vow to share your gifts with the world for as long as God gives you the power to do so. After all, the best way to say "Thank You" for God's gifts is to use them.

One thing taught large in the Holy Scriptures is that while God gives His gifts freely, He will require a strict accounting of them at the end of the road.

A. W. Tozer

BUILDING A BETTER YOU

God has given you a unique array of talents and opportunities. If you use your gifts wisely, they're multiplied. If you misuse your gifts—or ignore them altogether—they are lost. God is anxious for you to use your gifts . . . are you?

OBEY AND BE BLESSED

Now by this we know that we know Him,
if we keep His commandments.
1 John 2:3 NKJV

God gave us His commandments for a reason: so that we might obey them and be blessed. Oswald Chambers, the author of the Christian classic devotional text *My Utmost for His Highest*, advised, "Never support an experience which does not have God as its source, and faith in God as its result." These words serve as a powerful reminder that, as Christians, we are called to walk with God and obey His commandments. But, we live in a world that presents us with countless temptations to stray far from God's path. We Christians, when confronted with sin, have clear instructions: Walk—or better yet run—in the opposite direction.

Let us remember therefore this lesson: That to worship our God sincerely we must evermore begin by hearkening to His voice, and by giving ear to what He commands us. For if every man goes after his own way, we shall wander. We may well run, but we shall never be a whit nearer to the right way, but rather farther away from it.

John Calvin

A LESSON FOR THE HEART AND SOUL

Remember that God has given us His commandments for a reason: to obey them. These commandments are not suggestions, helpful hints, or friendly reminders—they are rules we must live by . . . or else!

NEED COURAGE?
GOD CAN GIVE IT

*Do not be afraid or discouraged, for the LORD is the one
who goes before you. He will be with you;
he will neither fail you nor forsake you.*
Deuteronomy 31:8 NLT

As you take the next step on your life's journey, you may discover that life can be difficult and discouraging at times. During our darkest moments, God offers us courage and strength if we turn our hearts and our prayers to Him.

As believing Christians, we have every reason to live courageously. After all, the ultimate battle has already been fought and won on the cross at Calvary. But sometimes, because we are imperfect human beings who possess imperfect faith, we fall prey to fear and doubt. The answer to our fears, of course, is God.

The next time you find your courage tested to the limit, remember that God is as near as your next breath. He is your shield and your strength; He is your protector and your deliverer. Call upon Him in your hour of need and then be comforted. Whatever your challenge, whatever your trouble, God can handle it.

Our Lord is searching for people who will make a difference. Christians dare not dissolve into the background or blend into the neutral scenery of the world.

Charles Swindoll

BUILDING A BETTER YOU

Is your courage being tested? Cling tightly to God's promises, and pray. God can give you the strength to meet any challenge, and that's exactly what you should ask Him to do.

AS YOU BEGIN ANEW, ASK FOR DIRECTIONS

But if any of you lacks wisdom, let him ask of God,
who gives to all generously and without reproach,
and it will be given to him.

James 1:5 NASB

Jesus made it clear to His disciples: They should petition God to meet their needs. So should we. Genuine, heartfelt prayer produces powerful changes in us and in our world. When we lift our hearts to God, we open ourselves to a never-ending source of divine wisdom and infinite love.

Do you have questions about your future that you simply can't answer? Do you have needs that you simply can't meet by yourself? Do you sincerely seek to know God's unfolding plans for your life? If so, ask Him for direction, for protection, and for strength—and then keep asking Him every day that you live. Whatever your need, no matter how great or small, pray about it and never lose hope. God is not just near; He is here, and He's perfectly capable of answering your prayers. Now, it's up to you to ask.

All we have to do is to acknowledge our need, move from self-sufficiency to dependence, and ask God to become our hiding place.

Bill Hybels

BUILDING A BETTER YOU

If you want more from life, ask more from God. If you're seeking a worthy goal, ask for God's help—and keep asking—until He answers your prayers.

INFINITE POSSIBILITIES

Is anything too hard for the LORD?
Genesis 18:14 KJV

Ours is a God of infinite possibilities. But sometimes, because of limited faith and limited understanding, we wrongly assume that God cannot or will not intervene in the affairs of mankind. Such assumptions are simply wrong.

Are you afraid to ask God to do big things in your life? Is your faith threadbare and worn? If so, it's time to abandon your doubts and reclaim your faith in God's promises.

God's Holy Word makes it clear: absolutely nothing is impossible for the Lord. And since the Bible means what it says, you can be comforted in the knowledge that the Creator of the universe can do miraculous things in your own life and in the lives of your loved ones. Your challenge, as a believer, is to take God at His word, and to expect the miraculous.

God has power and He's willing to share it if we step out in faith and believe that He will.

Bill Hybels

So God's patience is His power over Himself. Great is that God who, having all power, yet keeps all power subject to Himself.

Jim Elliot

A LESSON FOR THE HEART AND SOUL

When you place your faith in God, life becomes a grand adventure energized by the power of God.

RELY UPON HIM

Therefore humble yourselves under the mighty hand of God,
that He may exalt you at the proper time,
casting all your anxiety on Him, because He cares for you.
1 Peter 5:6–7 NASB

God is a never-ending source of support and courage for those of us who call upon Him. When we are weary, He gives us strength. When we see no hope, God reminds us of His promises. When we grieve, God wipes away our tears.

Do the demands of this day threaten to overwhelm you? If so, you must rely not only upon your own resources but also upon the promises of your Father in Heaven. God will hold your hand and walk with you every day of your life if you let Him. So even if your circumstances are difficult, trust the Father. His love is eternal and His goodness endures forever.

Ask Christ to come into your heart to forgive you and help you. When you do, Christ will take up residence in your life by His Holy Spirit, and when you face temptations and trials, you will no longer face them alone.

Billy Graham

Faith is not merely you holding on to God—it is God holding on to you.

E. Stanley Jones

A LESSON FOR THE HEART AND SOUL

Whatever your weaknesses, God is stronger. And His strength will help you measure up to His tasks.

GROWING IN CHRIST

When I was a child, I spoke as a child, I understood as a child,
I thought as a child; but when I became a man,
I put away childish things.
1 Corinthians 13:11 NKJV

The journey toward spiritual maturity lasts a lifetime. As Christians, we can and should continue to grow in the love and the knowledge of our Savior as long as we live. Norman Vincent Peale had the following advice for believers of all ages: "Ask the God who made you to keep remaking you." That advice, of course, is perfectly sound, but often ignored.

When we cease to grow, either emotionally or spiritually, we do ourselves a profound disservice. But, if we study God's Word, if we obey His commandments, and if we live in the center of His will, we will not be "stagnant" believers; we will, instead, be growing Christians . . . and that's exactly what God wants for our lives.

Being a Christian means accepting the terms of creation, accepting God as our maker and redeemer, and growing day by day into an increasingly glorious creature in Christ, developing joy, experiencing love, maturing in peace.

Eugene Peterson

BUILDING A BETTER YOU

Your future depends, to a very great extent, upon you. So keep learning and keep growing personally, professionally, and spiritually.

CALMING YOUR FEARS

Be not afraid; only believe.
Mark 5:36 NKJV

Most of the things we worry about will never come to pass, yet we worry still. We worry about the future and the past; we worry about finances and relationships. As we survey the landscape of our lives, we observe all manner of molehills and imagine them to be mountains.

Are you concerned about the inevitable challenges that make up the fabric of everyday life? If so, why not ask God to help you regain a clear perspective about the problems (and opportunities) that confront you? When you petition your Heavenly Father sincerely and seek His guidance, He can touch your heart, clear your vision, renew your mind, and calm your fears.

God alone can give us songs in the night.

C. H. Spurgeon

Despair is a greater sin than any of the sins which provoke it.

C. S. Lewis

BUILDING A BETTER YOU

If you're feeling fearful or anxious, you must trust God to solve the problems that are simply too big for you to solve.

ALWAYS WITH US

For unto us a Child is born, unto us a Son is given;
and the government will be upon His shoulder.
And His name will be called Wonderful, Counselor, Mighty God,
Everlasting Father, Prince of Peace.
Isaiah 9:6 NKJV

Are you facing difficult circumstances or unwelcome changes? If so, please remember that God is far bigger than any problem you may face. So, instead of worrying about life's inevitable challenges, put your faith in the Father and His only begotten Son: "Jesus Christ is the same yesterday, today, and forever" (Hebrews 13:8 NKJV). And remember: it is precisely because your Savior does not change that you can face your challenges with courage for today and hope for tomorrow.

Life is often challenging, but as Christians, we should not be afraid. God loves us, and He will protect us. In times of hardship, He will comfort us; in times of change, He will guide our steps. When we are troubled, or weak, or sorrowful, God is always with us. We must build our lives on the rock that cannot be moved . . . we must trust in God. Always.

Conditions are always changing; therefore, I must not be dependent upon conditions. What matters supremely is my soul and my relationship to God.

Corrie ten Boom

BUILDING A BETTER YOU

Change is inevitable . . . you can either roll with it or be rolled over by it. Choose the former.

TOMORROW'S OPPORTUNITIES BEGIN TODAY

Do not remember the former things, nor consider the things of old.
Behold, I will do a new thing.
Isaiah 43:18–19 NKJV

Each new day offers countless opportunities to serve God, to seek His will, and to obey His teachings. But each day also offers countless opportunities to stray from God's commandments and to wander far from His path.

Sometimes, we wander aimlessly in a wilderness of our own making, but God has better plans for us. And, whenever we ask Him to renew our strength and guide our steps, He does so.

Consider this day a new beginning. Consider it a fresh start, a renewed opportunity to serve your Creator with willing hands and a loving heart. Ask God to renew your sense of purpose as He guides your steps. Today is a glorious opportunity to serve your Father in Heaven. Seize that opportunity while you can; tomorrow may indeed be too late.

Don't be intimidated by your past, good or bad. Face it, deal with it and then get over it and let it go. Begin a new day and new tradition for those who follow after you. Realize that God will always be with you.

Dennis Swanberg

BUILDING A BETTER YOU

Optimism pays. Pessimism does not. Guard your thoughts and your words accordingly.

DON'T BE DISCOURAGED

But thanks be to God, who gives us the victory through
our Lord Jesus Christ. Therefore, my beloved brethren,
be steadfast, immovable, always abounding in the work of the Lord,
knowing that your labor is not in vain in the Lord.

1 Corinthians 15:57–58 NKJV

As you continue to seek God's purpose for your life, you will undoubtedly experience your fair share of disappointments, detours, false starts, and failures. When you do, don't become discouraged: God's not finished with you yet.

The old saying is as true today as it was when it was first spoken: "Life is a marathon, not a sprint." That's why wise travelers select a traveling companion who never tires and never falters. That partner, of course, is your Heavenly Father. So pray as if everything depended upon God, and work as if everything depended upon you. And trust God to do the rest.

Perseverance is more than endurance. It is endurance combined with absolute assurance and certainty that what we are looking for is going to happen.

Oswald Chambers

Stand still and refuse to retreat. Look at it as God looks at it and draw upon his power to hold up under the blast.

Charles Swindoll

BUILDING A BETTER YOU

Life is difficult and success requires effort—so perseverance pays big dividends.

LET GOD DECIDE

A man's heart plans his way, but the Lord directs his steps.
Proverbs 16:9 NKJV

Are you facing a difficult decision, a troubling circumstance, or a powerful temptation? If so, it's time to step back, to stop focusing on the world, and to focus, instead, on the will of your Father in Heaven. The world will often lead you astray, but God will not. His counsel leads you to Himself, which, of course, is the path He has always intended for you to take.

Everyday living is an exercise in decision-making. Today and every day you must make choices: choices about what you will do, what you will worship, and how you will think. When in doubt, make choices that you sincerely believe will bring you to a closer relationship with God. And if you're uncertain of your next step, pray about it. When you do, answers will come—the right answers for you.

Good and evil both increase at compound interest. That is why the little decisions you and I make every day are of such infinite importance.

C. S. Lewis

God always gives His best to those who leave the choice with Him.

Jim Elliot

BUILDING A BETTER YOU

When you're about to make an important decision, take your time and talk to your Creator.

DILIGENCE NOW

Never be lazy in your work, but serve the Lord enthusiastically.
Romans 12:11 NLT

God's Word reminds us again and again that our Creator expects us to lead disciplined lives. God doesn't reward laziness, misbehavior, or apathy. To the contrary, He expects believers to behave with dignity and discipline.

We live in a world in which leisure is glorified and indifference is often glamorized. But God has other plans. He did not create us for lives of mediocrity; He created us for far greater things.

Life's greatest rewards seldom fall into our laps; to the contrary, our greatest accomplishments usually require lots of work, which is perfectly fine with God. After all, He knows that we're up to the task, and He has big plans for us. May we, as disciplined believers, always be worthy of those plans.

Discipline is training that develops and corrects.

Charles Stanley

He will clothe you in rags if you clothe yourself with idleness.

C. H. Spurgeon

BUILDING A BETTER YOU

When you take a disciplined approach to your life and your responsibilities, God will reward your good judgment.

AN INTENSELY BRIGHT FUTURE: YOURS

I came so they can have real and eternal life,
more and better life than they ever dreamed of.
John 10:10 MSG

Are you excited about the opportunities of today and thrilled by the possibilities of tomorrow? Do you confidently expect God to lead you to a place of abundance, peace, and joy? And, when your days on earth are over, do you expect to receive the priceless gift of eternal life? If you trust God's promises, and if you have welcomed God's Son into your heart, then you believe that your future is intensely and eternally bright.

It takes courage to dream big dreams. You will discover that courage when you do three things: accept the past, trust God to handle the future, and make the most of the time He has given you today. No dreams are too big for God—not even yours. So start living—and dreaming—accordingly.

Set goals so big that unless God helps you, you will be a miserable failure.

Bill Bright

BUILDING A BETTER YOU

Making your dreams come true requires work. John Maxwell writes, "The gap between your vision and your present reality can only be filled through a commitment to maximize your potential." Enough said.

LET THE CELEBRATION BEGIN

I've told you these things for a purpose:
that my joy might be your joy, and your joy wholly mature.
John 15:11 MSG

Oswald Chambers correctly observed, "Joy is the great note all throughout the Bible." C. S. Lewis echoed that thought when he wrote, "Joy is the serious business of Heaven." But, even the most dedicated Christians can, on occasion, forget to celebrate each day for what it is: a priceless gift from God.

Today, let us be joyful Christians with smiles on our faces and kind words on our lips. After all, this is God's day, and He has given us clear instructions for its use. We are commanded to rejoice and be glad. So, with no further ado, let the celebration begin.

The joy of God is experienced as I love, trust, and obey God—no matter the circumstances—and as I allow Him to do in and through me whatever He wishes, thanking Him that in every pain there is pleasure, in every suffering there is satisfaction, in every aching there is comfort, in every sense of loss there is the surety of the Savior's presence, and in every tear there is the glistening eye of God.

Bill Bright

A LESSON FOR THE HEART AND SOUL

Joy begins with a choice—the choice to establish a genuine relationship with God and His Son. Joy does not depend upon your circumstances, but upon your relationship with God.

IN HIS HANDS

Do not boast about tomorrow,
for you do not know what a day may bring forth.
Proverbs 27:1 NKJV

The old saying is both familiar and true: "Man proposes and God disposes." Our world unfolds according to God's plans, not our wishes. Thus, boasting about future events is to be avoided by those who acknowledge God's sovereignty over all things.

Are you planning for a better tomorrow for yourself and your family? If so, you are to be congratulated: God rewards forethought in the same way that He often punishes impulsiveness. But as you make your plans, do so with humility, with gratitude, and with trust in your Heavenly Father. His hand directs the future; to think otherwise is both arrogant and naïve.

The Christian believes in a fabulous future.

Billy Graham

That we may not complain of what is, let us see God's hand in all events; and, that we may not be afraid of what shall be, let us see all events in God's hand.

Matthew Henry

BUILDING A BETTER YOU

The future isn't some pie-in-the-sky dream. Hope for the future is simply one aspect of trusting God.

LIFE ABUNDANT

I have come that they may have life,
and that they may have it more abundantly.
John 10:10 NKJV

God sent His Son so that mankind might enjoy the abundant life that Jesus describes in the familiar words of John 10:10. But, God's gifts are not guaranteed; they must be claimed by those who choose to follow Christ.

As you plan for your own new beginnings, you may be asking yourself, "What kind of life does God intend for me?" The answer can be found in God's promise of abundance: those who accept that promise and live according to God's commandments are eternally blessed.

What, exactly, did Jesus mean when He promised "life . . . more abundantly"? Was He referring to material possessions or financial wealth? Hardly. Jesus offers a different kind of abundance: a spiritual richness that extends beyond the temporal boundaries of this world. This everlasting abundance is available to all who seek it and claim it.

Instead of living a black-and-white existence, we'll be released into a Technicolor world of vibrancy and emotion when we more accurately reflect His nature to the world around us.

Bill Hybels

BUILDING A BETTER YOU

Don't miss out on God's abundance. Every day is a beautifully wrapped gift from God. Unwrap it. Use it. And give thanks to the Giver.

THIS IS HIS DAY

This is the day the LORD has made. We will rejoice and be glad in it.
Psalm 118:24 NLT

The 118th Psalm reminds us that today, like every other day, is a cause for celebration. God gives us this day; He fills it to the brim with possibilities, and He challenges us to use it for His purposes. The day is presented to us fresh and clean at midnight, free of charge, but we must beware: Today is a non-renewable resource—once it's gone, it's gone forever. Our responsibility, of course, is to use this day in the service of God's will and according to His commandments.

Today, treasure the time that God has given you. Give Him the glory and the praise and the thanksgiving that He deserves. And search for the hidden possibilities that God has placed along your path. This day is a priceless gift from God, so use it joyfully and encourage others to do likewise. After all, this is the day the Lord has made . . . .

I choose joy. I will refuse the temptation to be cynical; cynicism is the tool of a lazy thinker. I will refuse to see people as anything less than human beings, created by God. I will refuse to see any problem as anything less than an opportunity to see God.

Max Lucado

A LESSON FOR THE HEART AND SOUL

God has given you the gift of life (here on earth) and the promise of eternal life (in Heaven). Now, He wants you to celebrate those gifts.

A PATTERN OF GOOD WORKS

In all things showing yourself to be a pattern of good works;
in doctrine showing integrity, reverence, incorruptibility....
Titus 2:7 NKJV

It has been said that character is what we are when nobody is watching. How true. When we do things that we know aren't right, we try to hide them from our families and friends. But even then, God is watching.

If you sincerely wish to walk with God, you must seek, to the best of your ability, to follow His commandments. When you do, your character will take care of itself . . . and you won't need to look over your shoulder to see who, besides God, is watching.

A person's character is determined by his motives, and motive is always a matter of the heart.

John Eldredge

If God can fashion the mountains, if God can keep the sun in its orbit, if God can split a sea and dry the ground beneath it so an entire nation can cross, do you doubt that he can transform your character?

Bill Hybels

BUILDING A BETTER YOU

When your words are honest and your intentions are pure, you have nothing to fear.

TOO BUSY

Careful planning puts you ahead in the long run;
hurry and scurry puts you further behind.
Proverbs 21:5 MSG

Are you one of those people who is simply too busy for your own good? Has the hectic pace of life robbed you of the peace that might otherwise be yours through Jesus Christ? If so, you're doing a disservice to yourself and your family.

Through His Son Jesus, God offers you a peace that passes human understanding, but He won't force His peace upon you; in order to experience it, you must slow down long enough to sense His presence and His love.

Today, as a gift to yourself, to your family, and to the world, be still and claim the inner peace that is your spiritual birthright—the peace of Jesus Christ. It is offered freely; it has been paid for in full; it is yours for the asking. So ask. And then share.

This day's bustle and hurly-burly would too often and too soon call us away from Jesus' feet. These distractions must be immediately dismissed, or we shall know only the "barrenness of busyness."

A. W. Tozer

BUILDING A BETTER YOU

Do first things first, and keep your focus on high-priority tasks. And remember this: Your highest priority should be your relationship with God and His Son.

RESPECTING YOUR BODY

*And so, dear brothers and sisters, I plead with you to give
your bodies to God. Let them be a living and holy sacrifice—
the kind he will accept. When you think of what he has
done for you, is this too much to ask?*
Romans 12:1 NLT

In the 12th chapter of Romans, Paul encourages us to take special care of the bodies God has given us. But it's tempting to do otherwise.

We live in a fast-food world where unhealthy choices are convenient, inexpensive, and tempting. And, we live in a digital world filled with modern conveniences that often rob us of the physical exercise needed to maintain healthy lifestyles. As a result, too many of us find ourselves glued to the television, with a snack in one hand and a clicker in the other. The results are as unfortunate as they are predictable.

God's Word teaches us that our bodies are "temples" that belong to God (1 Corinthians 6:19-20). We are commanded (not encouraged, not advised—we are commanded!) to treat our bodies with respect and honor. We do so by making wise choices and by making those choices consistently: day by day.

Food ought to be a refreshment to the body, and not a burden.

St. Bonaventure

BUILDING A BETTER YOU

Take a few minutes to examine your eating habits. If your habits are healthy, congratulations. If not, it's time to form some new ones. Poor eating habits are usually well established, so they won't be easy to change, but change them you must if you want to enjoy the benefits of a healthy lifestyle.

THE LESSONS OF TOUGH TIMES

I waited patiently for the Lord; and He inclined to me,
and heard my cry. He also brought me up out of a horrible pit,
out of the miry clay, and set my feet upon a rock,
and established my steps. He has put a new song in my mouth—
praise to our God; many will see it and fear,
and will trust in the Lord.
Psalm 40:1–3 NKJV

Have you experienced a recent setback? If so, look for the lesson that God is trying to teach you. Instead of complaining about life's sad state of affairs, learn what needs to be learned, change what needs to be changed, and move on. View failure as an opportunity to reassess God's will for your life. View life's inevitable disappointments as opportunities to learn more about yourself and your world.

Life can be difficult at times. And everybody makes mistakes. Your job is to make them only once.

Lord, when we are wrong, make us willing to change; and when we are right, make us easy to live with.

Peter Marshall

BUILDING A BETTER YOU

When you make a mistake, the time to make things better is now, not later. The sooner you address your problem, the better.

A ONE-OF-A-KIND TREASURE

Every word of God is pure;
He is a shield to those who put their trust in Him.
Proverbs 30:5 NKJV

God's Word is a roadmap for life here on earth and for life eternal. As Christians, we are called upon to study God's Holy Word, to trust its promises, to follow its commandments, and to share its Good News with the world.

As believers, we must study the Bible and meditate upon its meaning for our lives. Otherwise, we deprive ourselves of a priceless gift from our Creator. God's Holy Word is, indeed, a transforming, life-changing, one-of-a-kind treasure. And, a passing acquaintance with the Good Book is insufficient for Christians who seek to obey God's Word and to understand His will. After all, neither man nor woman should live by bread alone.

God meant that we adjust to the Gospel—not the other way around.

Vance Havner

Light is stronger than darkness—darkness cannot "comprehend" or "overcome" it.

Anne Graham Lotz

A LESSON FOR THE HEART AND SOUL

Trust God's Word: Charles Swindoll writes, "There are four words I wish we would never forget, and they are, 'God keeps his word.'" And remember: When it comes to studying God's Word, school is always in session.

THE WORLD'S BEST FRIEND

Greater love has no one than this,
that he lay down his life for his friends.
John 15:13 NIV

Who's the best friend this world has ever had? Jesus, of course! When you invite Him into your heart, Jesus will be your friend, too . . . your friend forever.

Jesus has offered to share the gifts of everlasting life and ever-lasting love with the world . . . and with you. If you make mistakes, He'll still be your friend. If you behave badly, He'll still love you. If you feel sorry or sad, He can help you feel better.

Jesus wants you to have a happy, healthy life. He wants you to be generous and kind. He wants you to follow His example. And the rest is up to you. You can do it! And with a friend like Jesus, you will.

Jesus was the perfect reflection of God's nature in every situation He encountered during His time here on earth.

Bill Hybels

The dearest friend on earth is but a mere shadow compared with Jesus Christ.

Oswald Chambers

A LESSON FOR THE HEART AND SOUL

What a friend you have in Jesus: Jesus loves you, and He offers you eternal life with Him in Heaven. Welcome Him into your heart now! And once you've done so, begin to use His teachings to help you prioritize every aspect of your life.

HIS JOY . . . AND OURS

Rejoice in the Lord always; again I will say, rejoice!
Philippians 4:4 NASB

Christ made it clear: He intends that His joy should become our joy. Yet sometimes, amid the inevitable hustle and bustle of daily life, we can forfeit—albeit temporarily—the joy of Christ as we wrestle with the challenges of daily living.

Billy Graham correctly observed, "When Jesus Christ is the source of our joy, no words can describe it." And C. S. Lewis noted that, "Joy is the serious business of Heaven." So here's a prescription for better spiritual health: Open the door of your soul to Christ. When you do, He will give you peace and joy.

Our joy ends where love of the world begins.

C. H. Spurgeon

You have to look for the joy. Look for the light of God that is hitting your life, and you will find sparkles you didn't know were there.

Barbara Johnson

A LESSON FOR THE HEART AND SOUL

Joy does not depend upon your circumstances; it depends upon your thoughts and upon your relationship with God.

PRIORITIES . . .
MOMENT BY MOMENT

You can't go wrong when you love others. When you add up
everything in the law code, the sum total is love.
But make sure that you don't get so absorbed and exhausted
in taking care of all your day-by-day obligations that
you lose track of the time and doze off, oblivious to God.
Romans 13:10–11 MSG

Each waking moment holds the potential to think a creative thought or offer a heartfelt prayer. So even if you're a person with too many demands and too few hours in which to meet them, don't panic. Instead, be comforted in the knowledge that when you sincerely seek to discover God's priorities for your life, He will provide answers in marvelous and surprising ways.

This is the day that God has made and He has filled it with countless opportunities to love, to serve, and to seek His guidance. Seize those opportunities. And as a gift to yourself, to your family, and to the world, slow down and claim the inner peace that is your spiritual birthright: the peace of Jesus Christ. It is yours for the asking. So ask . . . and be thankful.

There is no work more likely to crowd out the quiet hour than the very work that draws its strength from the quiet hour.

Vance Havner

A LESSON FOR THE HEART AND SOUL

If you don't feel like celebrating, start counting your blessings. Before long, you'll realize that you have plenty of reasons to celebrate.

THE WISDOM OF MODERATION

Moderation is better than muscle,
self-control better than political power.
Proverbs 16:32 MSG

Moderation and wisdom are traveling companions. If we are wise, we must learn to temper our appetites, our desires, and our impulses. When we do, we are blessed, in part, because God has created a world in which temperance is rewarded and intemperance is inevitably punished.

Would you like to improve your life? Then harness your appetites and restrain your impulses. Moderation is difficult, of course; it is especially difficult in a prosperous society such as ours. But the rewards of moderation are numerous and long-lasting. Claim those rewards today. No one can force you to moderate your appetites. The decision to live temperately (and wisely) is yours and yours alone. And so are the consequences.

The key to healthy eating is moderation and managing what you eat every day.

John Maxwell

BUILDING A BETTER YOU

God's Word instructs us to be moderate and disciplined as we guard our bodies, our minds, and our hearts. Your job is to follow those instructions.

THE BATTLE HAS BEEN WON

*Cast your burden upon the Lord and He will sustain you:
He will never allow the righteous to be shaken.*
Psalm 55:22 NASB

Christians have every reason to live courageously. After all, the ultimate battle has already been won on the cross at Calvary. But even dedicated followers of Christ may find their courage tested by the inevitable disappointments and fears that visit the lives of believers and non-believers alike.

When you find yourself worried about the challenges of today or the uncertainties of tomorrow, you must ask yourself whether or not you are ready to place your concerns and your life in God's all-powerful, all-knowing, all-loving hands. If the answer to that question is yes—as it should be—then you can draw courage today from the source of strength that never fails: your Heavenly Father.

The Lord is glad to open the gate to every knocking soul. It opens very freely; its hinges are not rusted, no bolts secure it. Have faith and enter at this moment through holy courage. If you knock with a heavy heart, you shall yet sing with joy of spirit. Never be discouraged!

C. H. Spurgeon

BUILDING A BETTER YOU

If you trust God completely and without reservation, you have every reason on earth—and in Heaven—to live courageously. And that's precisely what you should do.

GOD'S FORGIVENESS

*If we confess our sins, He is faithful and just to forgive us
our sins and to cleanse us from all unrighteousness.*
1 John 1:9 NKJV

The Bible promises you this: When you ask God for forgiveness, He will give it. No questions asked; no explanations required.

God's power to forgive, like His love, is infinite. Despite your sins, God offers immediate forgiveness. And it's time to take Him up on His offer.

When it comes to forgiveness, God doesn't play favorites and neither should you. You should forgive all the people who have harmed you (not just the people who have asked for forgiveness or the ones who have made restitution). Complete forgiveness is God's way, and it should be your way, too. Anything less is not enough.

God's heart of mercy provides for us not only pardon from sin but also a daily provision of spiritual food to strengthen us.

Jim Cymbala

When God forgives, He forgets. He buries our sins in the sea and puts a sign on the shore saying, "No Fishing Allowed."

Corrie ten Boom

A LESSON FOR THE HEART AND SOUL

For most of people, forgiveness doesn't come naturally. It's your job to keep practicing until it does.

IN GOD WE TRUST

And my God shall supply all your need
according to His riches in glory by Christ Jesus.
Philippians 4:19 NKJV

All of us experience adversity, disappointments, and hardship. Sometimes we bring these hardships upon ourselves, and sometimes we are victimized by circumstances that we cannot control and cannot fully understand. As human beings with limited insight, we can never completely comprehend the will of our Father in Heaven. But as believers in a benevolent God, we must always trust His providence. When Jesus went to the Mount of Olives, as described in Luke 22, He poured out His heart to God. Jesus knew of the agony that He was destined to endure, but He also knew that God's will must be done. We, like our Savior, face trials that bring fear and trembling to the very depths of our souls, but like Christ, we, too, must seek God's will, not our own.

Have you been touched by a personal tragedy that you cannot understand? If so, it's time to accept the unchangeable past . . . and it's time to trust God completely. When you do, you'll reclaim the peace—His peace—that can and should be yours.

If you work hard and maintain an attitude of gratitude, you'll find it easier to manage your finances every day.

John Maxwell

A LESSON FOR THE HEART AND SOUL

Don't fall in love with stuff. We live in a society that worships stuff—please don't fall into that trap. Remember this: material possessions are highly overrated. Worship God almighty, not the almighty dollar (Proverbs 11:28).

A WALK WITH GOD

For I have given you an example,
that you should do as I have done to you.
John 13:15 NKJV

Each day, we are confronted with countless opportunities to serve God and to follow in the footsteps of His Son. When we do, our Heavenly Father guides our steps and blesses our endeavors. As citizens of a fast-changing world, we face challenges that sometimes leave us feeling overworked, over-committed, and overwhelmed. But God has different plans for us. He intends that we slow down long enough to praise Him and to glorify His Son. When we do, He lifts our spirits and enriches our lives.

Today provides a glorious opportunity to place yourself in the service of the One who is the Giver of all blessings. May you seek His will, may you trust His Word, and may you walk in the footsteps of His Son.

The heaviest end of the cross lies ever on His shoulders. If He bids us carry a burden, He carries it also.

C. H. Spurgeon

Teach a man a rule and you help him solve a problem; teach a man to walk with God and you help him solve the rest of his life.

John Eldredge

A LESSON FOR THE HEART AND SOUL

If you want to follow in Christ's footsteps . . . welcome Him into your heart, obey His commandments, and share His never-ending love.

FORGIVING AND FORGETTING

But the wisdom that is from above is first pure,
then peaceable, gentle, willing to yield, full of mercy and good fruits,
without partiality and without hypocrisy.
James 3:17 NKJV

Do you have a tough time forgiving and forgetting? If so, welcome to the club. Most of us find it difficult to forgive the people who have hurt us. And that's too bad because life would be much simpler if we could forgive people "once and for all" and be done with it. Yet forgiveness is seldom that easy. Usually, the decision to forgive is straightforward, but the process of forgiving is more difficult. Forgiveness is a journey that requires time, perseverance, and prayer.

If you sincerely wish to forgive someone, pray for that person. And then pray for yourself by asking God to heal your heart. Don't expect forgiveness to be easy or quick, but rest assured: with God as your partner, you can forgive . . . and you will.

There are some facts that will never change. One fact is that you are forgiven. He sees you better than you see yourself. And that is a glorious fact of your life.

Max Lucado

A LESSON FOR THE HEART AND SOUL

Forgive . . . and keep forgiving! Sometimes, you may forgive someone once and then, at a later time, become angry at the very same person again. If so, you must forgive that person again and again . . . until it sticks!

THE GREATEST OF THESE

And now abide faith, hope, love, these three;
but the greatest of these is love.
1 Corinthians 13:13 NKJV

The beautiful words of 1st Corinthians 13 remind us that love is God's commandment: Faith is important, of course. So, too, is hope. But, love is more important still. We are commanded (not advised, not encouraged . . . commanded!) to love one another just as Christ loved us (John 13:34). That's a tall order, but as Christians, we are obligated to follow it.

Christ showed His love for us on the cross, and we are called upon to return Christ's love by sharing it. Today, let us spread Christ's love to our families, friends, and even strangers, so that through us, others might come to know Him.

It is important to know that you have to work to keep love alive; you have to protect it and maintain it, just like you would a delicate flower.

James Dobson

God calls upon the loved not just to love but to be loving. God calls upon the forgiven not just to forgive but to be forgiving.

Beth Moore

A LESSON FOR THE HEART AND SOUL

God loves you, and He wants you to reflect His love to those around you.

FINDING HOPE

These things I have spoken to you, that in Me you may have peace.
In the world you will have tribulation;
but be of good cheer, I have overcome the world.
John 16:33 NKJV

There are few sadder sights on earth than the sight of a person who has lost all hope. In difficult times, hope can be elusive, but Christians need never lose it. After all, God is good; His love endures; He has promised His children the gift of eternal life.

If you find yourself falling into the spiritual traps of worry and discouragement, consider the words of Jesus. It was Christ who promised, "In the world you will have tribulation; but be of good cheer, I have overcome the world." This world is indeed a place of trials and tribulations, but as believers, we are secure. God has promised us peace, joy, and eternal life. And, of course, God always keeps His promises.

Without the certainty of His resurrection, we would come to the end of this life without hope, with nothing to anticipate except despair and doubt. But because He lives, we rejoice, knowing soon we will meet our Savior face to face, and the troubles and trials of this world will be behind us.

Bill Bright

A LESSON FOR THE HEART AND SOUL

Since God has promised to guide and protect you—now and forever—you should never lose hope.

LOOK UP AND MOVE ON

Let all bitterness, wrath, anger, clamor, and evil speaking be put away
from you, with all malice. And be kind to one another, tenderhearted,
forgiving one another, just as God in Christ forgave you.
Ephesians 4:31–32 NKJV

Are you mired in the quicksand of bitterness or regret? If so, you are not only disobeying God's Word, you are also wasting your time. The world holds few, if any, rewards for those who remain angrily focused upon the past. Still, the act of forgiveness is difficult for all but the most saintly men and women.

Being frail, fallible, imperfect human beings, most of us are quick to anger, quick to blame, slow to forgive, and even slower to forget. Yet as Christians, we are commanded to forgive others, just as we, too, have been forgiven.

If there exists even one person—alive or dead—against whom you hold bitter feelings, it's time to forgive. Or, if you are embittered against yourself for some past mistake or shortcoming, it's finally time to forgive yourself and move on. Hatred, bitterness, and regret are not part of God's plan for your life. Forgiveness is.

Bitterness is the greatest barrier to friendship with God.

Rick Warren

A LESSON FOR THE HEART AND SOUL

You can never fully enjoy the present if you're bitter about the past.
Instead of living in the past, make peace with it . . . and move on.

IN TIMES OF ADVERSITY

For whatever is born of God overcomes the world.
And this is the victory that has overcome the world—our faith.
1 John 5:4 NKJV

All of us face times of adversity. On occasion, we all must endure the disappointments and tragedies that befall believers and nonbelievers alike. The reassuring words of 1 John 5:4 remind us that when we accept God's grace, we overcome the passing hardships of this world by relying upon His strength, His love, and His promise of eternal life.

When we face the inevitable difficulties of life-here-on-earth, God stands ready to protect us. Our responsibility, of course, is to ask Him for protection. When we call upon Him in heartfelt prayer, He will answer—in His own time and according to His own plan—and He will heal us. And while we are waiting for God's plans to unfold and for His healing touch to restore us, we can be comforted in the knowledge that our Creator can overcome any obstacle, even if we cannot. Let us take God at His word, and let us trust Him.

Adversity is always unexpected and unwelcomed. It is an intruder and a thief, and yet in the hands of God, adversity becomes the means through which His supernatural power is demonstrated.

Charles Stanley

A LESSON FOR THE HEART AND SOUL

Remember that tough times are simply opportunities to trust God completely and to find strength in Him.

ACCEPTING HIS GIFTS

*You fathers—if your children ask for a fish, do you give them
a snake instead? Or if they ask for an egg, do you give them
a scorpion? Of course not! If you sinful people know how to give
good gifts to your children, how much more will your
heavenly Father give the Holy Spirit to those who ask him.*
Luke 11:11–13 NLT

God gives the gifts; we, as believers, should accept them—
but oftentimes, we don't. Why? Because we fail to trust our
Heavenly Father completely, and because we are, at times, surprisingly stubborn. Luke 11 teaches us that God does not withhold
spiritual gifts from those who ask. Our obligation, quite simply, is
to ask for them.

Are you asking God to move mountains in your life, or are
you expecting Him to stumble over molehills? Whatever the size
of your challenges, God is big enough to handle them. Ask for His
help today, with faith and with fervor, and then watch in amazement as your mountains begin to move.

We honor God by asking for great things when they are a part of
His promise. We dishonor Him and cheat ourselves when we ask
for molehills where He has promised mountains.

Vance Havner

BUILDING A BETTER YOU

If you sincerely want to rise above the stresses and complications of
everyday life, ask for God's help many times each day.

MEASURING YOUR WORDS

The heart of the wise teaches his mouth,
and adds learning to his lips.
Proverbs 16:23 NKJV

God's Word reminds us that "Reckless words pierce like a sword, but the tongue of the wise brings healing" (Proverbs 12:18 NIV). If you seek to be a source of encouragement to friends, to family members, and to coworkers, then you must measure your words carefully. And that's exactly what God wants you to do.

Today, make this promise to yourself: Vow to be an honest, effective, encouraging communicator at work, at home, and everyplace in between. Speak wisely, not impulsively. Use words of kindness and praise, not words of anger or derision. Learn how to be truthful without being cruel. Remember that you have the power to heal others or to injure them, to lift others up or to hold them back. And when you learn how to lift them up, you'll soon discover that you've lifted yourself up, too.

We should ask ourselves three things before we speak: Is it true? Is it kind? Does it glorify God?

Billy Graham

A LESSON FOR THE HEART AND SOUL

Want to be a better communicator? Try being a briefer communicator. Longwinded monologues, although satisfying to the speaker, are usually torture for the listener. So when in doubt, say less and listen more.

DECISION-MAKING 101

Such doubters are thinking two different things at the same time,
and they cannot decide about anything they do.
They should not think they will receive anything from the Lord.
James 1:8 NCV

From the instant you wake in the morning until the moment you nod off to sleep at night, you have the opportunity to make countless decisions: decisions about the things you do, decisions about the words you speak, and decisions about the thoughts you choose to think.

If you're facing one of life's major decisions, here are some things you can do: 1. Gather as much information as you can. 2. Don't be too impulsive. 3. Rely on the advice of trusted friends and mentors. 4. Pray for guidance. 5. Trust the quiet inner voice of your conscience. 6. When the time for action arrives, act. Procrastination is the enemy of progress; don't let it defeat you.

People who can never quite seem to make up their minds usually make themselves miserable. So when in doubt, be decisive. It's the decent way to live.

There is no need to fear the decisions of life when you know Jesus Christ, for His name is Counselor.

Warren Wiersbe

BUILDING A BETTER YOU

Slow down! If you're about to make an important decision, don't be impulsive. Remember: big decisions have big consequences, and if you don't think about those consequences now, you may pay a big price later.

FINDING ENCOURAGEMENT

Have I not commanded you? Be strong and of good courage;
do not be afraid, nor be dismayed,
for the Lord your God is with you wherever you go.
Joshua 1:9 NKJV

God offers us the strength to meet our challenges, and He offers us hope for the future. One way that He shares His message of hope is through the words of encouraging friends and family members.

Hope, like other human emotions, is contagious. If we associate with hope-filled, enthusiastic people, their enthusiasm will have a tendency to lift our spirits. But if we find ourselves spending too much time in the company of naysayers, pessimists, or cynics, our thoughts—like the naysayers'—will tend to be negative.

Are you a hopeful, optimistic Christian? And do you associate with like-minded people? If so, then you're both wise and blessed.

If I am asked how we are to get rid of discouragements, I can only say, as I have had to say of so many other wrong spiritual habits, we must give them up. It is never worth while to argue against discouragement. There is only one argument that can meet it, and that is the argument of God.

Hannah Whitall Smith

A LESSON FOR THE HEART AND SOUL

When things go wrong, it's easy to become discouraged. But those who follow Jesus need never be discouraged because God's promises are true . . . and Heaven is eternal.

ENERGIZED FOR LIFE

*Be energetic in your life of salvation, reverent and sensitive
before God. That energy is God's energy, an energy
deep within you, God himself willing and working
at what will give him the most pleasure.*
Philippians 2:12–13 MSG

A re you fired with enthusiasm for Christ? If so, congratulations, and keep up the good work! But, if your spiritual batteries are running low, then perhaps you're spending too much energy working for yourself and not enough energy working for God.

If you're feeling tired, or troubled, or both, don't despair. Instead, seek strength from the source that never fails; that source, of course, is your Heavenly Father. And rest assured—when you sincerely petition Him, He will give you all the strength you need to live victoriously for Him.

God does not dispense strength and encouragement like a druggist fills your prescription. The Lord doesn't promise to give us something to take so we can handle our weary moments. He promises us Himself. That is all. And that is enough.

Charles Swindoll

BUILDING A BETTER YOU

Feeling exhausted? Try this: Start getting more sleep each night; begin a program of regular, sensible exercise; avoid harmful food and drink; and turn your problems over to God . . . and the greatest of these is "turn your problems over to God."

THE POWER OF FAITH

Have faith in the LORD your God and you will be upheld;
have faith in his prophets and you will be successful.
2 Chronicles 20:20 NIV

Every life—including yours—is a series of successes and failures, celebrations and disappointments, joys and sorrows. Every step of the way, through every triumph and tragedy, God will stand by your side and strengthen you . . . if you have faith in Him. Jesus taught His disciples that if they had faith, they could move mountains. You can too.

When you place your faith, your trust, indeed your life in the hands of Christ Jesus, you'll be amazed at the marvelous things He can do with you and through you. So strengthen your faith through praise, through worship, through Bible study, and through prayer. And trust God's plans. With Him, all things are possible, and He stands ready to open a world of possibilities to you . . . if you have faith.

Let your faith in Christ be in the quiet confidence that He will, every day and every moment, give you the strength you need.

Andrew Murray

Faith never means gullibility. The man who believes everything is as far from God as the man who refuses to believe anything.

A. W. Tozer

BUILDING A BETTER YOU

Today, dare to place your hopes, your dreams, and your future in God's hands.

GOD'S GIFT OF FAMILY

You must choose for yourselves today whom you will serve...
as for me and my family, we will serve the Lord.
Joshua 24:15 NCV

In the life of every family, there are moments of frustration and disappointment. Lots of them. But, for those who are lucky enough to live in the presence of a close-knit, caring clan, the rewards far outweigh the frustrations.

No family is perfect, and neither is yours. But, despite the inevitable challenges and hurt feelings of family life, your clan is God's gift to you. That little band of men, women, kids, and babies is a priceless treasure on temporary loan from the Father above. Give thanks to the Giver for the gift of family . . . and act accordingly.

The only true source of meaning in life is found in love for God and his son Jesus Christ, and love for mankind, beginning with our own families.

James Dobson

Apart from religious influence, the family is the most important influence on society.

Billy Graham

A LESSON FOR THE HEART AND SOUL

Your family is a precious gift from above, a gift that should be treasured, nurtured, and loved.

THE FINANCIAL GUIDE

The blessing of the Lord makes one rich....
Proverbs 10:22 NKJV

God's Word is not only a roadmap to eternal life, it is also an indispensable guidebook for life here on earth. As such, the Bible has much to say about your life and your finances.

God's Word can be a roadmap to a place of righteousness and abundance. Make it your roadmap. God's wisdom can be a light to guide your steps. Claim it as your light. God's Word can be an invaluable tool for crafting a better day and a better life. Make it your tool. And finally, God's Word can help you organize your financial life in such a way that you have less need to worry and more time to celebrate His glorious creation. If that sounds appealing, open your Bible, read its instructions, and follow them.

It is easy to determine the importance money plays in God's plan by the abundance of Scripture that relates to it—more than seven hundred verses directly refer to its use.

Larry Burkett

Sadly, family problems and even financial problems are seldom the real problem, but often the symptom of a weak or nonexistent value system.

Dave Ramsey

BUILDING A BETTER YOU

Don't buy impulsively. Savvy salespeople want you to buy "right now." But savvy buyers take their time (Proverbs 21:5).

THE JOYS OF FRIENDSHIP

I thank my God upon every remembrance of you.
Philippians 1:3 NKJV

What is a friend? The dictionary defines the word *friend* as "a person who is attached to another by feelings of affection or personal regard." This definition is accurate, as far as it goes, but when we examine the deeper meaning of friendship, so many more descriptors come to mind: trustworthiness, loyalty, helpfulness, kindness, encouragement, humor, and cheerfulness, to mention but a few.

Today, as you consider the many blessings that God has given you, remember to thank Him for the friends He has chosen to place along your path. May you be a blessing to them, and may they richly bless you today, tomorrow, and every day that you live.

True friends don't spend time gazing into each other's eyes. They show great tenderness toward each other, but they face in the same direction, toward common projects, interest, goals, and above all, toward a common Lord.

C. S. Lewis

A friend who loves will be more concerned about what is best for you than being accepted by you.

Charles Stanley

A LESSON FOR THE HEART AND SOUL

Take the time to reconnect with old friends. They'll be glad you did, and so, too, will you.

HIS GENEROSITY . . . AND YOURS

But God demonstrates His own love toward us,
in that while we were still sinners, Christ died for us.
Romans 5:8 NKJV

Christ showed His love for us by willingly sacrificing His own life so that we might have eternal life. We, as Christ's followers, are challenged to share His love. And, when we walk each day with Jesus—and obey the commandments found in God's Holy Word—we are worthy ambassadors for Him.

Just as Christ has been—and will always be—the ultimate friend to His flock, so should we be Christ-like in our love and generosity to those in need. When we share the love of Christ, we share a priceless gift. As His servants, we must do no less.

If we have the true love of God in our hearts, we will show it in our lives. We will not have to go up and down the earth proclaiming it. We will show it in everything we say or do.

D. L. Moody

A LESSON FOR THE HEART AND SOUL

Would you like to be a little happier? Try sharing a few more of the blessings that God has bestowed upon you. In other words, if you want to be happy, be generous. And if you want to be unhappy, be greedy.

HIS CALLING

But as God has distributed to each one,
as the Lord has called each one, so let him walk.
1 Corinthians 7:17 NKJV

It is terribly important that you heed God's calling by discovering and developing your talents and your spiritual gifts. If you seek to make a difference—and if you seek to bear eternal fruit—you must discover your gifts and begin using them for the glory of God.

Every believer has at least one gift. In John 15:16, Jesus says, "You did not choose Me, but I chose you and appointed you that you should go and bear fruit, and that your fruit should remain, that whatever you ask the Father in My name He may give you." Have you found your special calling? If not, keep searching and keep praying until you find it. God has important work for you to do, and the time to begin that work is now.

We can all humbly say in the sincerity of faith, "I am loved; I am called; I am secure."

Franklin Graham

If God's Word, your circumstances, and the counsel of others line up, and if you sense his provision, I'd say go for it.

Luci Swindoll

BUILDING A BETTER YOU

God calls you to a life that is perfectly suited for you, a life that will bring happiness and satisfaction to yourself and to others.

GOD IS LOVE

He who does not love does not know God, for God is love.
1 John 4:8 NKJV

God loves you. He loves you more than you can imagine; His affection is deeper than you can fathom. God made you in His own image and gave you salvation through the person of His Son Jesus Christ. And as a result, you have an important decision to make. You must decide what to do about God's love: you can return it . . . or not.

When you accept the love that flows from the heart of God, you are transformed. When you embrace God's love, you feel differently about yourself, your neighbors, your community, your church, and your world. When you open your heart to God's love, you will feel compelled to share God's message—and His compassion—with others. God's heart is overflowing—accept His love; return His love; and share His love. Today.

The love of God is one of the great realities of the universe, a pillar upon which the hope of the world rests. But it is a personal, intimate thing too. God does not love populations. He loves people. He loves not masses, but men.

A. W. Tozer

BUILDING A BETTER YOU

When you invite the love of God into your heart, everything changes . . . including you.

WHERE IS GOD LEADING?

Consider it pure joy, my brothers, whenever you face trials of many kinds, because you know that the testing of your faith develops perseverance. Perseverance must finish its work so that you may be mature and complete, not lacking anything.

James 1:2–4 NIV

Whether we realize it or not, times of adversity can be times of intense personal and spiritual growth. Our difficult days are also times when we can learn and relearn some of life's most important lessons.

The next time you experience a difficult moment, a difficult day, or a difficult year, ask yourself this question: Where is God leading me? In times of struggle and sorrow, you can be certain that God is leading you to a place of His choosing. Your duty is to watch, to pray, to listen, and to follow.

A tried Christian grows rich by his losses, he rises by his falls, he lives by dying, and he becomes full by being emptied.

C. H. Spurgeon

BUILDING A BETTER YOU

If you're having tough times, don't hit the panic button and don't keep everything bottled up inside. Find a person you can really trust, and talk things over. A second opinion (or, for that matter, a third, fourth, or fifth opinion) is usually helpful.

THE POWER OF PRAYER

*The earnest prayer of a righteous person has
great power and wonderful results.*
James 5:16 NLT

"The power of prayer": these words are so familiar, yet sometimes we forget what they mean. Prayer is a powerful tool for communicating with our Creator; it is an opportunity to commune with the Giver of all things good. Prayer helps us find strength for today and hope for the future. Prayer is not a thing to be taken lightly or to be used infrequently.

The quality of your spiritual life will be in direct proportion to the quality of your prayer life. Prayer changes things, and it changes you. Today, instead of turning things over in your mind, turn them over to God in prayer. Instead of worrying about your next decision, ask God to lead the way. Pray constantly about things great and small. God is listening, and He wants to hear from you now.

Our prayers are the link between God's inexhaustible resources and people's need. When we intercede, we stand in the gap between the need and the satisfaction of that need.

Charles Stanley

Where there is much prayer, there will be much of the Spirit; where there is much of the Spirit, there will be ever-increasing power.

Andrew Murray

BUILDING A BETTER YOU

Prayer changes things and it changes you. So pray.

THE VOICE INSIDE YOUR HEAD

This being so, I myself always strive to have
a conscience without offense toward God and men.
Acts 24:16 NKJV

When you're about to do something that you know is wrong, a little voice inside your head has a way of speaking up. That voice, of course, is your conscience: an early-warning system designed to keep you out of trouble. If you listen to that voice, you'll be okay; if you ignore it, you're asking for headaches, or heartbreaks, or both.

Whenever you're about to make an important decision, you should listen carefully to the quiet voice inside. Sometimes, of course, it's tempting to do otherwise. From time to time, you'll be tempted to abandon your better judgment by ignoring your conscience. But remember: a conscience is a terrible thing to waste. So instead of ignoring that quiet little voice, pay careful attention to it. If you do, your conscience will lead you in the right direction—in fact, it's trying to lead you right now. So listen . . . and learn.

To go against one's conscience is neither safe nor right. Here I stand. I cannot do otherwise.

Martin Luther

BUILDING A BETTER YOU

The more important the decision . . . the more carefully you should listen to your conscience.

EVERY NEW DAY IS A FRESH OPPORTUNITY

*When we were baptized, we were buried with Christ
and shared his death. So, just as Christ was raised from
the dead by the wonderful power of the Father,
we also can live a new life.*

Romans 6:4 NCV

God's Word is clear: When we genuinely invite Him to reign over our hearts, and when we accept His transforming love, we are forever changed. When we welcome Christ into our hearts, an old life ends and a new way of living—along with a completely new way of viewing the world—begins.

Each morning offers a fresh opportunity to invite Christ, yet once again, to rule over our hearts and our days. Each morning presents yet another opportunity to take up His cross and follow in His footsteps. Today, let us rejoice in the new life that is ours through Christ, and let us follow Him, step by step, on the path that He first walked.

Salvation is not just a repairing of the original self. It is a new self created of God.

Billy Graham

A LESSON FOR THE HEART AND SOUL

If you're a thoughtful believer, you'll make it a habit to praise God many times each day, beginning with your morning devotional.

SOLVING THE RIDDLES

*If you need wisdom—if you want to know what
God wants you to do—ask him, and he will gladly tell you.
He will not resent your asking.*

James 1:5 NLT

Life presents each of us with countless questions, conundrums, doubts, and problems. Thankfully, the riddles of everyday living are not too difficult to solve if we look for answers in the right places. When we have questions, we should consult God's Word, we should seek the guidance of the Holy Spirit, and we should trust the counsel of God-fearing friends and family members.

Are you facing a difficult decision? Take your concerns to God and avail yourself of the messages and mentors that He has placed along your path. When you do, God will speak to you in His own way and in His own time, and when He does, you can most certainly trust the answers that He gives.

God does not give His counsel to the curious or the careless; He reveals His will to the concerned and to the consecrated.

Warren Wiersbe

BUILDING A BETTER YOU

Never take on a major obligation of any kind without first taking sufficient time to carefully consider whether or not you should commit to it. The bigger the obligation, the more days you should take to decide. If someone presses you for an answer before you are ready, your automatic answer should always be "No."

THE REMEDY FOR UNCERTAINTY

And Jesus answered, "Why are you afraid? You have so little faith!"
Then he stood up and rebuked the wind and waves,
and suddenly all was calm.
Matthew 8:26 NLT

Sometimes, like Jesus' disciples, we feel threatened by the storms of life. During these moments, when our hearts are flooded with uncertainty, we must remember that God is not simply near, He is here.

Have you ever felt your faith in God slipping away? If so, you are in good company. Even the most faithful Christians are, at times, beset by occasional bouts of discouragement and doubt. But even when you feel far removed from God, God never leaves your side. He is always with you, always willing to calm the storms of life. When you sincerely seek His presence—and when you genuinely seek to establish a deeper, more meaningful relationship with His Son—God will calm your fears, answer your prayers, and restore your soul.

Seldom do you enjoy the luxury of making decisions that are based on enough evidence to absolutely silence all skepticism.

Bill Hybels

A LESSON FOR THE HEART AND SOUL

Are you sincerely looking for a way to address your doubts? Try Bible Study, prayer, and worship.

SHARING WORDS OF HOPE

*Let's see how inventive we can be in encouraging love
and helping out, not avoiding worshipping together
as some do but spurring each other on.*
Hebrews 10:24–25 MSG

Hope, like other human emotions, is contagious. When we associate with hope-filled Christians, we are encouraged by their faith and optimism. But, if we spend too much time in the company of naysayers and pessimists, our attitudes, like theirs, tend to be cynical and negative.

Are you a hopeful, optimistic, encouraging believer? And do you associate with like-minded people? Hopefully so. As a faithful follower of the One from Galilee, you have every reason to be hopeful, and you have every reason to share your hopes with others. So today, look for reasons to celebrate God's endless blessings. And while you're at it, look for people who will join you in the celebration. You'll be better for their company, and they'll be better for yours.

A lot of people have gone further than they thought they could because someone else thought they could.

Zig Ziglar

A LESSON FOR THE HEART AND SOUL

Today, challenge your faith by finding at least three people who need your encouragement, and then give them as much encouragement as you can. Be generous with your words, with pats on the back, and with your prayers. And remember: encouragement is contagious. You can't lift other people up without lifting yourself up, too.

EXCELLENCE, NOT EXCUSES

Do you see any truly competent workers?
They will serve kings rather than ordinary people.
Proverbs 22:29 NLT

Excuses are everywhere . . . excellence is not. If you seek excellence (and the rewards that accompany it), you must avoid the bad habit of making excuses.

Whatever your job description, it's up to you, and no one else, to become a master of your craft. It's up to you to do your job right—and to do it right now. When you do, you'll discover that excellence is its own reward . . . but not its only reward.

Rationalization: It's what we do when we substitute false explanations for true reasons, when we cloud our actual motives with a smoke screen of nice-sounding excuses.

Charles Swindoll

Few things fire up a person's commitment like dedication to excellence.

John Maxwell

BUILDING A BETTER YOU

Today, think of something important that you've been putting off. Then think of the excuses you've used to avoid that responsibility. Finally, ask yourself what you can do today to finish the work you've been avoiding.

CARING FOR YOUR FAMILY

*But if anyone does not provide for his own,
and especially for those of his household,
he has denied the faith and is worse than an unbeliever.*
1 Timothy 5:8 NASB

The words of 1 Timothy 5:8 are unambiguous: If God has blessed us with families, then He expects us to care for them. Sometimes, this profound responsibility seems daunting. And sometimes, even for the most dedicated Christian, family life holds moments of frustration and disappointment. But, for those who are lucky enough to live in the presence of a close-knit, caring clan, the rewards far outweigh the demands.

No family is perfect, and neither is yours. Despite the inevitable challenges of caring for your family, and despite the occasional hurt feelings of family life, your clan is God's gift to you. Give thanks to the Giver for the gift of family . . . and act accordingly.

When God asks someone to do something for Him entailing sacrifice, He makes up for it in surprising ways. Though He has led Bill all over the world to preach the gospel, He has not forgotten the little family in the mountains of North Carolina.

Ruth Bell Graham

A LESSON FOR THE HEART AND SOUL

Let your family and friends know that you love them by the things you say and the things you do. And, never take your family for granted; they deserve your very best treatment!

THE WORLD . . . AND YOU

Don't copy the behavior and customs of this world,
but let God transform you into a new person by
changing the way you think.
Romans 12:2 NLT

We live in the world, but we must not worship it. Our duty is to place God first and everything else second. But because we are fallible beings with imperfect faith, placing God in His rightful place is often difficult. In fact, at every turn, or so it seems, we are tempted to do otherwise.

The world is a noisy, distracting place filled with countless opportunities to stray from God's will. The world seems to cry, "Worship me with your time, your money, your energy, and your thoughts!" But God commands otherwise: He commands us to worship Him and Him alone; everything else must be secondary.

A fish would never be happy living on land, because it was made for water. An eagle could never feel satisfied if it wasn't allowed to fly. You will never feel completely satisfied on earth, because you were made for more.

Rick Warren

A LESSON FOR THE HEART AND SOUL

The world's power to distract, detour, and destroy is formidable. Thankfully, God's power is even greater.

THE LOVE OF MONEY

For the love of money is a root of all kinds of evil,
for which some have strayed from the faith in their greediness,
and pierced themselves through with many sorrows.
1 Timothy 6:10 NKJV

Our society is in love with money and the things that money can buy. God is not. God cares about people, not possessions, and so must we. We must, to the best of our abilities, love our neighbors as ourselves, and we must, to the best of our abilities, resist the mighty temptation to place possessions ahead of people.

Money, in and of itself, is not evil; worshipping money is. So today, as you prioritize matters of importance for you and yours, remember that God is almighty, but the dollar is not. If we worship God, we are blessed. But if we worship "the almighty dollar," we are punished because of our misplaced priorities—and our punishment inevitably comes sooner rather than later.

There is nothing wrong with people possessing riches. The wrong comes when riches possess people.

Billy Graham

When money is in your possession, what you do with it screams loudly who you are.

Dave Ramsey

A LESSON FOR THE HEART AND SOUL

When you realize that this world is not your home, that realization changes the way you think about money . . . and the way you spend it.

THE MIRACLE WORKER

Jesus said to them, "I have shown you many
great miracles from the Father."
John 10:32 NIV

God is a miracle worker. Throughout history, He has intervened in the course of human events in ways that cannot be explained by science or human rationale. And He's still doing so today.

God's miracles are not limited to special occasions, nor are they witnessed by a select few. God is crafting His wonders all around us: the miracle of the birth of a new baby; the miracle of a world renewing itself with every sunrise; the miracle of lives transformed by God's love and grace. Each day, God's handiwork is evident for all to see and experience.

Today, seize the opportunity to inspect God's hand at work. His miracles come in a variety of shapes and sizes, so keep your eyes and your heart open. Be watchful, and you'll soon be amazed.

We have a God who delights in impossibilities.

Andrew Murray

Only God can move mountains, but faith and prayer can move God.

E. M. Bounds

A LESSON FOR THE HEART AND SOUL

God is in the business of doing miraculous things. You should never be afraid to ask Him for a miracle.

CONSTANT PRAISE

Through Him then, let us continually offer up
a sacrifice of praise to God, that is,
the fruit of lips that give thanks to His name.
Hebrews 13:15 NASB

The Bible makes it clear: it pays to praise God. But sometimes, we allow ourselves to become so preoccupied with the demands of daily life that we forget to say "Thank You" to the Giver of all good gifts.

Worship and praise should be a part of everything we do. Otherwise, we quickly lose perspective as we fall prey to the demands of the moment.

Do you sincerely desire to be a worthy servant of your Heavenly Father, who has given you eternal love and eternal life? Then praise Him for who He is and for what He has done for you. Praise Him all day long, every day, for as long as you live . . . and then for all eternity.

This is my story, this is my song, praising my Savior all the day long; this is my story, this is my song, praising my Savior all the day long.

Fanny Crosby

BUILDING A BETTER YOU

Thoughtful believers (like you) make it a habit to carve out quiet moments throughout the day to praise God.

A TIME TO REST

Come to me, all you who are weary and burdened,
and I will give you rest. Take my yoke upon you and learn from me,
for I am gentle and humble in heart, and you will find rest for
your souls. For my yoke is easy and my burden is light.
Matthew 11:28–30 NIV

Sometimes, the struggles of life can drain us of our strength. When we find ourselves tired, discouraged, or worse, there is a source from which we can draw the power needed to recharge our spiritual batteries. That source, of course, is God.

God expects us to work hard, but He also intends for us to rest. When we fail to take the rest that we need, we do a disservice to ourselves and to our families.

Is your spiritual battery running low? Is your energy on the wane? Are your emotions frayed? If so, it's time to turn your thoughts and your prayers to God. And when you're finished, it's time to rest.

Prescription for a happier and healthier life: resolve to slow down your pace; learn to say no gracefully; resist the temptation to chase after more pleasure, more hobbies, and more social entanglements.

James Dobson

A LESSON FOR THE HEART AND SOUL

God wants you to get enough rest. The world wants you to burn the candle at both ends. Trust God.

THE SHEPHERD'S GIFT

My cup runs over. Surely goodness and mercy
shall follow me all the days of my life;
and I will dwell in the house of the Lord forever.
Psalm 23:5–6 NKJV

The Word of God is clear: Christ came in order that we might have life abundant and life eternal. Eternal life is the priceless possession of all who invite Christ into their hearts, but God's abundance is optional: He does not force it upon us.

When we entrust our hearts and our days to the One who created us, we experience abundance through the grace and sacrifice of His Son. But, when we turn our thoughts and direct our energies away from God's commandments, we inevitably forfeit the spiritual abundance that might otherwise be ours.

Do you sincerely seek the riches that our Savior offers to those who give themselves to Him? Then follow Him completely and obey Him without reservation. When you do, you will receive the love and the abundance that He has promised. Seek first the salvation that is available through a personal relationship with Jesus Christ, and then claim the joy, the peace, and the spiritual abundance that the Shepherd offers His sheep.

The Bible says that being a Christian is not only a great way to die, but it's also the best way to live.

Bill Hybels

BUILDING A BETTER YOU

God offers you His abundance—the rest is up to you.

FACE-TO-FACE
WITH OLD MAN TROUBLE

When you pass through the waters, I will be with you;
and through the rivers, they shall not overflow you.
When you walk through the fire, you shall not be burned,
nor shall the flame scorch you. For I am the Lord your God,
The Holy One of Israel, your Savior.
Isaiah 43:2–3 NKJV

As life-here-on-earth unfolds, all of us encounter occasional setbacks: Those occasional visits from Old Man Trouble are simply a fact of life, and none of us are exempt. When tough times arrive, we may be forced to rearrange our plans and our priorities. But even on our darkest days, we must remember that God's love remains constant.

The fact that we encounter adversity is not nearly so important as the way we choose to deal with it. When tough times arrive, we have a clear choice: we can begin the difficult work of tackling our troubles . . . or not. When we summon the courage to look Old Man Trouble squarely in the eye, an amazing thing usually happens: He blinks.

God will never let you sink under your circumstances. He always provides a safety net and His love always encircles.

Barbara Johnson

BUILDING A BETTER YOU

When tough times arrive, you should work as if everything depended on you and pray as if everything depended on God.

FIT TO SERVE

Whatever you eat or drink or whatever you do,
you must do all for the glory of God.
1 Corinthians 10:31 NLT

We live in a world in which leisure is glorified and consumption is commercialized. But God has other plans. He did not create us for lives of gluttony or laziness; He created us for far greater things.

God has a plan for every aspect of your life, and His plan includes provisions for your physical health. But, He expects you to do your fair share of the work! In a world that is chock-full of tasty temptations, you may find it all too easy to make unhealthy choices. Your challenge, of course, is to resist those unhealthy temptations by every means you can, including prayer. And rest assured: when you ask for God's help, He will give it.

People are funny. When they are young, they will spend their health to get wealth. Later, they will gladly pay all they have trying to get their health back.

John Maxwell

BUILDING A BETTER YOU

Simply put, it's up to you to assume the ultimate responsibility for your health. So if you're fighting the battle of the bulge (the bulging waistline, that is), don't waste your time blaming the fast food industry—or anybody else, for that matter. It's your body, and it's your responsibility to take care of it.

FORGIVE: IT'S GOD'S WAY

Be kind to one another, tender-hearted, forgiving each other,
just as God in Christ also has forgiven you.
Ephesians 4:32 NASB

To forgive others is difficult. Being frail, fallible, imperfect human beings, we are quick to anger, quick to blame, slow to forgive, and even slower to forget. No matter. Forgiveness, no matter how difficult, is God's way, and it must be our way, too.

God's commandments are not intended to be customized for the particular whims of particular believers. God's Word is not a menu from which each of us may select items à la carte, according to our own desires. Far from it. God's Holy Word is a book that must be taken in its entirety; all of God's commandments are to be taken seriously. And, so it is with forgiveness. So, if you hold bitterness against even a single person, forgive. Then, to the best of your abilities, forget. It's God's way for you to live.

Looking back over my life, all I can see is mercy and grace written in large letters everywhere. May God help me have the same kind of heart toward those who wound or offend me.

Jim Cymbala

BUILDING A BETTER YOU

Make a list of people whom you have not yet forgiven. Then, challenge yourself to forgive each and every one of them today. And what should you do if you simply cannot find it in your heart to forgive? Ask for God's help. He can give you the wisdom and courage you need to forgive everybody, including yourself.

RICHLY BLESSED

So let each one give as he purposes in his heart,
not grudgingly or of necessity; for God loves a cheerful giver.
2 Corinthians 9:7 NKJV

God's Word commands us to be generous, compassionate servants to those who need our support. As believers, we have
been richly blessed by our Creator. We, in turn, are called to share
our gifts, our possessions, our testimonies, and our talents.

The theme of generosity is one of the cornerstones of Christ's
teachings. If we are to be disciples of Christ, we, too, must be
cheerful, generous, courageous givers. Our Savior expects no less
from us. And He deserves no less.

Giving to God and, in His name, to others, is not something that
we do; it the result of what we are.

Warren Wiersbe

Think of the blessings we so easily take for granted: Life itself;
preservation from danger; every bit of health we enjoy; every hour
of liberty; the ability to see, to hear, to speak, to think, and to
imagine all this comes from the hand of God.

Billy Graham

A LESSON FOR THE HEART AND SOUL

There is a direct relationship between generosity and joy—the
more you give to others, the more joy you will experience for
yourself.

THE GIFT OF SALVATION

For it is by grace you have been saved, through faith—
and this not from yourselves, it is the gift of God—
not by works, so that no one can boast.

Ephesians 2:8–9 NIV

God has given us so many gifts, but none can compare with the gift of salvation. We have not earned our salvation; it is a gift from God. When we accept Christ into our hearts, we are saved by His grace.

God's grace is the ultimate gift, and we owe to Him the ultimate in thanksgiving. Let us praise the Creator for His priceless gift, and let us share the Good News with all who cross our paths. We return our Father's love by accepting His grace and by sharing His message and His love. When we do, we are eternally blessed . . . and the Father smiles.

The grace of God is sufficient for all our needs, for every problem, and for every difficulty, for every broken heart, and for every human sorrow.

Peter Marshall

A LESSON FOR THE HEART AND SOUL

God's grace is always available. Jim Cymbala writes, "No one is beyond his grace. No situation, anywhere on earth, is too hard for God." If you sincerely seek God's grace, He will give it freely. So ask, and you will receive.

SENSING HIS PRESENCE

*Where can I go from Your Spirit? Or where can I flee from
Your presence? If I ascend into heaven, You are there;
if I make my bed in hell, behold, You are there. If I take the wings of
the morning, and dwell in the uttermost parts of the sea,
even there Your hand shall lead me, and Your right hand shall hold me.*

Psalm 139:7–10 NKJV

If God is everywhere, why does He sometimes seem so far away? The answer to that question, of course, has nothing to do with God and everything to do with us.

When we begin each day on our knees, in praise and worship to Him, God often seems very near indeed. But, if we ignore God's presence or—worse yet—rebel against it altogether, the world in which we live becomes a spiritual wasteland.

Today, and every day hereafter, thank God and praise Him. He is the Giver of all things good. Wherever you are, whether you are happy or sad, victorious or vanquished, celebrate God's presence. And be comforted. For He is here.

The Lord Jesus by His Holy Spirit is with me, and the knowledge of His presence dispels the darkness and allays any fears.

Bill Bright

BUILDING A BETTER YOU

God is here, and He wants to establish an intimate relationship with you. When you sincerely reach out to Him, you will sense His presence.

THANKSGIVING YES . . . ENVY NO!

Stop your anger! Turn from your rage!
Do not envy others—it only leads to harm.
Psalm 37:8 NLT

As the recipient of God's grace, you have every reason to celebrate life. After all, God has promised you the opportunity to receive His abundance and His joy—in fact, you have the opportunity to receive those gifts right now. But if you allow envy to gnaw away at the fabric of your soul, you'll find that joy remains elusive. So do yourself an enormous favor: Rather than succumbing to the sin of envy, focus on the marvelous things that God has done for you—starting with Christ's sacrifice. Thank the Giver of all good gifts, and keep thanking Him for the wonders of His love and the miracles of His creation. Count your own blessings and let your neighbors count theirs. It's the godly way to live.

Contentment comes when we develop an attitude of gratitude for the important things we do have in our lives that we tend to take for granted if we have our eyes staring longingly at our neighbor's stuff.

Dave Ramsey

A LESSON FOR THE HEART AND SOUL

You can be envious, or you can be happy, but you can't be both. Envy and happiness can't live at the same time in the same brain.

TO JUDGE OR NOT TO JUDGE

When they continued to ask Jesus their question,
he raised up and said, "Anyone here who has never sinned
can throw the first stone at her."
John 8:7 NCV

The warning of Matthew 7:1 is clear: "Judge not, that ye be not judged" (KJV). Yet even the most devoted Christians may fall prey to a powerful yet subtle temptation: the temptation to judge others. But as obedient followers of Christ, we are commanded to refrain from such behavior.

As Jesus came upon a young woman who had been condemned by the Pharisees, He spoke not only to the crowd that was gathered there, but also to all generations when He warned, "He that is without sin among you, let him first cast a stone at her" (John 8:7 KJV). Christ's message is clear, and it applies not only to the Pharisees of ancient times, but also to us.

An individual Christian may see fit to give up all sorts of things for special reasons—marriage, or meat, or beer, or cinema; but the moment he starts saying these things are bad in themselves, or looking down his nose at other people who do use them, he has taken the wrong turn.

C. S. Lewis

A LESSON FOR THE HEART AND SOUL

To the extent you judge others, so, too, will you be judged. So you must, to the best of your ability, refrain from judgmental thoughts and words.

ACTIONS THAT REFLECT OUR BELIEFS

*If the way you live isn't consistent with
what you believe, then it's wrong.*
Romans 14:23 MSG

As Christians, we must do our best to ensure that our actions are accurate reflections of our beliefs. Our theology must be demonstrated, not only by our words but, more importantly, by our actions. In short, we should be practical believers, quick to act whenever we see an opportunity to serve God.

Are you the kind of practical Christian who is willing to dig in and do what needs to be done when it needs to be done? If so, congratulations: God acknowledges your service and blesses it. But if you find yourself more interested in the fine points of theology than in the needs of your neighbors, it's time to rearrange your priorities. God needs believers who are willing to roll up their sleeves and go to work for Him. Count yourself among that number. Theology is a good thing unless it interferes with God's work. And it's up to you to make certain that your theology doesn't.

Do noble things, do not dream them all day long.

Charles Kingsley

A LESSON FOR THE HEART AND SOUL

Because actions do speak louder than words, it's always a good time to let your actions speak for themselves.

A PRESCRIPTION FOR PANIC

Anxiety in the heart of man causes depression,
but a good word makes it glad.
Proverbs 12:25 NKJV

We live in a world that sometimes seems to shift beneath our feet. We live in an uncertain world, a world where tragedies can befall even the most godly among us. And we are members of an anxious society, a society in which the changes we face threaten to outpace our abilities to make adjustments. No wonder we sometimes find ourselves beset by feelings of anxiety and panic.

At times, our anxieties may stem from physical causes—chemical imbalances in the brain that result in severe emotional distress or relentless panic attacks. In such cases, modern medicine offers hope to those who suffer. But oftentimes, our anxieties result from spiritual deficits, not physical ones. And when we're spiritually depleted, the best prescription is found not in the medicine cabinet but deep inside the human heart. What we need is a higher daily dose of God's love, God's peace, God's assurance, and God's presence. And how do we acquire these blessings from our Creator? Through prayer, through meditation, through worship, and through trust.

Anxiety is the natural result when our hopes are centered on anything short of God and His will for us.

Billy Graham

BUILDING A BETTER YOU

Remembering God's faithfulness in the past can give you peace for today and hope for tomorrow.

THE RIGHT KIND OF BEHAVIOR

By this we know that we have come to know Him,
if we keep His commandments.
1 John 2:3 NASB

When we seek righteousness in our own lives—and when we seek the companionship of those who do likewise—we reap the spiritual rewards that God intends for us to enjoy. When we behave ourselves as godly men and women, we honor God. When we live righteously and according to God's commandments, He blesses us in ways that we cannot fully understand.

Today, as you fulfill your responsibilities, hold fast to that which is good, and associate yourself with believers who behave themselves in like fashion. When you do, your good works will serve as a powerful example for others and as a worthy offering to your Creator.

Christianity says we were created by a righteous God to flourish and be exhilarated in a righteous environment. God has "wired" us in such a way that the more righteous we are, the more we'll actually enjoy life.

Bill Hybels

A LESSON FOR THE HEART AND SOUL

When it comes to telling the world about your relationship with God . . . your actions speak much more loudly than your words . . . so behave accordingly.

A RELATIONSHIP THAT HONORS GOD

I am always praising you; all day long I honor you.
Psalm 71:8 NCV

As you think about the nature of your relationship with God, remember this: you will always have some type of relationship with Him—it is inevitable that your life must be lived in relationship to God. The question is not if you will have a relationship with Him; the burning question is whether that relationship will be one that seeks to honor Him . . . or not.

Are you willing to place God first in your life? And, are you willing to welcome God's Son into your heart? Unless you can honestly answer these questions with a resounding yes, then your relationship with God isn't what it could be or should be. Thankfully, God is always available, He's always ready to forgive, and He's waiting to hear from you now. The rest, of course, is up to you.

God shows unbridled delight when He sees people acting in ways that honor Him: when He receives worship, when He sees faith demonstrated in the most trying of circumstances, and when He sees tender love shared among His people.

Bill Hybels

A LESSON FOR THE HEART AND SOUL

The difference between theological dogma and faith with works is the difference between stagnant religion and joyful Christianity.

THE SOURCE OF ALL COMFORT

When doubts filled my mind,
your comfort gave me renewed hope and cheer.
Psalm 94:19 NLT

In times of adversity, we are wise to remember the words of Jesus, who, when He walked on the waters, reassured His disciples, saying, "Take courage! It is I. Don't be afraid" (Matthew 14:27 NIV). Then, with Christ on His throne—and with trusted friends and loving family members at our sides—we can face our fears with courage and with faith.

Are you facing a difficult challenge? If so, remember that no problem is too big for God . . . not even yours.

Deep in the dark night of the suffering soul comes a moment when nothing intellectual or psychological matters. It is the time of the touch, the tender touch, a hand held, a cheek kissed, a holy embrace that conveys more to the human spirit than anything from tongue or pen.

Bill Bright

A LESSON FOR THE HEART AND SOUL

When talking to a person who's enduring obvious pain, don't assume that you know how he or she feels. To say, "I know how you must feel" is to assume that you can know the inner workings of another person's heart. Those words are often better left unsaid.

GOD'S VOICE

*For this is commendable, if because of conscience toward
God one endures grief, suffering wrongfully.*
1 Peter 2:19 NKJV

Billy Graham correctly observed, "Most of us follow our conscience as we follow a wheelbarrow. We push it in front of us in the direction we want to go." To do so, of course, is a profound mistake. Yet all of us, on occasion, have failed to listen to the voice that God planted in our hearts, and all of us have suffered the consequences.

God gave you a conscience for a very good reason: to make your path conform to His will. Wise believers make it a practice to listen carefully to that quiet internal voice. Count yourself among that number. When your conscience speaks, listen and learn. In all likelihood, God is trying to get His message through. And in all likelihood, it is a message that you desperately need to hear.

The beginning of backsliding means your conscience does not answer to the truth.

Oswald Sanders

BUILDING A BETTER YOU

Trust the quiet inner voice of your conscience: Treat your conscience as you would a trusted advisor.

MOUNTAINTOPS AND VALLEYS

I sought the Lord, and He heard me,
and delivered me from all my fears.
Psalm 34:4 NKJV

Every life (including yours) is an unfolding series of events: some fabulous, some not-so-fabulous, and some downright disheartening. When you reach the mountaintops of life, praising God is easy. But, when the storm clouds form overhead, your faith will be tested, sometimes to the breaking point. As a believer, you can take comfort in this fact: Wherever you find yourself, whether at the top of the mountain or the depths of the valley, God is there, and because He cares for you, you can live courageously.

The next time you find your courage tested to the limit, remember that God is your shield and your strength; He is your protector and your deliverer. Call upon Him in your hour of need and He will protect you.

There comes a time when we simply have to face the challenges in our lives and stop backing down.

John Eldredge

A LESSON FOR THE HEART AND SOUL

With God as your partner, you have nothing to fear. Why? Because you and God, working together, can handle absolutely anything that comes your way. So the next time you'd like an extra measure of courage, recommit yourself to a true one-on-one relationship with your Creator. When you sincerely turn to Him, He will never fail you.

TODAY'S OPPORTUNITIES

But encourage each other every day while it is "today."
Help each other so none of you will become
hardened because sin has tricked you.
Hebrews 3:13 NCV

The 118th Psalm reminds us, "This is the day which the Lord hath made; we will rejoice and be glad in it" (v. 24 KJV). As we rejoice in this day that the Lord has given us, let us remember that an important part of today's celebration is the time we spend celebrating others. Each day provides countless opportunities to encourage others and to praise their good works. When we do, we not only spread seeds of joy and happiness, we also follow the commandments of God's Holy Word.

How can we build others up? By celebrating their victories and their accomplishments. So look for the good in others and celebrate the good that you find. When you do, you'll be a powerful force of encouragement in the world . . . and a worthy servant to your God.

Discouraged people don't need critics. They hurt enough already. They don't need more guilt or piled-on distress. They need encouragement. They need a refuge, a willing, caring, available someone.

Charles Swindoll

A LESSON FOR THE HEART AND SOUL

Think carefully about the things you say so that your words can be a "gift of encouragement" to others. Your friends and family members need encouraging words . . . from you.

CONTAGIOUS FAITH

Whatever you do, do your work heartily,
as for the Lord rather than for men.
Colossians 3:23 NASB

Genuine, heartfelt Christianity is contagious. If you enjoy a life-altering relationship with God, that relationship will have an impact on others—perhaps a profound impact.

Are you genuinely excited about your faith? And do you make your enthusiasm known to those around you? Or are you a "silent ambassador" for Christ? God's preference is clear: He intends that you stand before others and proclaim your faith.

Does Christ reign over your life? Then share your testimony and your excitement. The world needs both.

There seems to be a chilling fear of holy enthusiasm among the people of God. We try to tell how happy we are—but we remain so well-controlled that there are very few waves of glory experienced in our midst.

A. W. Tozer

A LESSON FOR THE HEART AND SOUL

Be enthusiastic about your faith. John Wesley wrote, "You don't have to advertise a fire. Get on fire for God and the world will come to watch you burn." When you allow yourself to become extremely enthusiastic about your faith, other people will notice—and so will God.

THE STORMS OF LIFE

But Jesus immediately said to them:
"Take courage! It is I. Don't be afraid."
Matthew 14:27 NIV

A storm rose quickly on the Sea of Galilee, and the disciples were afraid. Although they had seen Jesus perform many miracles, the disciples feared for their lives, so they turned to their Savior, and He calmed the waters and the wind.

Sometimes, we, like the disciples, feel threatened by the inevitable storms of life. And when we are fearful, we, too, can turn to Christ for courage and for comfort.

From time to time, all of us, even the most devout believers, experience fear. But, as believers, we can live courageously in the promises of our Lord . . . and we should.

As you take the next step on your life's journey, you can be comforted: Wherever you find yourself, God is there. And, because He cares for you, you can live courageously.

Down through the centuries, in times of trouble and trial, God has brought courage to the hearts of those who love Him. The Bible is filled with assurances of God's help and comfort in every kind of trouble.

Billy Graham

A LESSON FOR THE HEART AND SOUL

If you are a disciple of the risen Christ, you have every reason on earth—and in Heaven—to live courageously. And that's precisely what you should do.

HIS INTIMATE LOVE

As the Father loved Me, I also have loved you; abide in My love.
John 15:9 NKJV

St. Augustine observed, "God loves each of us as if there were only one of us." Do you believe those words? Do you seek an intimate, one-on-one relationship with your Heavenly Father, or are you satisfied to keep Him at a "safe" distance?

Sometimes, in the crush of our daily duties, God may seem far away, but He is not. God is everywhere we have ever been and everywhere we will ever go. He is with us night and day; He knows our thoughts and our prayers. And, when we earnestly seek Him, we will find Him because He is here, waiting patiently for us to reach out to Him. May we reach out to Him today and always. And may we praise Him for the glorious gifts that have transformed us today and forever.

God wants to emancipate his people; he wants to set them free. He wants his people to be not slaves but sons. He wants them governed not by law but by love.

Max Lucado

A LESSON FOR THE HEART AND SOUL

When all else fails, God's love does not. You can always depend upon God's love . . . and He is always your ultimate protection.

BEING PATIENT WITH OURSELVES

Knowing God leads to self-control. Self-control leads to patient endurance, and patient endurance leads to godliness.
2 Peter 1:6 NLT

Being patient with other people can be difficult. But sometimes, we find it even more difficult to be patient with ourselves. We have high expectations and lofty goals. We want to accomplish things now, not later. And, of course, we want our lives to unfold according to our own timetables, not God's.

Throughout the Bible, we are instructed that patience is the companion of wisdom. God's message, then, is clear: we must be patient with all people, beginning with that particular person who stares back at us each time we gaze into the mirror.

Two signposts of faith: "Slow Down" and "Wait Here."

Charles Stanley

Be patient. God is using today's difficulties to strengthen you for tomorrow. He is equipping you. The God who makes things grow will help you bear fruit.

Max Lucado

BUILDING A BETTER YOU

When you learn to be more patient with yourself and with others, you'll make your world—and your heart—a more peaceful and less stressful place.

YOUR REAL RICHES

He said, "I came naked from my mother's womb, and I will be stripped
of everything when I die. The LORD gave me everything I had,
and the LORD has taken it away. Praise the name of the LORD!"
Job 1:21 NLT

Martin Luther observed, "Many things I have tried to grasp and have lost. That which I have placed in God's hands I still have." How true. Earthly riches are transitory; spiritual riches are not.

In our demanding world, financial security can be a good thing, but spiritual prosperity is profoundly more important. Certainly we all need the basic necessities of life, but once we've acquired those necessities, enough is enough. Why? Because our real riches are not of this world. We are never really rich until we are rich in spirit.

The characteristic of the life of a saint is essentially elemental simplicity.

Oswald Chambers

He is no fool who gives what he cannot keep to gain what he cannot lose.

Jim Elliot

A LESSON FOR THE HEART AND SOUL

The world says, "Buy more stuff." God says, "Stuff isn't important." Believe God.

REAL REPENTANCE

*I preached that they should repent and turn to God
and prove their repentance by their deeds.*
Acts 26:20 NIV

Who among us has sinned? All of us. But the good news is this: When we do ask God's forgiveness and turn our hearts to Him, He forgives us absolutely and completely.

Genuine repentance requires more than simply offering God apologies for our misdeeds. Real repentance may start with feelings of sorrow and remorse, but it ends only when we turn away from the sin that has heretofore distanced us from our Creator. In truth, we offer our most meaningful apologies to God, not with our words, but with our actions. As long as we are still engaged in sin, we may be "repenting," but we have not fully "repented." So, if there is an aspect of your life that is distancing you from your God, ask for His forgiveness, and—just as importantly—stop sinning. Now.

Repentance is among other things a sincere apology to God for distrusting Him so long, and faith is throwing oneself upon Christ in complete confidence.

A. W. Tozer

A LESSON FOR THE HEART AND SOUL

If you're engaged in behavior that is displeasing to God, repent today—tomorrow may be too late.

CONQUERING EVERYDAY FRUSTRATIONS

A hot-tempered man stirs up dissension,
but a patient man calms a quarrel.
Proverbs 15:18 NIV

Life is full of frustrations: some great and some small. On occasion, you, like Jesus, will confront evil, and when you do, you may respond as He did: vigorously and without reservation. But, more often your frustrations will be of the more mundane variety. As long as you live here on earth, you will face countless opportunities to lose your temper over small, relatively insignificant events: a traffic jam, a spilled cup of coffee, an inconsiderate comment, a broken promise. When you are tempted to lose your temper over the minor inconveniences of life, don't. Turn away from anger, hatred, bitterness, and regret. Turn instead to God. When you do, you'll be following His commandments and giving yourself a priceless gift . . . the gift of peace.

Anger's the anaesthetic of the mind.

C. S. Lewis

Anger breeds remorse in the heart, discord in the home, bitterness in the community, and confusion in the state.

Billy Graham

A LESSON FOR THE HEART AND SOUL

God's Word warns against the folly and the futility of anger. It's a warning you should take seriously.

GIVE ME PATIENCE, LORD, RIGHT NOW!

Now we exhort you, brethren, warn those who are unruly,
comfort the fainthearted, uphold the weak, be patient with all.
1 Thessalonians 5:14 NKJV

Most of us are impatient for God to grant us the desires of our heart. Usually, we know what we want, and we know precisely when we want it: right now, if not sooner. But God may have other plans. And when God's plans differ from our own, we must trust in His infinite wisdom and in His infinite love.

As busy people living in a fast-paced world, many of us find that waiting quietly for God is difficult. But God instructs us to be patient in all things. We must be patient with our families, our friends, and our associates. We must also be patient with our Creator as He unfolds His plan for our lives. And that's as it should be. After all, think about how patient God has been with us.

It is wise to wait because God gives clear direction only when we are willing to wait.

Charles Stanley

Our challenge is to wait in faith for the day of God's favor and salvation.

Jim Cymbala

A LESSON FOR THE HEART AND SOUL

Patience pays. Impatience costs. Behave accordingly.

A PASSIONATE PURSUIT OF GOD'S TRUTH

But grow in the grace and knowledge of our Lord and Savior
Jesus Christ. To Him be the glory both now and forever. Amen.
2 Peter 3:18 NKJV

Have you established a passionate relationship with God's Holy Word? Hopefully so. The words of Matthew 4:4 remind us that, "Man shall not live by bread alone but by every word that proceedeth out of the mouth of God" (KJV). As believers, we must study the Bible and meditate upon its meaning for our lives. Otherwise, we deprive ourselves of a priceless gift from our Creator.

Martin Luther observed, "The Bible is alive, it speaks to me; it has feet, it runs after me; it has hands, it lays hold of me. The Bible is not antique or modern. It is eternal." God's Holy Word is, indeed, an eternal, transforming, one-of-a-kind treasure. And, a passing acquaintance with the Good Book is insufficient for Christians who seek to obey God's Word and to understand His will.

We should approach the Bible with the assurance that here we have God-breathed literature, that it is our privilege and joy to find out what He has to say.

Billy Graham

BUILDING A BETTER YOU

God intends for you to use His Word as your guidebook for life . . . your intentions should be the same.

TAKING UP THE CROSS

Then He said to them all, "If anyone desires to come after Me,
let him deny himself, and take up his cross daily, and follow Me.
For whoever desires to save his life will lose it,
but whoever loses his life for My sake will save it."
Luke 9:23–24 NKJV

When we have been saved by Christ, we can, if we choose, become passive Christians. We can sit back, secure in our own salvation, and let other believers spread the healing message of Jesus. But to do so is wrong. Instead, we are commanded to become disciples of the One who has saved us, and to do otherwise is a sin of omission with terrible consequences.

When Jesus addressed His disciples, He warned them that each one must, "take up his cross daily and follow me" (Luke 9:23 NIV). Christ's message was clear: in order to follow Him, Christ's disciples must deny themselves and, instead, trust Him completely. Nothing has changed since then.

Do you seek to fulfill God's purpose for your life? Then follow Christ. Follow Him by picking up His cross today and every day that you live. Then, you will quickly discover that Christ's love has the power to change everything, including you.

Being a disciple involves becoming a learner, a student of the Master.

Charles Stanley

BUILDING A BETTER YOU

Today, think of at least one single step that you can take to become a better disciple for Christ. Then, take that step.

FOR ALL ETERNITY

Most assuredly, I say to you, he who hears My word and believes in Him who sent Me has everlasting life, and shall not come into judgment, but has passed from death into life.

John 5:24 NKJV

Our vision for the future, like our life here on earth, is limited. God's vision is not burdened by such limitations: His plans extend throughout all eternity. Thus, God's plans for you are not limited to the ups and downs of everyday life. Your Heavenly Father has bigger things in mind . . . much bigger things.

Let us praise the Creator for His priceless gift, and let us share the Good News with all who cross our paths. We return our Father's love by accepting His grace and by sharing His message and His love. When we do, we are blessed here on earth and throughout all eternity.

Teach us to set our hopes on heaven, to hold firmly to the promise of eternal life, so that we can withstand the struggles and storms of this world.

Max Lucado

A LESSON FOR THE HEART AND SOUL

People love talking about religion, and everybody has their own opinions, but ultimately only one opinion counts . . . God's. Talk to your friends about God's promise of eternal life—what that promise means to you and what it should mean to them.

A POSITIVE INFLUENCE

*Be an example to the believers in word, in conduct,
in love, in spirit, in faith, in purity.*
1 Timothy 4:12 NKJV

As followers of Christ, we must each ask ourselves an important question: "What kind of example am I?" The answer to that question determines, in large part, whether or not we are positive influences on our own little corners of the world.

Are you the kind of man or woman whose life serves as a powerful example of righteousness? Are you a person whose behavior serves as a positive role model for young people? Are you the kind of Christian whose actions, day in and day out, are based upon integrity, fidelity, and a love for the Lord? If so, you are not only blessed by God, you are also a powerful force for good in a world that desperately needs positive influences such as yours.

For one man who can introduce another to Jesus Christ by the way he lives and by the atmosphere of his life, there are a thousand who can only talk jargon about him.

Oswald Chambers

A LESSON FOR THE HEART AND SOUL

As a Christian, the most important light you shine is the light that your own life shines on the lives of others. May your light shine brightly, righteously, obediently, and eternally!

TROUBLED TIMES

He shall not be afraid of evil tidings:
his heart is fixed, trusting in the LORD.
Psalm 112:7 KJV

We live in a fear-based world, a world where bad news travels at light speed and good news doesn't. These are troubled times, times when we have legitimate fears for the future of our nation, our world, and our families. But as Christians, we have every reason to live courageously. After all, the ultimate battle has already been fought and won on that faraway cross at Calvary.

Perhaps you, like countless other believers, have found your courage tested by the anxieties and fears that are an inevitable part of life. If so, God wants to have a little chat with you. The next time you find your courage tested to the limit, God wants to remind you that He is not just near, He is here.

Your Heavenly Father is your Protector and your Deliverer. Call upon Him in your hour of need, and be comforted. Whatever your challenge, whatever your trouble, God can handle it. And will.

When we submit difficult and alarming situations to God, he promises that his peace will be like military garrison to guard our hearts from fear.

Dennis Swanberg

BUILDING A BETTER YOU

If you're too afraid of failure, you may not live up to your potential. Remember that failing isn't nearly as bad as failing to try.

NOURISHED BY THE WORD

You will be a good servant of Christ Jesus,
constantly nourished on the words of the faith and of the sound
doctrine which you have been following.
1 Timothy 4:6 NASB

Do you read your Bible a lot . . . or not? The answer to this simple question will determine, to a surprising extent, the quality of your life and the direction of your faith.

As you establish priorities for life, you must decide whether God's Word will be a bright spotlight that guides your path every day or a tiny nightlight that occasionally flickers in the dark. The decision to study the Bible—or not—is yours and yours alone. But make no mistake: how you choose to use your Bible will have a profound impact on you and your loved ones.

The Bible is the ultimate guide for life; make it your guidebook as well. When you do, you can be comforted in the knowledge that your steps are guided by a Source of wisdom and truth that never fails.

Decisions which are made in the light of God's Word are stable and show wisdom.

Vonette Bright

BUILDING A BETTER YOU

Never stop studying God's Word. Even if you've been studying the Bible for many years, you've still got lots to learn. Bible study should be a lifelong endeavor; make it your lifelong endeavor.

ALWAYS FORGIVING

Then Peter came to him and asked,
"Lord, how often should I forgive someone who sins against me?
Seven times?" "No!" Jesus replied, "seventy times seven!"
Matthew 18:21–22 NLT

How often should we forgive other people? More times than we can count (Matthew 18:21-22). That's a mighty tall order, but we must remember that it's an order from God—an order that must be obeyed.

In God's curriculum, forgiveness isn't optional; it's a required course. Sometimes, of course, we have a very difficult time forgiving the people who have hurt us, but if we don't find it in our hearts to forgive them, we not only hurt ourselves, we also disobey our Father in Heaven. So we must forgive—and keep forgiving—as long as we live.

What makes a Christian a Christian is not perfection but forgiveness.

Max Lucado

By not forgiving, by not letting wrongs go, we aren't getting back at anyone. We are merely punishing ourselves by barricading our own hearts.

Jim Cymbala

A LESSON FOR THE HEART AND SOUL

If you're having trouble forgiving someone else . . . think about how many times other people have forgiven you!

A TERRIFIC TOMORROW

"I say this because I know what I am planning for you,"
says the Lord. "I have good plans for you, not plans to hurt you.
I will give you hope and a good future."
Jeremiah 29:11 NCV

How bright do you believe your future to be? Well, if you're a faithful believer, God has plans for you that are so bright that you'd better pack several pairs of sunglasses and a lifetime supply of sunblock!

The way that you think about your future will play a powerful role in determining how things turn out (it's called the "self-fulfilling prophecy," and it applies to everybody, including you). So here's another question: Are you expecting a terrific tomorrow, or are you dreading a terrible one? The answer to that question will have a powerful impact on the way tomorrow unfolds.

Today, as you live in the present and look to the future, remember that God has an amazing plan for you. Act—and believe—accordingly. And one more thing: don't forget the sunblock.

The pages of your past cannot be rewritten, but the pages of your tomorrows are blank.

Zig Ziglar

A LESSON FOR THE HEART AND SOUL

Even when the world seems dark, the future is bright for those who look to the Son.

OFFERING THANKS

In everything give thanks; for this is the will of
God in Christ Jesus for you.
1 Thessalonians 5:18 NKJV

Sometimes, life can be complicated, demanding, and frustrating. When the demands of life leave us rushing from place to place with scarcely a moment to spare, we may fail to pause and thank our Creator for His gifts. But, whenever we neglect to give proper thanks to the Father, we suffer because of our misplaced priorities.

Today, begin making a list of your blessings. You most certainly will not be able to make a complete list, but take a few moments and jot down as many blessings as you can. Then, give thanks to the Giver of all good things: God. His love for you is eternal, as are His gifts. And it's never too soon to offer Him thanks.

Grace is an outrageous blessing bestowed freely on a totally undeserving recipient.

Bill Hybels

It is when we give ourselves to be a blessing that we can specially count on the blessing of God.

Andrew Murray

BUILDING A BETTER YOU

Carve out time to thank God for His blessings. Take time out of every day (not just on Sundays) to praise God and thank Him for His gifts.

TRANSCENDENT LOVE

Who will separate us from the love of Christ?
Will tribulation, or distress, or persecution, or famine,
or nakedness, or peril, or sword? . . . But in all these things
we overwhelmingly conquer through Him who loved us.
Romans 8:35, 37 NASB

Where can we find God's love? Everywhere. God's love transcends space and time. It reaches beyond the Heavens, and it touches the darkest, smallest corner of every human heart. When we become passionate in our devotion to the Father, when we sincerely open our minds and hearts to Him, His love does not arrive "some day"—it arrives immediately.

Today, take God at His word and welcome His Son into your heart. When you do, God's transcendent love will surround you and transform you, now and forever.

The grace of God transcends all our feeble efforts to describe it. It cannot be poured into any mental receptacle without running over.

Vance Havner

God has pursued us from farther than space and longer than time.

John Eldredge

BUILDING A BETTER YOU

God's love makes everything better, including you.

YOUR PLANS AND GOD'S PLANS

A man's heart plans his way, but the Lord directs his steps.
Proverbs 16:9 NKJV

If you're like most people, you like being in control. Period. You want things to happen according to your wishes and according to your timetable. But sometimes, God has other plans . . . and He always has the final word. Are you embittered by a personal tragedy that you did not deserve and cannot understand? If so, it's time to make peace with life. It's time to forgive others, and, if necessary, to forgive yourself. It's time to accept the unchangeable past, to embrace the priceless present, and to have faith in the promise of tomorrow. It's time to trust God completely. And it's time to reclaim the peace—His peace—that can and should be yours.

So if you've encountered unfortunate circumstances that are beyond your power to control, accept those circumstances . . . and trust God. When you do, you can be comforted in the knowledge that your Creator is both loving and wise, and that He understands His plans perfectly, even when you do not.

Acceptance is resting in God's goodness, believing that He has all things under His control.

Charles Swindoll

A LESSON FOR THE HEART AND SOUL

When you encounter situations that you cannot change, you must learn the wisdom of acceptance . . . and you must learn to trust God.

OUR ROCK IN TURBULENT TIMES

And he said: "The Lord is my rock and my fortress and my deliverer; the God of my strength, in whom I will trust."
2 Samuel 22:2–3 NKJV

Psalm 145 promises, "The Lord is near to all who call on him, to all who call on him in truth. He fulfills the desires of those who fear him; he hears their cry and saves them" (vv. 18-20 NIV). And the words of Jesus offer us comfort: "These things I have spoken to you, that in Me you may have peace. In the world you will have tribulation; but be of good cheer, I have overcome the world" (John 16:33 NKJV).

As believers, we know that God loves us and that He will protect us. In times of hardship, He will comfort us; in times of sorrow, He will dry our tears. When we are troubled, or weak, or sorrowful, God is always with us. We must build our lives on the rock that cannot be shaken: We must trust in God. And then, we must get on with the hard work of tackling our problems . . . because if we don't, who will? Or should?

In order to realize the worth of the anchor, we need to feel the stress of the storm.

Corrie ten Boom

A LESSON FOR THE HEART AND SOUL

When times are tough, you should guard your heart by turning it over to God.

ASK AND RECEIVE

Ask, and it will be given to you; seek, and you will find;
knock, and it will be opened to you. For everyone who asks receives,
and he who seeks finds, and to him who knocks it will be opened.
Matthew 7:7–8 NKJV

Are you a person who asks God for guidance and strength? If so, then you're continually inviting your Creator to reveal Himself in a variety of ways. As a follower of Christ, you must do no less.

Jesus made it clear to His disciples: they should petition God to meet their needs. So should we. Genuine, heartfelt prayer produces powerful changes in us and in our world. When we lift our hearts to God, we open ourselves to a never-ending source of divine wisdom and infinite love.

Do you have questions about your future that you simply can't answer? Do you have needs that you simply can't meet by yourself? Do you sincerely seek to know God's purpose for your life? If so, ask Him for direction, for protection, and for strength—and then keep asking Him every day that you live. Whatever your need, no matter how great or small, pray about it and never lose hope. God is not just near; He is here, and He's perfectly capable of answering your prayers. Now, it's up to you to ask.

God's help is always available, but it is only given to those who seek it.

Max Lucado

A LESSON FOR THE HEART AND SOUL

Today, think of a specific need that is weighing heavily on your heart. Then, spend a few quiet moments asking God for His guidance and for His help.

THE GUIDEBOOK

All Scripture is given by inspiration of God,
and is profitable for doctrine, for reproof, for correction,
for instruction in righteousness, that the man of God may be complete,
thoroughly equipped for every good work.
2 Timothy 3:16–17 NKJV

God has given us a guidebook for righteous living called the Holy Bible. It contains thorough instructions which, if followed, lead to fulfillment, righteousness, and salvation. But, if we choose to ignore God's commandments, the results are as predictable as they are tragic.

God has given us the Bible for the purpose of knowing His promises, His power, His commandments, His wisdom, His love, and His Son. As we study God's teachings and apply them to our lives, we live by the Word that shall never pass away.

Today, let us follow God's commandments, and let us conduct our lives in such a way that we might be shining examples to our families, and, most importantly, to those who have not yet found Christ.

The Bible is a Christian's guidebook, and I believe the knowledge it sheds on pain and suffering is the great antidote to fear for suffering people. Knowledge can dissolve fear as light destroys darkness.

Philip Yancey

BUILDING A BETTER YOU

If you have a choice to make, the Bible can help you make it. If you've got questions, the Bible has answers.

A GODLY LEADER

But the noble man makes noble plans, and by noble deeds he stands.
Isaiah 32:8 NIV

Our world needs Christian leaders who willingly honor God with their words and their deeds, but not necessarily in that order.

If you seek to be a godly leader, then you must begin by being a worthy example to your family, to your friends, to your church, and to your community. After all, your words of instruction will never ring true unless you yourself are willing to follow them.

Are you the kind of leader whom you would want to follow? If so, congratulations. But if the answer to that question is no, then it's time to improve your leadership skills, beginning with the words that you speak and the example that you set, but not necessarily in that order.

People who inspire others are those who see invisible bridges at the end of dead-end streets.

Charles Swindoll

Great leaders understand that the right attitude will set the right atmosphere, which enables the right response from others.

John Maxwell

BUILDING A BETTER YOU

Leadership comes in many forms, and you can lead others in your own way using your own style.

COURAGE FOR CHANGING TIMES

Therefore do not worry about tomorrow, for tomorrow will worry about itself. Each day has enough trouble of its own.
Matthew 6:34 NIV

If you're graduating to another phase of life, everything around you may seem to be in a state of flux. And you may be required to make lots of adjustments. If all these events have left your head spinning and your heart pounding, don't worry. Although the world is in a state of constant change, God is not.

Are you anxious about situations that you cannot control? Take your anxieties to God. Are you troubled about changes that threaten to disrupt your life? Take your troubles to Him. Does your corner of the world seem to be trembling beneath your feet? Seek protection from the One who cannot be moved.

The same God who created the universe will protect you if you ask Him . . . so ask Him . . . and then serve Him with willing hands and a trusting heart. And rest assured that the world may change moment by moment, but God's love endures—unfathomable and unchanging—forever.

With God, it isn't who you were that matters; it's who you are becoming.

Liz Curtis Higgs

BUILDING A BETTER YOU

If a big change is called for, don't be afraid to make a big change—sometimes, one big leap is better than a thousand baby steps.

SAYING YES TO GOD

Fear thou not; for I am with thee.
Isaiah 41:10 KJV

Your decision to seek a deeper relationship with God will not remove all problems from your life; to the contrary, it will bring about a series of personal crises as you constantly seek to say "yes" to God although the world encourages you to do otherwise. Each time you are tempted to distance yourself from the Creator, you will face a spiritual crisis. A few of these crises may be monumental in scope, but most will be the small, everyday decisions of life. In fact, life here on earth can be seen as one test after another—and with each crisis comes yet another opportunity to grow closer to God . . . or to distance yourself from His plan for your life.

Today, you will face many opportunities to say "yes" to your Creator—and you will also encounter many opportunities to say "no" to Him. Your answers will determine the quality of your day and the direction of your life, so answer carefully . . . very carefully.

Adversity is not simply a tool. It is God's most effective tool for the advancement of our spiritual lives. The circumstances and events that we see as setbacks are oftentimes the very things that launch us into periods of intense spiritual growth. Once we begin to understand this, and accept it as a spiritual fact of life, adversity becomes easier to bear.

Charles Stanley

BUILDING A BETTER YOU

If you want to be more like Jesus, follow in His footsteps every day, obey His commandments every day, and share His never-ending love—every day.

COMFORTING OTHERS

Carry each other's burdens,
and in this way you will fulfill the law of Christ.
Galatians 6:2 NIV

We live in a world that is, on occasion, a frightening place. Sometimes, we sustain life-altering losses that are so profound and so tragic that it seems we could never recover. But, with God's help and with the help of encouraging family members and friends, we can recover.

In times of need, God's Word is clear: as believers, we must offer comfort to those in need by sharing not only our courage but also our faith. As the renowned revivalist Vance Havner observed, "No journey is complete that does not lead through some dark valleys. We can properly comfort others only with the comfort wherewith we ourselves have been comforted of God." Enough said.

God's promises are medicine for the broken heart. Let Him comfort you. And, after He has comforted you, try to share that comfort with somebody else. It will do both of you good.

Warren Wiersbe

When action-oriented compassion is absent, it's a tell-tale sign that something's spiritually amiss.

Bill Hybels

A LESSON FOR THE HEART AND SOUL

Never confuse encouragement with pity. Pity parties are best left unattended by you and by your family and friends.

THE INNER VOICE

*Let us draw near to God with a sincere heart in full assurance
of faith, having our hearts sprinkled to cleanse us from
a guilty conscience and having our bodies washed with pure water.*
Hebrews 10:22 NIV

American humorist Josh Billings observed, "Reason often makes mistakes, but conscience never does." How true. Even when we deceive our neighbors, and even when we attempt to deceive ourselves, God has given each of us a conscience, a small, quiet voice that tells us right from wrong. We must listen to that inner voice . . . or else we must accept the consequences that inevitably befall those who choose to rebel against God.

When we learn to listen to Christ's voice for the details of our daily decisions, we begin to know Him personally.

Catherine Marshall

Most of us follow our conscience as we follow a wheelbarrow. We push it in front of us in the direction we want to go.

Billy Graham

A LESSON FOR THE HEART AND SOUL

That quiet little voice inside your head will guide you down the right path if you listen carefully. Very often, your conscience will actually tell you what God wants you to do. So listen, learn, and behave accordingly.

COURTESY MATTERS

Out of respect for Christ, be courteously reverent to one another.
Ephesians 5:21 MSG

Did Christ instruct us in matters of etiquette and courtesy? Of course He did. Christ's instructions are clear: "In everything, therefore, treat people the same way you want them to treat you, for this is the Law and the Prophets" (Matthew 7:12 NASB). Jesus did not say, "In some things, treat people as you wish to be treated." And, He did not say, "From time to time, treat others with kindness." Christ said that we should treat others as we wish to be treated in every aspect of our daily lives. This, of course, is a tall order indeed, but as Christians, we are commanded to do our best.

Today, be a little kinder than necessary to family members, friends, and total strangers. And, as you consider all the things that Christ has done in your life, honor Him with your words and with your deeds. He expects no less, and He deserves no less.

Only the courteous can love, but it is love that makes them courteous.

C. S. Lewis

A LESSON FOR THE HEART AND SOUL

Remember: courtesy isn't optional. If you disagree, do so without being disagreeable; if you're angry, hold your tongue; if you're frustrated or tired, don't argue . . . take a nap.

HE REIGNS

In all your ways acknowledge Him, and He shall direct your paths.
Proverbs 3:6 NKJV

God is sovereign. He reigns over the entire universe, and He reigns over your little corner of that universe. Your challenge is to recognize God's sovereignty and live in accordance with His commandments. Sometimes, of course, this is easier said than done.

Your Heavenly Father may not always reveal Himself as quickly (or as clearly) as you would like. But rest assured: God is in control, God is here, and God intends to use you in wonderful, unexpected ways. He desires to lead you along a path of His choosing. Your challenge is to watch, to listen, to learn . . . and to follow.

He proves His sovereignty, not by intervening constantly and preventing these events, but by ruling and overruling them so that even tragedies end up accomplishing His ultimate purposes.

Warren Wiersbe

We do not understand the intricate pattern of the stars in their course, but we know that He Who created them does, and that just as surely as he guides them, He is charting a safe course for us.

Billy Graham

A LESSON FOR THE HEART AND SOUL

God is in control of our world . . . and your world. When something is beyond your control, place your total trust in Him.

SEEKING HIS WILL

Teach me to do Your will, for You are my God; Your Spirit is good.
Lead me in the land of uprightness.
Psalm 143:10 NKJV

God has a plan for our world and our lives. God does not do things by accident; He is willful and intentional. Unfortunately for us, we cannot always understand the will of God. Why? Because we are mortal beings with limited understanding. Although we cannot fully comprehend the will of God, we should always trust the will of God.

As this day unfolds, seek God's will and obey His Word. When you entrust your life to Him without reservation, He will give you the courage to meet any challenge, the strength to endure any trial, and the wisdom to live in His righteousness and in His peace.

"If the Lord will" is not just a statement on a believer's lips; it is the constant attitude of his heart.

Warren Wiersbe

He has the right to interrupt your life. He is Lord. When you accepted Him as Lord, you gave Him the right to help Himself to your life anytime He wants.

Henry Blackaby

BUILDING A BETTER YOU

When you place yourself in the center of God's will . . . He will provide for your needs and direct your path.

A HELPING HAND

Then a Samaritan traveling down the road came to where the hurt man was. When he saw the man, he felt very sorry for him. The Samaritan went to him, poured olive oil and wine on his wounds, and bandaged them. Then he put the hurt man on his own donkey and took him to an inn where he cared for him.

Luke 10:33–34 NCV

Sometimes we would like to help make the world a better place, but we're not sure how to do it. Jesus told the story of the "Good Samaritan," a man who helped a fellow traveler when no one else would. We, too, should be good Samaritans when we find people who need our help.

When bad things happen in our world, there's always something we can do. So what can you do to make God's world a better place? You can start by making your own corner of the world a little nicer place to live (by sharing kind words and good deeds). And then, you can take your concerns to God in prayer. Whether you've offered a helping hand or a heartfelt prayer, you've done a lot.

Do all the good you can. By all the means you can. In all the ways you can. In all the places you can. At all the times you can. To all the people you can. As long as ever you can.

John Wesley

A LESSON FOR THE HEART AND SOUL

Someone very near you may need a helping hand or a kind word, so keep your eyes open, and look for people who need your help, whether at home, at church, at work, or anywhere in between.

BEYOND ANXIETY

In the multitude of my anxieties within me,
Your comforts delight my soul.
Psalm 94:19 NKJV

God calls us to live above and beyond anxiety. God calls us to live by faith, not by fear. He instructs us to trust Him completely, this day and forever. But sometimes, trusting God is difficult, especially when we become caught up in the incessant demands of an anxious world.

When you feel anxious—and you will—return your thoughts to God's love. Then, take your concerns to Him in prayer, and to the best of your ability, leave them there. Whatever "it" is, God is big enough to handle it. Let Him. Now.

Worry and anxiety are sand in the machinery of life; faith is the oil.

E. Stanley Jones

Man without God is always torn between two urges. His nature prompts him to do wrong, and his conscience urges him to do right. Christ can rid you of that inner conflict.

Billy Graham

BUILDING A BETTER YOU

Divide your areas of concern into two categories: those you can control and those you cannot. Resolve never to waste time or energy worrying about the latter.

WHY DO BAD THINGS HAPPEN?

They won't be afraid of bad news;
their hearts are steady because they trust the Lord.
Psalm 112:7 NCV

If God is good, and if He made the world, why do bad things happen? Part of that question is easy to answer, and part of it isn't. Let's get to the easy part first: Sometimes, bad things happen because people disobey God's commandments and invite sadness and heartache into God's beautiful world.

But on other occasions, bad things happen, and it's nobody's fault. So who is to blame? Sometimes, nobody is to blame. Sometimes, things just happen and we simply cannot know why. Thankfully, all our questions will be answered . . . some day. The Bible promises that in Heaven we will understand all the reasons behind God's plans. But until then, we must simply trust that God is good, and that, in the end, He will make things right.

There is but one good; that is God. Everything else is good when it looks to Him and bad when it turns from Him.

C. S. Lewis

A LESSON FOR THE HEART AND SOUL

The grieving process takes time. God does not promise instantaneous healing, but He does promise healing: "I have heard your prayer, I have seen your tears; surely I will heal you" (2 Kings 20:5 NKJV).

BEYOND BITTERNESS

Don't insist on getting even; that's not for you to do.
"I'll do the judging," says God. "I'll take care of it."
Romans 12:19 MSG

Bitterness is a spiritual sickness. It will consume your soul; it is dangerous to your emotional health. It can destroy you if you let it . . . so don't let it!

If you are caught up in intense feelings of anger or resentment, you know all too well the destructive power of these emotions. How can you rid yourself of these feelings? First, you must prayerfully ask God to cleanse your heart. Then, you must learn to catch yourself whenever thoughts of bitterness or hatred begin to attack you. Your challenge is this: You must learn to resist negative thoughts before they hijack your emotions.

Matthew 5:22 teaches us that if we judge our brothers and sisters, we, too, will be subject to judgment. Let us refrain, then, from judging our neighbors. Instead, let us forgive them and love them, while leaving their judgment to a far more capable authority: the One who sits on His throne in Heaven.

Forgiveness is the key which unlocks the door of resentment and the handcuffs of hatred. It breaks the chains of bitterness and the shackles of selfishness.

Corrie ten Boom

A LESSON FOR THE HEART AND SOUL

Blaming others is easy . . . but it's usually wrong. Fixing mistakes is harder . . . but it's usually right.

UNBENDING TRUTH

Therefore, putting away lying, "Let each one of you speak truth with his neighbor," for we are members of one another.
Ephesians 4:25 NKJV

Oswald Chambers advised, "Never support an experience which does not have God as its source, and faith in God as its result." These words serve as a powerful reminder that as Christians we are called to walk with God and to obey His commandments. But, we live in a world that presents us with countless temptations to wander far from God's path. These temptations have the potential to destroy us, in part, because they cause us to be dishonest with ourselves and with others.

Dishonesty is a habit. Once we start bending the truth, we're likely to keep bending it. A far better strategy, of course, is to acquire the habit of being completely forthright with God, with other people, and with ourselves.

Honesty is also a habit, a habit that pays powerful dividends for those who place character above convenience. So, the next time you're tempted to bend the truth—or to break it—ask yourself this simple question: "What does God want me to do?" Then listen carefully to your conscience. When you do, your actions will be honorable, and your character will take care of itself.

It is the thoughts and intents of the heart that shape a person's life.
John Eldredge

A LESSON FOR THE HEART AND SOUL

Character matters. Your ability to witness for Christ depends more upon your actions than your words.

A SERIES OF CHOICES

But seek first his kingdom and his righteousness,
and all these things will be given to you as well.
Matthew 6:33 NIV

Face facts: Your life is a series of choices. From the instant you wake up in the morning until the moment you nod off to sleep at night, you make countless decisions—decisions about the things you do, decisions about the words you speak, and decisions about the way that you choose to direct your thoughts.

As a believer who has been transformed by the love of Jesus, you have every reason to make wise choices. But sometimes, when the daily grind threatens to grind you up and spit you out, you may make choices that are displeasing to God. When you do, you'll pay a price because you'll forfeit the happiness and the peace that might otherwise have been yours.

So, as you pause to consider the kind of Christian you are—and the kind of Christian you want to become—ask yourself whether you're sitting on the fence or standing in the light. The choice is yours . . . and so are the consequences.

Every time you make a choice, you are turning the central part of you, the part that chooses, into something a little different from what it was before.

C. S. Lewis

BUILDING A BETTER YOU

Wise choices bring you happiness; unwise choices don't. So whenever you have a choice to make, choose wisely and prayerfully.

IMPERFECT BEINGS, IMPERFECT FAITH

He who heeds the word wisely will find good,
and whoever trusts in the Lord, happy is he.
Proverbs 16:20 NKJV

Why are we humans plagued by worry? Because we are imperfect beings with imperfect faith. Even though we are Christians who have been given the assurance of salvation—even though we are Christians who have received the promise of God's love and protection—we find ourselves fretting over the countless details of everyday life. Jesus understood our concerns when He spoke the reassuring words found in Matthew 6: "Therefore I tell you, do not worry about your life . . ."

As you consider the promises of Jesus, remember that God still sits in His Heaven and you are His beloved child. Then, perhaps, you will worry a little less and trust God a little more, and that's as it should be because God is trustworthy . . . and you are protected.

Remember always that there are two things which are more utterly incompatible even than oil and water, and these two are trust and worry.

Hannah Whitall Smith

BUILDING A BETTER YOU

Focus on your work, not your worries. Worry is never a valid substitute for work, so get out there, do your best, and turn your worries over to God.

COMPASSIONATE SERVANTS

Finally, all of you be of one mind, having compassion for one another; love as brothers, be tenderhearted, be courteous.
1 Peter 3:8 NKJV

God's Word commands us to be compassionate, generous servants to those who need our support. As believers, we have been richly blessed by our Creator. We, in turn, are called to share our gifts, our possessions, our testimonies, and our talents.

Concentration camp survivor Corrie ten Boom correctly observed, "The measure of a life is not its duration but its donation." These words remind us that the quality of our lives is determined not by what we are able to take from others, but instead by what we are able to share with others.

The thread of compassion is woven into the very fabric of Christ's teachings. If we are to be disciples of Christ, we, too, must be zealous in caring for others. Our Savior expects no less from us. And He deserves no less.

Our Lord worked with people as they were, and He was patient—not tolerant of sin, but compassionate.

Vance Havner

A LESSON FOR THE HEART AND SOUL

It's good to feel compassion for others . . . but it's better to do something to ease their suffering. Martin Luther wrote, "Faith never asks whether good works are to be done, but has done them before there is time to ask the question, and it is always doing them." So when in doubt, do something good for somebody.

FIRST THINGS FIRST

Steep your life in God-reality, God-initiative, God-provisions.
Don't worry about missing out.
You'll find all your everyday human concerns will be met.
Matthew 6:33 MSG

Have you fervently asked God to help prioritize your life? Have you asked Him for guidance and for the courage to do the things that you know need to be done? If so, then you're continually inviting your Creator to reveal Himself in a variety of ways. As a follower of Christ, you must do no less.

When you make God a full partner in every aspect of your life, He will lead you along the proper path: His path. When you allow God to reign over your heart, He will honor you with spiritual blessings that are simply too numerous to count. So, as you plan for the day ahead, make God's will your ultimate priority. When you do, your daily to-do list will take care of itself.

Give to us clear vision that we may know where to stand and what to stand for. Let us not be content to wait and see what will happen, but give us the determination to make the right things happen.

Peter Marshall

BUILDING A BETTER YOU

Make time for God. Even if your day is filled to the brim with obligations and priorities, no priority is greater than your obligation to your Creator. Make sure to give Him the time He deserves, not only on Sundays, but also on every other day of the week.

CRITICS BEWARE

Don't pick on people, jump on their failures, criticize their faults—
unless, of course, you want the same treatment.
Don't condemn those who are down; that hardness can boomerang.
Be easy on people; you'll find life a lot easier.
Luke 6:37 MSG

From experience, we know that it is easier to criticize than to correct. And we know that it is easier to find faults than solutions. Yet the urge to criticize others remains a powerful temptation for most of us. Our task, as obedient believers, is to break the twin habits of negative thinking and critical speech.

Negativity is highly contagious. We give it to others who, in turn, give it back to us. This cycle can be broken by positive thoughts, heartfelt prayers, and encouraging words. As thoughtful servants of a loving God, we can use the transforming power of Christ's love to break the chains of negativity. And we should.

Never be afraid of the world's censure; its praise is much more to be dreaded.

C. H. Spurgeon

The scrutiny we give other people should be for ourselves.

Oswald Chambers

A LESSON FOR THE HEART AND SOUL

If you're tempted to be critical of others, remember that your ability to judge others requires a level of insight that you simply don't have. So do everybody (including yourself) a favor: don't criticize.

WHEN PEOPLE BEHAVE BADLY

Bad temper is contagious—don't get infected.
Proverbs 22:25 MSG

Face it: sometimes people can be rude . . . very rude. When other people are unkind to you, you may be tempted to strike back, either verbally or in some other way. Don't do it! Instead, remember that God corrects other people's behaviors in His own way, and He doesn't need your help (even if you're totally convinced that He does).

So, when other people behave cruelly, foolishly, or impulsively—as they will from time to time—don't be hotheaded. Instead, speak up for yourself as politely as you can, and walk away. Then, forgive everybody as quickly as you can, and leave the rest up to God.

We are all fallen creatures and all very hard to live with.

C. S. Lewis

Some folks cause happiness wherever they go, others whenever they go.

Barbara Johnson

A LESSON FOR THE HEART AND SOUL

Unless the person you're trying to change is a young child, and unless you are that child's parent or guardian, don't try to change him or her. Why? Because teenagers and adults change when they want to, not when you want them to.

DOUBT AND THE TRUE BELIEVER

Immediately the father of the child cried out and said with tears,
"Lord, I believe; help my unbelief!"
Mark 9:24 NKJV

Even the most faithful Christians are overcome by occasional bouts of fear and doubt. You are no different. When you feel that your faith is being tested to its limits, seek the comfort and assurance of the One who sent His Son as a sacrifice for you.

Have you ever felt your faith in God slipping away? If so, you are not alone. Every life—including yours—is a series of successes and failures, celebrations and disappointments, joys and sorrows, hopes and doubts. But even when you feel very distant from God, God is never distant from you. When you sincerely seek His presence, He will touch your heart, calm your fears, and restore your faith in the future . . . and your faith in Him.

There is a difference between doubt and unbelief. Doubt is a matter of mind: we cannot understand what God is doing or why He is doing it. Unbelief is a matter of will: we refuse to believe God's Word and obey what He tells us to do.

Warren Wiersbe

BUILDING A BETTER YOU

Doubts creeping in? Increase the amount of time you spend in Bible Study, prayer, and worship.

STANDING ON THE ROCK

He heals the brokenhearted and binds up their wounds.
Psalm 147:3 NIV

God loves us and protects us. In times of trouble, He comforts us; in times of sorrow, He dries our tears. Psalm 147 promises, "He heals the brokenhearted, and binds their wounds" (v. 3, NASB). When we are troubled, we must call upon God, and—in His own time and according to His own plan—He will heal us.

Do you feel fearful, or weak, or sorrowful? Are you discouraged or bitter? Do you feel "stuck" in a place that is uncomfortable for you? If so, remember that God is as near as your next breath. So trust Him and turn to Him for solace, for security, and for salvation. And build your life on the rock that cannot be shaken . . . that rock is God.

Under heaven's lock and key, we are protected by the most efficient security system available: the power of God.

Charles Swindoll

When you fall and skin your knees and skin your heart, He'll pick you up.

Charles Stanley

A LESSON FOR THE HEART AND SOUL

Earthly security is an illusion. Your only real security comes from the loving heart of God.

A LIGHT TO MY PATH

Your word is a lamp to my feet and a light to my path.
Psalm 119:105 NKJV

Are you a person who trusts God's Word without reservation? Hopefully so, because the Bible is unlike any other book—it is a guidebook for life here on earth and for life eternal. The Psalmist describes God's Word as, "a light to my path." Is the Bible your lamp? If not, you are depriving yourself of a priceless gift from the Creator.

Vance Havner observed, "It takes calm, thoughtful, prayerful meditation on the Word to extract its deepest nourishment." How true. God's Word can be a roadmap to a place of righteousness and abundance. Make it your roadmap. God's wisdom can be a light to guide your steps. Claim it as your light today, tomorrow, and every day of your life—and then walk confidently in the footsteps of God's only begotten Son.

Weave the unveiling fabric of God's word through your heart and mind. It will hold strong, even if the rest of life unravels.

Gigi Graham Tchividjian

A LESSON FOR THE HEART AND SOUL

God's wisdom is found in God's Word. When you pick up your Bible and read it, you tune into that wisdom. So do the wise thing: make Bible reading an important part of your day. Every day.

HAPPINESS AND HOLINESS

Happy are the people who live at your Temple . . . .
Happy are those whose strength comes from you.
Psalm 84:4–5 NKJV

Do you seek happiness, abundance, and contentment? If so, here are some things you should do: Love God and His Son; depend upon God for strength; try, to the best of your abilities, to follow God's will; and strive to obey His Holy Word. When you do these things, you'll discover that happiness goes hand-in-hand with righteousness. The happiest people are not those who rebel against God; the happiest people are those who love God and obey His commandments.

What does life have in store for you? A world full of possibilities (of course it's up to you to seize them) and God's promise of abundance (of course it's up to you to accept it). Your Creator has blessed you beyond measure. Honor Him with your prayers, your words, your deeds, and your joy.

No man should desire to be happy who is not at the same time holy. He should spend his efforts in seeking to know and do the will of God, leaving to Christ the matter of how happy he shall be.

A. W. Tozer

BUILDING A BETTER YOU

If you want to find lasting happiness, don't chase it. Instead, do your duty, obey your God, and wait for happiness to find you.

THE WISDOM TO BE HUMBLE

Don't be selfish....Be humble,
thinking of others as better than yourself.
Philippians 2:3 TLB

God's Word clearly instructs us to be humble. And that's good because, as fallible human beings, we have so very much to be humble about! Yet some of us continue to puff ourselves up, seeming to say, "Look at me!" To do so is wrong.

As Christians, we have been refashioned and saved by Jesus Christ, and that salvation came not because of our own good works but because of God's grace. How, then, can we be prideful? The answer, of course, is that, if we are honest with ourselves and with our God, we simply can't be boastful . . . we must, instead, be eternally grateful and exceedingly humble. The good things in our lives, including our loved ones, come from God. He deserves the credit— and we deserve the glorious experience of giving it to Him.

Because Christ Jesus came to the world clothed in humility, he will always be found among those who are clothed with humility. He will be found among the humble people.

A. W. Tozer

BUILDING A BETTER YOU

You must remain humble or face the consequences. Pride does go before the fall, but humility often prevents the fall.

THE ATTITUDE OF A LEADER

Those who are wise will shine like the brightness of the heavens,
and those who lead many to righteousness,
like the stars for ever and ever.
Daniel 12:3 NIV

John Maxwell writes, "Great leaders understand that the right attitude will set the right atmosphere, which enables the right response from others." If you are in a position of leadership—whether as a leader at your work, your church, or your school—it's up to you to set the right tone by maintaining the right attitude.

Our world needs Christian leaders, and so do your family members and coworkers. You can become a trusted, competent, thoughtful leader if you learn to maintain the right attitude: One that is realistic, optimistic, forward looking, and Christ-centered.

When God wants to accomplish something, He calls dedicated men and women to challenge His people and lead the way.

Warren Wiersbe

BUILDING A BETTER YOU

If you want to be a godly leader, you must first learn to be a faithful follower, a follower of the man from Galilee. Once you've learned to walk with Jesus, you'll be ready to lead others by your words and, more importantly, by your example.

ON A MISSION FOR GOD

But you are a chosen generation, a royal priesthood, a holy nation,
His own special people, that you may proclaim the praises
of Him who called you out of darkness into His marvelous light.
1 Peter 2:9 NKJV

Whether you realize it or not, you are on a personal mission for God. As a Christian, that mission is straightforward: Honor God, accept Christ as your personal Savior, and serve God's children.

Of course, you will encounter impediments as you attempt to discover the exact nature of God's purpose for your life, but you must never lose sight of the overriding purposes that God has established for all believers. You will encounter these overriding purposes again and again as you worship your Creator and study His Word.

Every day offers countless opportunities to serve God and to worship Him. When you do so, He will bless you in miraculous ways. May you continue to seek God's will, may you trust His Word, and may you place Him where He belongs: at the very center of your life.

The born-again Christian sees life not as a blurred, confused, meaningless mass, but as something planned and purposeful.

Billy Graham

BUILDING A BETTER YOU

God has a plan for your life, a definite purpose that you can fulfill . . . or not. Your challenge is to pray for God's guidance and to follow wherever He leads.

NEW BEGINNINGS AND GLORIOUS OPPORTUNITIES

Make the most of every opportunity.
Colossians 4:5 NIV

Are you excited about the opportunities of today and thrilled by the possibilities of tomorrow? Do you confidently expect God to lead you to a place of abundance, peace, and joy? And, when your days on earth are over, do you expect to receive the priceless gift of eternal life? If you trust God's promises, and if you have welcomed God's Son into your heart, then you believe that your future is intensely and eternally bright.

Today, as you prepare to meet the duties of everyday life, pause and consider God's promises. And then think for a moment about the wonderful future that awaits all believers, including you. God has promised that your future is secure. Trust that promise, and celebrate the life of abundance and eternal joy that is now yours through Christ.

With the right attitude and a willingness to pay the price, almost anyone can pursue nearly any opportunity and achieve it.

John Maxwell

BUILDING A BETTER YOU

God gives us opportunities for a reason: to use them. And, God wants you to make the most out of all the opportunities He sends your way. Billy Graham observed, "Life is a glorious opportunity." That's sound advice, so keep looking for your opportunities until you find them, and when you find them, take advantage of them sooner rather than later.

THE CHAINS OF PERFECTIONISM

Those who wait for perfect weather will never plant seeds;
those who look at every cloud will never harvest crops.
Ecclesiastes 11:4 NCV

The media delivers an endless stream of messages that tell you how to look, how to behave, and how to dress. The media's expectations are impossible to meet—God's are not. God doesn't expect perfection . . . and neither should you.

If you find yourself bound up by the chains of perfectionism, it's time to ask yourself who you're trying to impress, and why. If you're trying to impress other people, it's time to reconsider your priorities. Your first responsibility is to the Heavenly Father who created you and to His Son who saved you. Then, you bear a powerful responsibility to your family. But, when it comes to meeting society's unrealistic expectations, forget it! After all, pleasing God is simply a matter of obeying His commandments and accepting His Son. But as for pleasing everybody else? That's impossible!

What makes a Christian a Christian is not perfection but forgiveness.

Max Lucado

BUILDING A BETTER YOU

Accept your own imperfections: If you're caught up in the modern-day push toward perfection, grow up . . . and then lighten up on yourself.

THE GREATEST AMONG US

So think clearly and exercise self-control. Look forward to the special blessings that will come to you at the return of Jesus Christ.
1 Peter 1:13 NLT

Jesus teaches that the most esteemed men and women are not the leaders of society or the captains of industry. To the contrary, Jesus teaches that the greatest among us are those who choose to minister and to serve.

Today, you may feel the temptation to build yourself up in the eyes of your neighbors. Resist that temptation. Instead, serve your neighbors quietly and without fanfare. Then, when you have done your best to serve your community and to serve your God, you can rest comfortably knowing that in the eyes of God, you have achieved greatness. And God's eyes, after all, are the only ones that really count.

God will open up places of service for you as He sees you are ready. Meanwhile, study the Bible and give yourself a chance to grow.

Warren Wiersbe

Have thy tools ready; God will find thee work.

Charles Kingsley

A LESSON FOR THE HEART AND SOUL

Simplicity and peace are two concepts that are closely related. Complexity and peace are not.

THY WILL BE DONE

Shall I not drink from the cup the Father has given me?
John 18:11 NLT

All of us must, from time to time, endure days filled with suffering and pain. And as human beings with limited understanding, we can never fully understand the plans of our Father in Heaven. But as believers in a benevolent God, we must always trust Him.

When Jesus went to the Mount of Olives, He poured out His heart to God (Luke 22). Jesus knew of the agony that He was destined to endure, but He also knew that God's will must be done.

We, like our Savior, face trials that bring fear and trembling to the very depths of our souls, but like Christ, we, too, must seek God's will, not our own. When we learn to accept God's will without reservation, we experience the peace that He offers to wise believers who trust Him completely.

Our Lord never asks us to decide for Him; He asks us to yield to Him—a very different matter.

Oswald Chambers

BUILDING A BETTER YOU

You should learn from the past, but you should never allow yourself to become stuck there. Once you have made peace with the past, you are then free to live more fully in the present . . . and that's precisely what you should do.

LOOK BEFORE YOU LEAP

An impulsive vow is a trap; later you'll wish you could get out of it.
Proverbs 20:25 MSG

Are you, at times, just a little bit impulsive? Do you sometimes look before you leap? If so, God wants to have a little chat with you.

God's Word is clear: as believers, we are called to lead lives of discipline, diligence, moderation, and maturity. But the world often tempts us to behave otherwise. Everywhere we turn, or so it seems, we are faced with powerful temptations to behave in undisciplined, ungodly ways.

God's Word instructs us to be disciplined in our thoughts and our actions; God's Word warns us against the dangers of impulsive behavior. As believers in a just God, we should act and react accordingly.

Plan ahead—it wasn't raining when Noah built the ark.

Anonymous

The man who prays ceases to be a fool.

Oswald Chambers

BUILDING A BETTER YOU

If you can't seem to put the brakes on impulsive behavior . . . you're not praying hard enough.

NEVER-ENDING LOVE

And he has given us this command:
Whoever loves God must also love his brother.
1 John 4:21 NIV

C. S. Lewis observed, "A man's spiritual health is exactly proportional to his love for God." If we are to enjoy the spiritual health that God intends for us, we must praise Him, we must love Him, and we must obey Him.

When we worship God faithfully and obediently, we invite His love into our hearts. When we truly worship God, we allow Him to rule over our days and our lives. In turn, we grow to love God even more deeply as we sense His love for us.

Today, open your heart to the Father. And let your obedience be a fitting response to His never-ending love.

I love Him because He first loved me, and He still does love me, and He will love me forever and ever.

Bill Bright

A man's spiritual health is exactly proportional to his love for God.

C. S. Lewis

A LESSON FOR THE HEART AND SOUL

Because God first loved you, you should love Him. And one way that you demonstrate your love is by obeying Him.

YOUR SPIRITUAL JOURNEY

*Know the love of Christ which surpasses knowledge,
that you may be filled up to all the fullness of God.*
Ephesians 3:19 NASB

The journey toward spiritual maturity lasts a lifetime. As Christians, we can and should continue to grow in the love and the knowledge of our Savior as long as we live. When we cease to grow, either emotionally or spiritually, we do ourselves a profound disservice. But, if we study God's Word, if we obey His commandments, and if we live in the center of His will, we will not be "stagnant" believers; we will, instead, be healthy, growing Christians.

Life is a series of decisions. Each day, we make countless decisions that can bring us closer to God . . . or not. When we live according to the principles contained in God's Holy Word, we embark upon a journey of spiritual maturity that results in life abundant and life eternal.

I've never met anyone who became instantly mature. It's a painstaking process that God takes us through, and it includes such things as waiting, failing, losing, and being misunderstood—each calling for extra doses of perseverance.

Charles Swindoll

BUILDING A BETTER YOU

Today, think about the quality of the choices that you've made recently. Are these choices helping you become a more mature Christian? If so, don't change. If not, think about the quality of your decisions, the consequences of those decisions, and the steps that you can take to make better decisions.

MAKING PEACE WITH YOUR PAST

The Lord says, "Forget what happened before, and do not think
about the past. Look at the new thing I am going to do.
It is already happening. Don't you see it? I will make a road
in the desert and rivers in the dry land."
Isaiah 43:18–19 NCV

Have you made peace with your past? If so, congratulations. But, if you are mired in the quicksand of regret, it's time to plan your escape. How can you do so? By accepting what has been and by trusting God for what will be.

Because you are human, you may be slow to forget yesterday's disappointments. But, if you sincerely seek to focus your hopes and energies on the future, then you must find ways to accept the past, no matter how difficult it may be to do so. So, if you have not yet made peace with the past, today is the day to declare an end to all hostilities. When you do, you can then turn your thoughts to the wondrous promises of God and to the glorious future that He has in store for you.

Don't let yesterday use up too much of today.

Dennis Swanberg

BUILDING A BETTER YOU

The past is past, so don't invest all your energy there. If you're focused on the past, change your focus. If you're living in the past, it's time to stop living there.

PRAISE HIM

Praise the Lord! Oh, give thanks to the Lord, for He is good!
For His mercy endures forever.
Psalm 106:1 NKJV

Sometimes, in our rush "to get things done," we simply don't stop long enough to pause and thank our Creator for the countless blessings He has bestowed upon us. But when we slow down and express our gratitude to the One who made us, we enrich our own lives and the lives of those around us.

Thanksgiving should become a habit, a regular part of our daily routines. God has blessed us beyond measure, and we owe Him everything, including our eternal praise. Let us praise Him today, tomorrow, and throughout eternity.

The time for universal praise is sure to come some day. Let us begin to do our part now.

Hannah Whitall Smith

The Bible instructs—and experience teaches—that praising God results in our burdens being lifted and our joys being multiplied.

Jim Gallery

A LESSON FOR THE HEART AND SOUL

Remember that it always pays to praise your Creator. That's why thoughtful believers (like you) make it a habit to carve out quiet moments throughout the day to praise God.

SOLVING PROBLEMS

People who do what is right may have many problems,
but the Lord will solve them all.
Psalm 34:19 NCV

Life is an exercise in problem-solving. The question is not whether we will encounter problems; the real question is how we will choose to address them. When it comes to solving the problems of everyday living, we often know precisely what needs to be done, but we may be slow in doing it—especially if what needs to be done is difficult or uncomfortable for us. So we put off till tomorrow what should be done today.

The words of Psalm 34 remind us that the Lord solves problems for "people who do what is right." And usually, doing "what is right" means doing the uncomfortable work of confronting our problems sooner rather than later. So with no further ado, let the problem-solving begin . . . now.

We are all faced with a series of great opportunities, brilliantly disguised as unsolvable problems. Unsolvable without God's wisdom, that is.

Charles Swindoll

BUILDING A BETTER YOU

Everyone has problems, but not everyone deals with their problems in the same way. The way you address your problems—whether you choose to avoid them or confront them—determines how successfully—and how quickly—you overcome them.

BE STILL

Be still, and know that I am God.
Psalm 46:10 NKJV

D o you take time each day for an extended period of silence? And during those precious moments, do you sincerely open your heart to your Creator? If so, you are wise and you are blessed.

The world can be a noisy place, a place filled to the brim with distractions, interruptions, and frustrations. And if you're not careful, the struggles and stresses of everyday living can rob you of the peace that should rightfully be yours because of your personal relationship with Christ. So take time each day to quietly commune with your Savior. When you do, those moments of silence will enable you to participate more fully in the only source of peace that endures: God's peace.

Growth takes place in quietness, in hidden ways, in silence and solitude. The process is not accessible to observation.

Eugene Peterson

Noise and words and frenzied, hectic schedules dull our senses, closing our ears to His still, small voice and making us numb to His touch.

Charles Swindoll

A LESSON FOR THE HEART AND SOUL

You live in a noisy world filled with distractions, a world where silence is in short supply. But God wants you to carve out quiet moments with Him. Silence is, indeed, golden.

DISCIPLINE YOURSELF

Discipline yourself for the purpose of godliness.
1 Timothy 4:7 NASB

A re you a self-disciplined person? If so, congratulations . . . your disciplined approach to life can help you can build a more meaningful relationship with God. Why? Because God expects all His believers (including you) to lead lives of disciplined obedience to Him . . . and He rewards those believers who do.

Sometimes, it's hard to be dignified and disciplined. Why? Because you live in a world where many prominent people want you to believe that dignified, self-disciplined behavior is going out of style. But don't deceive yourself: self-discipline never goes out of style.

Your greatest accomplishments will probably require plenty of work and a heaping helping of self-discipline—which, by the way, is perfectly fine with God. After all, He knows that you're up to the task, and He has big plans for you. God will do His part to fulfill those plans, and the rest, of course, depends upon you.

Nothing of value is ever acquired without discipline.

Gordan MacDonald

BUILDING A BETTER YOU

A disciplined lifestyle gives you more control: The more disciplined you become, the more you can take control over your life (which, by the way, is far better than letting your life take control over you).

THE SEEDS OF GENEROSITY

Freely you have received, freely give.
Matthew 10:8 NKJV

Paul reminds us that when we sow the seeds of generosity, we reap bountiful rewards in accordance with God's plan for our lives. Thus, we are instructed to give cheerfully and without reservation: "But this I say, He which soweth sparingly shall reap also sparingly; and he which soweth bountifully shall reap also bountifully. Every man according as he purposeth in his heart, so let him give; not grudgingly, or of necessity: for God loveth a cheerful giver" (2 Corinthians 9:6-7 KJV).

Today, make this pledge and keep it: Be a cheerful, generous, courageous giver. The world needs your help, and you need the spiritual rewards that will be yours when you give it.

Two works of mercy set a man free: forgive and you will be forgiven, and give and you will receive.

St. Augustine

All the blessings we enjoy are divine deposits, committed to our trust on this condition: that they should be dispensed for the benefit of our neighbors.

John Calvin

A LESSON FOR THE HEART AND SOUL

God has given you countless blessings . . . and He wants you to share them.

HIS COMFORTING HAND

Nevertheless God, who comforts the downcast, comforted us . . . .
2 Corinthians 7:6 NKJV

If you have been touched by the transforming hand of Jesus, then you have every reason to live courageously. Still, even if you are a dedicated Christian, you may find yourself discouraged by the inevitable disappointments and tragedies that occur in the lives of believers and non-believers alike.

The next time you find your courage tested to the limit, lean upon God's promises. Trust His Son. Remember that God is always near and that He is your protector and your deliverer. When you are worried, anxious, or afraid, call upon Him and accept the touch of His comforting hand. Remember that God rules both mountaintops and valleys—with limitless wisdom and love—now and forever.

God's promises are medicine for the broken heart. Let Him comfort you. And, after He has comforted you, try to share that comfort with somebody else. It will do both of you good.

Warren Wiersbe

BUILDING A BETTER YOU

Perhaps you have become wrapped up in the world's problems or your own problems. If so, it's time to focus more on your spiritual blessings as you open yourself up to God. When you do, God will bless you and comfort you.

DISCOVERING GOD'S PLANS

For God is working in you, giving you the desire to obey him
and the power to do what pleases him.
Philippians 2:13 NLT

If you seek to live in accordance with God's will for your life—and you should—then you will live in accordance with His commandments. You will study God's Word, and you will be watchful for His signs. You will associate with fellow Christians who will encourage your spiritual growth, and you will listen to that inner voice that speaks to you in the quiet moments of your daily devotionals.

God intends to use you in wonderful, unexpected ways if you let Him. The decision to seek God's plan and to follow it is yours and yours alone. The consequences of that decision have implications that are both profound and eternal, so choose carefully.

The really committed leave the safety of the harbor, accept the risk of the open seas of faith, and set their compasses for the place of total devotion to God and whatever life adventures He plans for them.

Bill Hybels

BUILDING A BETTER YOU

God has a plan for the world and for you. When you discover His plan for your life—and when you follow in the footsteps of His Son—you will be rewarded. The place where God is leading you is the place where you must go.

WHEN ANGER IS OKAY

The face of the Lord is against those who do evil.
Psalm 34:16 NKJV

Sometimes, anger can be a good thing. In the 22nd chapter of Matthew, we see how Christ responded when He confronted the evildoings of those who invaded His Father's house of worship: "And Jesus entered the temple and drove out all those who were buying and selling in the temple, and overturned the tables of the moneychangers and the seats of those who were selling doves" (v. 12 NASB). Thus, Jesus proved that righteous indignation is an appropriate response to evil.

When you come face-to-face with the devil's handiwork, don't be satisfied to remain safely on the sidelines. Instead, follow in the footsteps of your Savior. Jesus never compromised with evil, and neither should you.

Anger unresolved will only bring you woe.

Kay Arthur

Bitterness and anger, usually over trivial things, make havoc of homes, churches, and friendships.

Warren Wiersbe

BUILDING A BETTER YOU

Angry words are dangerous to your emotional and spiritual health, not to mention your relationships. So treat anger as an uninvited guest, and usher it away as quickly—and as quietly—as possible.

THE RIGHT KIND OF ATTITUDE

Let the words of my mouth and the meditation of my heart
be acceptable in Your sight, O Lord,
my strength and my Redeemer.
Psalm 19:14 NKJV

What is your attitude today? Are you fearful or worried? Are you more concerned about pleasing your friends than about pleasing your God? Are you bitter, confused, cynical, or pessimistic? If so, it's time to have a little chat with your Father in Heaven.

God intends that your life be filled with spiritual abundance and joy—but God will not force His joy upon you—you must claim it for yourself. So do yourself this favor: accept God's gifts with a smile on your face, a song on your lips, and joy in your heart. Think optimistically about yourself and your future. Give thanks to the One who has given you everything, and trust in your heart that He wants to give you so much more.

The things we think are the things that feed our souls. If we think on pure and lovely things, we shall grow pure and lovely like them; and the converse is equally true.

Hannah Whitall Smith

A LESSON FOR THE HEART AND SOUL

If you're a Christian, you have every reason on earth—and in Heaven—to have a positive attitude.

BEHAVIOR REFLECTS BELIEF

As you have therefore received Christ Jesus the Lord, so walk in Him,
rooted and built up in Him and established in the faith,
as you have been taught, abounding in it with thanksgiving.
Colossians 2:6–7 NKJV

As Christians, we must do our best to make sure that our actions are accurate reflections of our beliefs. Our theology must be demonstrated, not only by our words but, more importantly, by our actions. In short, we should be practical believers, quick to act whenever we see an opportunity to serve God.

English clergyman Thomas Fuller observed, "He does not believe who does not live according to his beliefs." These words are most certainly true. Like it or not, your life is an accurate reflection of your creed. If this fact gives you cause for concern, don't bother talking about the changes that you intend to make—make them. And then, when your good deeds speak for themselves—as they most certainly will—don't interrupt.

The simple fact is that if we sow a lifestyle that is in direct disobedience to God's Word, we ultimately reap disaster.

Charles Swindoll

A LESSON FOR THE HEART AND SOUL

Ask yourself if your behavior has been radically changed by your unfolding relationship with God. If the answer to this question is unclear to you—or if the honest answer is a resounding no—think of a single step you can take, a positive change in your life, that will bring you closer to your Creator.

PATS ON THE BACK

So then we pursue the things which make for peace
and the building up of one another.
Romans 14:19 NASB

Life is a team sport, and all of us need occasional pats on the back from our teammates. In the book of Ephesians, Paul writes, "Do not let any unwholesome talk come out of your mouths, but only what is helpful for building others up according to their needs, that it may benefit those who listen" (4:29 NIV). Paul reminds us that when we choose our words carefully, we can have a powerful impact on those around us.

Since we don't always know who needs our help, the best strategy is to encourage all the people who cross our paths. So today, be a world-class source of encouragement to everyone you meet. Never has the need been greater.

How many people stop because so few say, "Go!"

Charles Swindoll

Make it a rule, and pray to God to help you to keep it, never to lie down at night without being able to say: "I have made at least one human being a little wiser, a little happier, or a little better this day."

Charles Kingsley

BUILDING A BETTER YOU

You should seek out encouraging friends who can lift you up, and you should strive to be an encouraging friend to others.

ENTHUSIASTIC SERVICE

Do your work with enthusiasm.
Work as if you were serving the Lord,
not as if you were serving only men and women.
Ephesians 6:7 NCV

Do you see each day as a glorious opportunity to serve God and to do His will? Are you enthused about life, or do you struggle through each day giving scarcely a thought to God's blessings? Are you constantly praising God for His gifts, and are you sharing His Good News with the world? And are you excited about the possibilities for service that God has placed before you, whether at home, at work, at church, or at school? You should be.

You are the recipient of Christ's sacrificial love. Accept it enthusiastically and share it fervently. Jesus deserves your enthusiasm; the world deserves it; and you deserve the experience of sharing it.

We must go out and live among them, manifesting the gentle, loving spirit of our Lord. We need to make friends before we can hope to make converts.

Lottie Moon

One of the great needs in the church today is for every Christian to become enthusiastic about his faith in Jesus Christ.

Billy Graham

A LESSON FOR THE HEART AND SOUL

If you become excited about life . . . life will become an exciting adventure.

FAITH TO SHARE

This and this only has been my appointed work:
getting this news to those who have never heard of God,
and explaining how it works by simple faith and plain truth.
1 Timothy 2:7 MSG

Genuine faith is never meant to be locked up in the heart of a believer; to the contrary, it is meant to be shared with the world. But, if you sincerely seek to share your faith, you must first find it.

When a suffering woman sought healing by merely touching the hem of His cloak, Jesus replied, "Daughter, be of good comfort; thy faith hath made thee whole" (Matthew 9:22 KJV). The message to believers of every generation is clear: live by faith today and every day.

How can you strengthen your faith? Through praise, through worship, through Bible study, and through prayer. And, as your faith becomes stronger, you will find ways to share it with your friends, your family, and with the world.

Do something that demonstrates faith, for faith with no effort is no faith at all.

Max Lucado

A LESSON FOR THE HEART AND SOUL

Don't be embarrassed to discuss your faith: You need not have attended seminary to have worthwhile opinions about your faith.

GOD'S PLAN FOR YOU AND YOUR FAMILY

Unless the Lord builds the house, they labor in vain who build it;
Unless the Lord guards the city, the watchman stays awake in vain.
Psalm 127:1 NKJV

As you consider God's purpose for your own life, you must also consider how your plans will effect the most important people whom God has entrusted to your care: your loved ones.

A loving family is a treasure from God. If you happen to be a member of a close knit, supportive clan, offer a word of thanks to your Creator. He has blessed you with one of His most precious earthly possessions. Your obligation, in response to God's gift, is to treat your family in ways that are consistent with His commandments. So, as you prayerfully seek God's direction, remember that He has important plans for your home life as well as your professional life. It's up to you to act—and to plan—accordingly.

Living life with a consistent spiritual walk deeply influences those we love most.

Vonette Bright

While you can't do much about your ancestors, you can influence your descendants greatly.

John Maxwell

A LESSON FOR THE HEART AND SOUL

Don't give up on God. And remember: He will never give up on you or your family.

A PEACE YOU CANNOT BUY

Peace, peace to you, and peace to your helpers!
For your God helps you.
1 Chronicles 12:18 NKJV

Sometimes, our financial struggles are simply manifestations of the inner conflict that we feel when we stray from God's path. The beautiful words of John 14:27 remind us that Jesus offers us peace, not as the world gives, but as He alone gives. Our challenge is to accept Christ's peace into our hearts and then, as best we can, to share His peace with our families and friends.

When we summon the courage and the determination to implement a sensible financial plan, we invite peace into our lives. But, we should never confuse earthly peace (with a small "p") with spiritual Peace (the Heavenly Peace—with a capital "P"—that flows from the Prince of Peace).

Have you found the genuine peace that can be yours through Christ? Or are you still rushing after the illusion of "peace and happiness" that the world promises but cannot deliver? Today, as a gift to yourself and to your loved ones, claim the inner peace that is your spiritual birthright: The peace of Jesus Christ. It is offered freely; it has been paid for in full; it is yours for the asking. So ask. And then share.

Financial peace can, and should, be yours. But the spiritual peace that stems from your personal relationship with Jesus must be yours if you are to receive the eternal abundance of our Lord. Claim that abundance today.

BUILDING A BETTER YOU

You can't fully enjoy financial peace . . . until you fully accept God's peace.

GOD IS LOVE

God is love; and he that dwelleth in love dwelleth in God,
and God in him.
1 John 4:16 KJV

The Bible makes this promise: God is love. It's a sweeping statement, a profoundly important description of what God is and how God works. God's love is perfect. When we open our hearts to His perfect love, we are touched by the Creator's hand, and we are transformed.

Today, even if you can only carve out a few quiet moments, offer sincere prayers of thanksgiving to your Creator. He loves you now and throughout all eternity. Open your heart to His presence and His love.

Even when we cannot see the why and wherefore of God's dealings, we know that there is love in and behind them, so we can rejoice always.

J. I. Packer

The life of faith is a daily exploration of the constant and countless ways in which God's grace and love are experienced.

Eugene Peterson

A LESSON FOR THE HEART AND SOUL

When all else fails, God's love does not. You can always depend upon God's love. And He is always your ultimate protection.

REJOICE!

Rejoice in the Lord always. Again I will say, rejoice!
Philippians 4:4 NKJV

Oswald Chambers correctly observed, "Joy is the great note all throughout the Bible." C. S. Lewis echoed that thought when he wrote, "Joy is the serious business of Heaven." But, even the most dedicated Christians can, on occasion, forget to celebrate each day for what it is: a priceless gift from God.

Today, let us celebrate life as God intended. Today, let us share the Good News of Jesus Christ. Today, let us put smiles on our faces, kind words on our lips, and songs in our hearts. Let us be generous with our praise and free with our encouragement. And then, when we have celebrated life to the fullest, let us invite others to do likewise. After all, this is God's day, and He has given us clear instructions for its use. We are commanded to rejoice and be glad. So, with no further ado, let the celebration begin.

God has a course mapped out for your life, and all the inadequacies in the world will not change His mind. He will be with you every step of the way. And though it may take time, He has a celebration planned for when you cross over the "Red Seas" of your life.

Charles Swindoll

BUILDING A BETTER YOU

Every day should be a cause for celebration. By celebrating the gift of life, you protect your heart from the dangers of pessimism, regret, hopelessness, and bitterness.

THE GIFT OF CHEERFULNESS

Anxiety in the heart of man causes depression,
but a good word makes it glad.
Proverbs 12:25 NKJV

Cheerfulness is a gift that we give to others and to ourselves. And, as believers who have been saved by a risen Christ, why shouldn't we be cheerful? The answer, of course, is that we have every reason to honor our Savior with joy in our hearts, smiles on our faces, and words of celebration on our lips.

Christ promises us lives of abundance and joy if we accept His love and His grace. Yet sometimes, even the most righteous among us are beset by fits of ill temper and frustration. During these moments, we may not feel like turning our thoughts and prayers to Christ, but that's precisely what we should do. When we do so, we simply can't stay grumpy for long.

The people whom I have seen succeed best in life have always been cheerful and hopeful people who went about their business with a smile on their faces.

Charles Kingsley

A LESSON FOR THE HEART AND SOUL

Do you need a little cheering up? If so, find somebody else who needs cheering up, too. Then, do your best to brighten that person's day. When you do, you'll discover that cheering up other people is a wonderful way to cheer yourself up, too.

OBEDIENCE NOW

Now by this we know that we know Him,
if we keep His commandments.
1 John 2:3 NKJV

In order to enjoy a deeper relationship with God, you must strive diligently to live in accordance with His commandments. But there's a problem—you live in a world that seeks to snare your attention and lead you away from God.

Because you are an imperfect mortal being, you cannot be perfectly obedient, nor does God expect you to be. What is required, however, is a sincere desire to be obedient coupled with an awareness of sin and a willingness to distance yourself from it as soon as you encounter it.

Are you willing to conform your behavior to God's rules? Hopefully, you can answer that question with a resounding yes. Otherwise, you'll never experience a full measure of the blessings that the Creator gives to those who obey Him.

The more you delve into the evidence for Christianity, the more your faith will grow.

Bill Hybels

A LESSON FOR THE HEART AND SOUL
Many people who call themselves Christians don't really invest much time or energy following Jesus. Don't be like them. Instead, make certain that you follow Jesus every day.

BUILDING HIS CHURCH

For we are God's fellow workers; you are God's field,
you are God's building.
1 Corinthians 3:9 NKJV

The church belongs to God; it is His just as certainly as we are His. When we help build God's church, we bear witness to the changes that He has made in our lives.

Today and every day, let us worship God with grateful hearts and helping hands as we support the church that He has created. Let us witness to our friends, to our families, and to the world. When we do so, we bless others—and we are blessed by the One who sent His Son to die so that we might have eternal life.

And how can we improve the church? Simply and only by improving ourselves.

A. W. Tozer

Only participation in the full life of a local church builds spiritual muscle.

Rick Warren

BUILDING A BETTER YOU

God intends for you to be actively involved in His church. Your intentions should be the same.

FINDING CONTENTMENT

I've learned by now to be quite content whatever my circumstances.
I'm just as happy with little as with much, with much as with little.
I've found the recipe for being happy
whether full or hungry, hands full or hands empty.
Philippians 4:11–12 MSG

Where can we find contentment? Is it a result of wealth, or power, or beauty, or fame? Hardly. Genuine contentment is a gift from God to those who trust Him and follow His commandments.

Our modern world seems preoccupied with the search for happiness. We are bombarded with messages telling us that happiness depends upon the acquisition of material possessions. These messages are false. Enduring peace is not the result of our acquisitions; it is a spiritual gift from God to those who obey Him and accept His will.

If we don't find contentment in God, we will never find it anywhere else. But, if we seek Him and obey Him, we will be blessed with an inner peace that is beyond human understanding. When God dwells at the center of our lives, peace and contentment will belong to us just as surely as we belong to God.

True contentment comes from godliness in the heart, not from wealth in the hand.

Warren Wiersbe

A LESSON FOR THE HEART AND SOUL

Be contented where you are, even if it's not exactly where you want to end up. God has something wonderful in store for you—and remember that God's timing is perfect—so be patient, trust God, do your best, and expect the best.

PROTECTED

Be of good courage, and He shall strengthen your heart,
all you who hope in the Lord.
Psalm 31:24 NKJV

Being a godly person in this difficult world is no easy task. Ours is a time of uncertainty and danger, a time when even the most courageous have legitimate cause for concern. But as believers we can live courageously, knowing that we have been saved by a loving Father and His only begotten Son.

Are you anxious? Take those anxieties to God. Are you troubled? Take your troubles to Him. Seek protection from the One who cannot be moved. And then live courageously, knowing that even in these troubled times, God is always as near as your next breath—and you are always protected.

There comes a time when we simply have to face the challenges in our lives and stop backing down.

John Eldredge

BUILDING A BETTER YOU

You can increase your supply of courage by sharing it. Courage is contagious, and courage inspired by a steadfast trust in a loving Heavenly Father is highly contagious. Today, as you interact with friends, family members, or co-workers, share your courage, your hopes, your dreams, and your enthusiasm. Your positive outlook will be almost as big a blessing to them as it is to you.

DEALING WITH DISAPPOINTMENT

For we do not want you to be ignorant, brethren, of our trouble which came to us in Asia: that we were burdened beyond measure, above strength, so that we despaired even of life. Yes, we had the sentence of death in ourselves, that we should not trust in ourselves but in God who raises the dead, who delivered us from so great a death, and does deliver us; in whom we trust that He will still deliver us.

2 Corinthians 1:8–10 NKJV

From time to time, all of us face life-altering disappointments that leave us breathless. Oftentimes, these disappointments come unexpectedly, leaving us with more questions than answers. But even when we don't have all the answers—or, for that matter, even when we don't seem to have any of the answers—God does. Whatever our circumstances, whether we stand atop the highest mountain or wander through the darkest valley, God is ready to protect us, to comfort us, and to heal us. Our task is to let Him.

Every achievement worth remembering is stained with the blood of diligence and scarred by the wounds of disappointment.

Charles Swindoll

BUILDING A BETTER YOU

Don't spend too much time asking, "Why me, Lord?" Instead, ask, "What now, Lord?" and then get to work. When you do, you'll feel much better.

DREAM BIG

*With God's power working in us, God can do
much, much more than anything we can ask or imagine.*
Ephesians 3:20 NCV

Are you willing to entertain the possibility that God has big plans in store for you? Hopefully so. Yet sometimes, especially if you've recently experienced a life-altering disappointment, you may find it difficult to envision a brighter future for yourself and your family. If so, it's time to reconsider your own capabilities . . . and God's.

Your Heavenly Father created you with unique gifts and untapped talents; your job is to tap them. When you do, you'll begin to feel an increasing sense of confidence in yourself and in your future. So even if you're experiencing difficult days, don't abandon your dreams. Instead, trust that God is preparing you for greater things.

It would be a dreadful thing to hang one's confidence in such a fragile thing as a dream.

C. H. Spurgeon

Always stay connected to people and seek out things that bring you joy. Dream with abandon. Pray confidently.

Barbara Johnson

BUILDING A BETTER YOU

You can dream big dreams, but you can never out-dream God. His plans for you are even bigger than you can imagine.

YOUR WAY OR GOD'S WAY

A man's heart plans his way, but the Lord directs his steps.
Proverbs 16:9 NKJV

The popular song "My Way" is a perfectly good tune, but it's not a perfect guide for life. If you're looking for life's perfect prescription, you'd better forget about doing things your way and start doing things God's way. The most important decision of your life is, of course, your commitment to accept Jesus Christ as your personal Lord and Savior. And once your eternal destiny is secured, you will undoubtedly ask yourself the question "What now, Lord?" If you earnestly seek God's will for your life, you will find it . . . in time.

Sometimes, God's plans are crystal clear; sometimes they are not. So be patient, keep searching, and keep praying. If you do, then in time, God will answer your prayers and make His plans known. You'll discover those plans by doing things His way . . . and you'll be eternally grateful that you did.

Almost 2000 years ago, Jesus Christ won the decisive battle against sin and Satan through His death and resurrection. Satan did his best to defeat God's plans, but he could not win against God's overwhelming power.

Billy Graham

BUILDING A BETTER YOU

God has a wonderful plan for your life. And the time to start looking for that plan—and living it—is now. And remember: Discovering God's plan begins with prayer.

THY WILL BE DONE

"Father, if it is Your will, take this cup away from Me;
nevertheless not My will, but Yours, be done."
Luke 22:42 NKJV

As human beings with limited understanding, we can never fully comprehend the will of God. But as believers in a benevolent God, we must always trust the will of our Heavenly Father.

Before His crucifixion, Jesus went to the Mount of Olives and poured out His heart to God. Jesus knew of the agony that He was destined to endure, but He also knew that God's will must be done. We, like our Savior, face trials that bring fear and trembling to the very depths of our souls, but like Christ, we, too, must ultimately seek God's will, not our own. When we entrust our lives to Him completely and without reservation, He gives us the strength to meet any challenge, the courage to face any trial, and the wisdom to live in His righteousness.

Faith is obedience at home and looking to the Master; obedience is faith going out to do His will.

Andrew Murray

BUILDING A BETTER YOU

Even when you cannot understand God's plans, you must trust them. If you place yourself in the center of God's will, He will provide for your needs and direct your path.

KEEPING UP APPEARANCES

We justify our actions by appearances; God examines our motives.
Proverbs 21:2 MSG

The world sees you as you appear to be; God sees you as you really are . . . He sees your heart, and He understands your intentions. The opinions of others should be relatively unimportant to you; however, God's view of you—His understanding of your actions, your thoughts, and your motivations—should be vitally important.

Few things in life are more futile than "keeping up appearances" for the sake of neighbors. What is important, of course, is pleasing your Father in Heaven. You please Him when your intentions are pure and your actions are just.

Outside appearances, things like the clothes you wear or the car you drive, are important to other people but totally unimportant to God. Trust God.

Jim Gallery

If the narrative of the Scriptures teaches us anything, from the serpent in the Garden to the carpenter in Nazareth, it teaches us that things are rarely what they seem, that we shouldn't be fooled by appearances.

John Eldredge

BUILDING A BETTER YOU

Don't be too worried about what you look like on the outside. Be more concerned about the kind of person you are on the inside.

BUILDING FELLOWSHIP

It is good and pleasant when God's people live together in peace!
Psalm 133:1 NCV

Fellowship with other believers should be an integral part of your everyday life. Your association with fellow Christians should be uplifting, enlightening, encouraging, and consistent.

Are you an active member of your own fellowship? Are you a builder of bridges inside the four walls of your church and outside it? Do you contribute to God's glory by contributing your time and your talents to a close-knit band of believers? Hopefully so. The fellowship of believers is intended to be a powerful tool for spreading God's Good News and uplifting His children. And God intends for you to be a fully contributing member of that fellowship. Your intentions should be the same.

The Bible knows nothing of solitary religion.

John Wesley

Christian brotherhood is not an ideal which we must realize; it is rather a reality created by God in Christ in which we may participate.

Dietrich Bonhoeffer

A LESSON FOR THE HEART AND SOUL

God intends for you to be an active member of your fellowship. Your intentions should be the same.

EXTREME CHANGES

Then he told them what they could expect for themselves:
"Anyone who intends to come with me has to let me lead."
Luke 9:23 MSG

Jesus made an extreme sacrifice for you. Are you willing to make extreme changes in your life for Him? Can you honestly say that you're passionate about your faith and that you're really following Jesus? Hopefully so. But if you're preoccupied with other things—or if you're strictly a one-day-a-week Christian—then you're in need of an extreme spiritual makeover!

Nothing is more important than your wholehearted commitment to your Creator and to His only begotten Son. Your faith must never be an afterthought; it must be your ultimate priority, your ultimate possession, and your ultimate passion. You are the recipient of Christ's love. Accept it enthusiastically and share it passionately. Jesus deserves your extreme enthusiasm; the world deserves it; and you deserve the experience of sharing it.

Will you, with a glad and eager surrender, hand yourself and all that concerns you over into his hands? If you will do this, your soul will begin to know something of the joy of union with Christ.

Hannah Whitall Smith

A LESSON FOR THE HEART AND SOUL

Think about your relationship with Jesus: what it is, and what it can be. Then, as you embark upon the next phase of your life's journey, be sure to walk with your Savior every step of the way.

FRIENDSHIPS THAT HONOR GOD

If your life honors the name of Jesus, he will honor you.
2 Thessalonians 1:12 MSG

Some friendships help us honor God; these friendships should be nurtured. Other friendships place us in situations where we are tempted to dishonor God by disobeying His commandments; friendships such as these have the potential to do us great harm.

Because we tend to become like our friends, we must choose our friends carefully. Because our friends influence us in ways that are both subtle and powerful, we must ensure that our friendships are pleasing to God. When we spend our days in the presence of godly believers, we are blessed, not only by those friends, but also by our Creator.

God has a plan for your friendships because He knows your friends determine the quality and direction of your life.

Charles Stanley

In a circle of true friends each man is simply what he is: stands for nothing but himself.

C. S. Lewis

A LESSON FOR THE HEART AND SOUL
The best rule for making friends . . . is the Golden one.

HIS RIGHTFUL PLACE

You shall have no other gods before Me.
Exodus 20:3 NKJV

When Jesus was tempted by Satan, the Master's response was unambiguous. Jesus chose to worship the Lord and serve Him only. We, as followers of Christ, must follow in His footsteps by placing God first.

When we place God in a position of secondary importance, we do ourselves great harm. When we allow temptations or distractions to come between us and our Creator, we suffer. But, when we imitate Jesus and place the Lord in His rightful place—at the center of our lives—then we claim spiritual treasures that will endure forever.

I am of the opinion that we should not be concerned about working for God until we have learned the meaning and delight of worshipping Him.

A. W. Tozer

You can't get second things by putting them first; you can get second things only be putting first things first.

C. S. Lewis

BUILDING A BETTER YOU

God deserves first place in your life . . . and you deserve the experience of putting Him there.

GOD'S GUIDANCE

The steps of a good man are ordered by the LORD.
Psalm 37:23 KJV

God is intensely interested in each of us, and He will guide our steps if we serve Him obediently.

When we sincerely offer heartfelt prayers to our Heavenly Father, He will give direction and meaning to our lives—but He won't force us to follow Him. To the contrary, God has given us the free will to follow His commandments . . . or not.

When we stray from God's commandments, we invite bitter consequences. But, when we follow His commandments, and when we genuinely and humbly seek His will, He touches our hearts and leads us on the path of His choosing.

Will you trust God to guide your steps? You should. When you entrust your life to Him completely and without reservation, God will give you the strength to meet any challenge, the courage to face any trial, and the wisdom to live in His righteousness and in His peace. So trust Him today and seek His guidance. When you do, your next step will be the right one.

We must always invite Jesus to be the navigator of our plans, desires, wills, and emotions, for He is the way, the truth, and the life.

Bill Bright

BUILDING A BETTER YOU

Pray for guidance. When you seek it, He will give it.

HIS PROMISES

Let's keep a firm grip on the promises that keep us going.
He always keeps his word.
Hebrews 10:23 MSG

The Christian faith is founded upon promises that are contained in a unique book. That book is the Holy Bible. The Bible is a roadmap for life here on earth and for life eternal. As Christians, we are called upon to study its meaning, to trust its promises, to follow its commandments, and to share its Good News. God's Holy Word is, indeed, a transforming, life-changing, one-of-a-kind treasure. And, a passing acquaintance with the Good Book is insufficient for Christians who seek to obey God's Word and understand His will.

God has made promises to you, and He intends to keep them. So take God at His word; trust His promises and share them with your family, with your friends, and with the world.

There are four words I wish we would never forget, and they are, "God keeps his word."

Charles Swindoll

A LESSON FOR THE HEART AND SOUL

God has made many promises to you, and He will keep every single one of them. Your job is to trust God's promises and live accordingly.

BEYOND GUILT

*There is therefore now no condemnation to those who are
in Christ Jesus, who do not walk according to the flesh,
but according to the Spirit.*
Romans 8:1 NKJV

All of us have sinned. Sometimes our sins result from our
own stubborn rebellion against God's commandments. And
sometimes, we are swept up in events that are beyond our abilities
to control. Under either set of circumstances, we may experience
intense feelings of guilt. But God has an answer for the guilt that
we feel. That answer, of course, is His forgiveness. When we confess our wrongdoings and repent from them, we are forgiven by the
One who created us.

Are you troubled by feelings of guilt or regret? If so, you must
repent from your misdeeds, and you must ask your Heavenly Father
for His forgiveness. When you do so, He will forgive you completely and without reservation. Then, you must forgive yourself just as
God has forgiven you: thoroughly and unconditionally.

Identify the sin. Confess it. Turn from it. Avoid it at all costs. Live
with a clean, forgiven conscience. Don't dwell on what God has
forgotten!

Max Lucado

A LESSON FOR THE HEART AND SOUL

If you've asked for God's forgiveness, He has given it. But have you
forgiven yourself? If not, the best moment to do so is this one.

EXPECTING THE BEST

This is the day the LORD has made; let us rejoice and be glad in it.
Psalm 118:24 NIV

What do you expect from the day ahead? Are you expecting God to do wonderful things, or are you living beneath a cloud of apprehension and doubt? The familiar words of Psalm 118:24 remind us of a profound yet simple truth: "This is the day which the LORD hath made; we will rejoice and be glad in it" (KJV).

For Christian believers, every day begins and ends with God's Son and God's promises. When we accept Christ into our hearts, God promises us the opportunity for earthly peace and spiritual abundance. But more importantly, God promises us the priceless gift of eternal life.

As we face the inevitable challenges of daily life, we must arm ourselves with the promises of God's Holy Word. When we do, we can expect the best, not only for the day ahead, but also for all eternity.

When I consider my existence beyond the grace, I am filled with confidence and gratitude because God has made an inviolable commitment to take me to heaven on the merits of Christ.

Bill Hybels

BUILDING A BETTER YOU

Today, think about the role that God's Word plays in your life, and think about ways that you can worry less and trust God more.

CONTENTED IN HIM

The LORD will give strength to His people;
The LORD will bless His people with peace.
Psalm 29:11 NKJV

Everywhere we turn, or so it seems, the world promises us contentment and happiness. But the contentment that the world offers is fleeting and incomplete. Thankfully, the contentment that God offers is all-encompassing and everlasting.

Happiness depends less upon our circumstances than upon our thoughts. When we turn our thoughts to God, to His gifts, and to His glorious creation, we experience the joy that God intends for His children. But, when we focus on the negative aspects of life—or when we disobey God's commandments—we cause ourselves needless suffering.

Do you sincerely want to be a contented Christian? Then set your mind and your heart upon God's love and His grace. Seek first the salvation that is available through a personal relationship with Jesus Christ, and then claim the joy, the contentment, and the spiritual abundance that the Shepherd offers His sheep.

Real contentment hinges on what's happening inside us, not around us.

Charles Stanley

A LESSON FOR THE HEART AND SOUL

Because you are loved and protected by God, you should be contented, whatever your circumstances.

BEYOND THE DIFFICULTIES

When you turn to the Lord your God and obey His voice
(for the Lord your God is a merciful God), He will not forsake you
nor destroy you, nor forget the covenant of
your fathers which He swore to them.
Deuteronomy 4:30–31 NKJV

Sometimes the traffic jams, and sometimes the dog gobbles the homework. But, when we find ourselves overtaken by the minor frustrations of life, we must catch ourselves, take a deep breath, and lift our thoughts upward. Although we are here on earth struggling to rise above the distractions of the day, we need never struggle alone. God is here—eternally and faithfully, with infinite patience and love—and, if we reach out to Him, He will restore perspective and peace to our souls.

If you find yourself enduring difficult circumstances, remember that God remains in His Heaven. If you become discouraged with the direction of your day or your life, lift your thoughts and prayers to Him. He will guide you through your difficulties and beyond them.

Whatever hallway you're in—no matter how long, how dark, or how scary—God is right there with you.

Bill Hybels

BUILDING A BETTER YOU

Difficult days come and go. Stay the course. The sun is shining somewhere, and will soon shine on you.

TEACHING DISCIPLINE

Whoever accepts correction is on the way to life, but whoever ignores correction will lead others away from life.

Proverbs 10:17 NCV

Wise parents teach their children the importance of discipline using both words and examples. If we are to hold true to that discipline, we need to understand that God doesn't reward laziness or misbehavior. To the contrary, God expects His believers to lead lives that are above reproach. And, He punishes those who disobey His commandments.

In Proverbs 28:19, God's message is clear: "He who works his land will have abundant food, but the one who chases fantasies will have his fill of poverty" (NIV). When we work diligently and consistently, we can expect a bountiful harvest. But we must never expect the harvest to precede the labor. First, we must lead lives of discipline and obedience; then, we will reap the never-ending rewards that God has promised.

True will power and courage are not only on the battlefield, but also in everyday conquests over our inertia, laziness, and boredom.

D. L. Moody

If one examines the secret behind a championship football team, a magnificent orchestra, or a successful business, the principal ingredient is invariably discipline.

James Dobson

BUILDING A BETTER YOU

If you're a disciplined person, you'll earn big rewards. If you're undisciplined, you won't.

CELEBRATING OTHERS

Therefore encourage one another and build up one another,
just as you also are doing.
1 Thessalonians 5:11 NASB

Do you delight in the victories of others? You should. Each day provides countless opportunities to encourage others and to praise their good works. When you do so, you not only spread seeds of joy and happiness, you also obey the commandments of God's Holy Word.

As Christians, we are called upon to spread the Good News of Christ, and we are also called to spread a message of encouragement and hope to the world.

Today, let us be cheerful Christians with smiles on our faces and encouraging words on our lips. By blessing others, we also bless ourselves, and, at the same time, we honor the One who gave His life for us.

The glory of friendship is not the outstretched hand, or the kindly smile, or the joy of companionship. It is the spiritual inspiration that comes to one when he discovers that someone else believes in him and is willing to trust him with his friendship.

Corrie ten Boom

BUILDING A BETTER YOU

Do you want to be successful and go far in life? Encourage others to do the same. You can't lift other people up without lifting yourself up, too. And remember the words of Oswald Chambers: "God grant that we may not hinder those who are battling their way slowly into the light."

ETERNAL PERSPECTIVE

Our Savior Jesus poured out new life so generously.
God's gift has restored our relationship with him and given us
back our lives. And there's more life to come—an eternity of life!
Titus 3:6–7 MSG

As mere mortals, our vision for the future, like our lives here on earth, is limited. God's vision is not burdened by such limitations: His plans extend throughout all eternity. Thus, God's plans for you are not limited to the ups and downs of everyday life. Your Heavenly Father has bigger things in mind . . . much bigger things.

Christ sacrificed His life on the cross so that we might have eternal life. This gift, freely given by God's only begotten Son, is the priceless possession of everyone who accepts Him as Lord and Savior. So, when you encounter troubles, keep things in perspective. Although you will experience occasional defeats in this world, you'll have all eternity to celebrate the ultimate victory in the next.

The damage done to us on this earth will never find its way into that safe city. We can relax, we can rest, and though some of us can hardly imagine it, we can prepare to feel safe and secure for all of eternity.

Bill Hybels

A LESSON FOR THE HEART AND SOUL

God has created Heaven and given you a way to get there. The rest is up to you.

IN HIS HANDS

For whatever is born of God overcomes the world.
And this is the victory that has overcome the world—our faith.
1 John 5:4 NKJV

The first element of a successful life is faith: faith in God, faith in His Son, and faith in His promises. If we place our lives in God's hands, our faith is rewarded in ways that we—as human beings with clouded vision and limited understanding—can scarcely comprehend. But, if we seek to rely solely upon our own resources, or if we seek earthly success outside the boundaries of God's commandments, we reap a bitter harvest for ourselves and for our loved ones.

Do you desire the abundance and success that God has promised? Then trust Him today and every day that you live. Then, when you have entrusted your future to the Giver of all things good, rest assured that your future is secure, not only for today, but also for all eternity.

Every man lives by faith, the nonbeliever as well as the saint; the one by faith in natural laws and the other by faith in God.

A. W. Tozer

A LESSON FOR THE HEART AND SOUL

If you don't have faith, you'll never move mountains. But if you do have faith, there's no limit to the things that you and God, working together, can accomplish.

AT PEACE WITH YOUR PURPOSE

But now in Christ Jesus you who once were far off have been brought near by the blood of Christ. For He Himself is our peace.
Ephesians 2:13–14 NKJV

Are you at peace with the direction of your life? If you're a Christian, you should be. Perhaps you seek a new direction or a sense of renewed purpose, but those feelings should never rob you of the genuine peace that can and should be yours through a personal relationship with Jesus.

Have you found the lasting peace that can be yours through Jesus, or are you still rushing after the illusion of "peace and happiness" that our world promises but cannot deliver? Today, as a gift to yourself, to your family, and to your friends, claim the inner peace that is your spiritual birthright: the peace of Jesus Christ.

Jesus gives us the ultimate rest, the confidence we need, to escape the frustration and chaos of the world around us.

Billy Graham

That peace, which has been described and which believers enjoy, is a participation of the peace which their glorious Lord and Master himself enjoys.

Jonathan Edwards

A LESSON FOR THE HEART AND SOUL

God's peace surpasses human understanding. When you accept His peace, it will revolutionize your life.

THE IMPORTANCE OF PRAYER

Be anxious for nothing, but in everything by prayer and supplication,
with thanksgiving, let your requests be made known to God.
Philippians 4:6 NKJV

Prayer is a powerful tool for communicating with our Creator; it is an opportunity to commune with the Giver of all things good. Prayer is not a thing to be taken lightly or to be used infrequently. Prayer should never be reserved for mealtimes or for bedtimes; it should be an ever-present focus in our daily lives.

In his first letter to the Thessalonians, Paul wrote, "Rejoice evermore. Pray without ceasing. In every thing give thanks: for this is the will of God in Christ Jesus concerning you" (5:17-18 KJV). Paul's words apply to every Christian of every generation. So, let us pray constantly about things great and small. God is listening, and He wants to hear from us. Now.

Each time, before you intercede, be quiet first and worship God in His glory. Think of what He can do and how He delights to hear the prayers of His redeemed people. Think of your place and privilege in Christ, and expect great things!

Andrew Murray

A LESSON FOR THE HEART AND SOUL

Give God your full attention by putting prayer at the very top of your daily to-do list.

LIVING RIGHTEOUSLY

Flee also youthful lusts; but pursue righteousness, faith, love, peace with those who call on the Lord out of a pure heart.
2 Timothy 2:22 NKJV

Do you sincerely desire to be a righteous person? Are you bound and determined—despite the inevitable temptations and distractions of our modern age—to be an example of godly behavior to your family, to your friends, to your coworkers, and to your community? If so, you must obey God's commandments. There are no shortcuts and no loopholes—to be a faithful Christian, you must be an obedient Christian.

You will never become righteous by accident. You must hunger for righteousness, and you must ask God to guide your steps. When you ask Him for guidance, He will give it. So, when you're faced with a difficult choice or a powerful temptation, seek God's counsel and trust the counsel He gives. Invite God into your heart and live according to His commandments. When you do, you will be blessed today, tomorrow, and forever.

We must appropriate the tender mercy of God every day after conversion, or problems quickly develop. We need his grace daily in order to live a righteous life.

Jim Cymbala

A LESSON FOR THE HEART AND SOUL

Because God is just, He rewards righteousness just as surely as He punishes sin.

SHARING THE WEALTH

If you give, you will receive. Your gift will return to you in full measure, pressed down, shaken together to make room for more, and running over. Whatever measure you use in giving—large or small—it will be used to measure what is given back to you.

Luke 6:38 NLT

The 10th chapter of John tells us that Christ came to earth so that our lives might be filled with abundance. But what, exactly, did Jesus mean when He promised "life . . . more abundantly"? Was He referring to material possessions or financial wealth? Hardly. Jesus offers a different kind of abundance: a spiritual richness that extends beyond the temporal boundaries of this world.

Is material abundance part of God's plan for our lives? Perhaps. But in every circumstance of life, during times of wealth or times of want, God will provide us what we need if we trust Him (Matthew 6). May we, as believers, claim the riches of Christ Jesus every day that we live, and may we share His blessings with all who cross our path.

Jesus wants Life for us, Life with a capital L.

John Eldredge

It would be wrong to have a "poverty complex," for to think ourselves paupers is to deny either the King's riches or to deny our being His children.

Catherine Marshall

BUILDING A BETTER YOU

God wants to shower you with abundance—your job is to let Him.

ONE MOUTH, TWO EARS

My dear brothers and sisters, be quick to listen,
slow to speak, and slow to get angry.
Your anger can never make things right in God's sight.
James 1:19–20 NLT

Perhaps God gave each of us one mouth and two ears in order that we might listen twice as much as we speak. Unfortunately, many of us do otherwise, especially when we become angry.

Anger is a natural human emotion that is sometimes necessary and appropriate. Even Jesus Himself became angered when He confronted the moneychangers in the temple. But, more often than not, our frustrations are of the more mundane variety. When you are tempted to lose your temper over the minor inconveniences of life, don't. Turn away from anger, and turn instead to God.

When you strike out in anger, you may miss the other person, but you will always hit yourself.

Jim Gallery

The fire of anger, if not quenched by loving forgiveness, will spread and defile and destroy the work of God.

Warren Wiersbe

A LESSON FOR THE HEART AND SOUL

Avoid angry outbursts: Sweet words usually work better than sour ones.

SPREADING KINDNESS

Don't be obsessed with getting your own advantage.
Forget yourselves long enough to lend a helping hand.
Philippians 2:4 MSG

The noted American theologian Phillips Brooks advised, "Be such a man, and live such a life, that if every man were such as you, and every life a life like yours, this earth would be God's Paradise." One tangible way to make the world a more godly place is to spread kindness wherever we go.

Sometimes, when we feel happy or generous, we find it easy to be kind. Other times, when we are discouraged or tired, we can scarcely summon the energy to utter a single kind word. But, God's commandment is clear: He intends that we make the conscious choice to treat others with kindness and respect, no matter our circumstances, no matter our emotions.

Today, as you consider all the things that Christ has done in your life, honor Him by following His commandment and obeying the Golden Rule. He expects no less, and He deserves no less.

The mark of a Christian is that he will walk the second mile and turn the other cheek. A wise man or woman gives the extra effort, all for the glory of the Lord Jesus Christ.

John Maxwell

A LESSON FOR THE HEART AND SOUL

Don't wait. The best time to do a good deed is as soon as you can do it.

BEHAVIOR THAT IS CONSISTENT WITH YOUR BELIEFS

If the way you live isn't consistent with what you believe,
then it's wrong.
Romans 14:23 MSG

In describing our beliefs, our actions are far better descriptors than our words. Yet far too many of us spend more energy talking about our beliefs than living by them—with predictably poor results.

As believers, we must beware: Our actions should always give credence to the changes that Christ can make in the lives of those who walk with Him.

Your beliefs shape your values, and your values shape your life. Is your life a clearly-crafted picture book of your creed? Are your actions always consistent with your beliefs? Are you willing to practice the philosophies that you preach? Hopefully so; otherwise, you'll be tormented by inconsistencies between your beliefs and your behaviors.

We must understand that the first and chief thing—for everyone who would do the work of Jesus—is to believe, and in doing so, to become linked to Him, the Almighty One . . . and then, to pray the prayer of faith in His Name.

Andrew Murray

BUILDING A BETTER YOU

When you live in accordance with your beliefs, God will guide your steps and protect your heart.

A LIFE OF INTEGRITY

People with integrity have firm footing,
but those who follow crooked paths will slip and fall.
Proverbs 10:9 NLT

Charles Swindoll correctly observed, "Nothing speaks louder or more powerfully than a life of integrity." Godly men and women agree.

Integrity is built slowly over a lifetime. It is a precious thing—difficult to build but easy to tear down. As believers in Christ, we must seek to live each day with discipline, honesty, and faith. When we do, at least two things happen: integrity becomes a habit, and God blesses us because of our obedience to Him.

Living a life of integrity isn't always the easiest way, but it is always the right way. And God clearly intends that it should be our way, too.

There's nothing like the power of integrity. It is a characteristic so radiant, so steady, so consistent, so beautiful, that it makes a permanent picture in our minds.

Franklin Graham

Integrity is a sign of maturity.

Charles Swindoll

A LESSON FOR THE HEART AND SOUL

The real test of integrity is being willing to tell the truth when it's hard.

SO LAUGH!

A happy heart makes the face cheerful,
but heartache crushes the spirit.
Proverbs 15:13 NIV

Laughter is God's gift, and He intends that we enjoy it. Yet sometimes, because of the inevitable stresses of everyday life, laughter seems only a distant memory. As Christians we have every reason to be cheerful and to be thankful. Our blessings from God are beyond measure, starting, of course, with a gift that is ours for the asking, God's gift of salvation through Christ Jesus.

Few things in life are more absurd than the sight of a grumpy Christian. So today, as you go about your daily activities, approach life with a grin and a chuckle. After all, God created laughter for a reason . . . to use it. So laugh!

Life goes on. Keep on smiling and the whole world smiles with you.

Dennis Swanberg

It is pleasing to the dear God whenever you rejoice or laugh from the bottom of your heart.

Martin Luther

BUILDING A BETTER YOU

Learn to laugh at life. Life has a lighter side—look for it, especially when times are tough. Laughter is medicine for the soul, so take your medicine early and often.

MENTORS THAT MATTER

The godly give good advice, but fools are destroyed
by their lack of common sense.
Proverbs 10:21 NLT

Here's a simple yet effective way to strengthen your faith: Choose role models whose faith in God is strong.

When you emulate godly people, you become a more godly person yourself. That's why you should seek out mentors who, by their words and their presence, make you a better person and a better Christian.

Today, as a gift to yourself, select, from your friends and family members, a mentor whose judgment you trust. Then listen carefully to your mentor's advice and be willing to accept that advice, even if accepting it requires effort, or pain, or both. Consider your mentor to be God's gift to you. Thank God for that gift, and use it for the glory of His kingdom.

The effective mentor strives to help a man or woman discover what they can be in Christ and then holds them accountable to become that person.

Howard Hendricks

A LESSON FOR THE HEART AND SOUL

When it comes to mentors, you need them. When it comes to mentoring, they need you.

BLESSED OBEDIENCE

Return to the Lord your God and obey His voice, according to
all that I command you today, you and your children, with all your
heart and with all your soul, that the Lord your God will bring you
back from captivity, and have compassion on you.

Deuteronomy 30:2–3 NKJV

We live in a world filled with temptations, distractions, and countless opportunities to disobey God. But as Christians who seek to be godly role models for our families, we must turn our thoughts and our hearts away from the evils of this world. We must turn instead to God.

Talking about God is easy; living by His laws is considerably harder. But unless we are willing to live obediently, all our righteous words ring hollow.

How can we best proclaim our love for the Lord? By obeying Him. We must seek God's counsel and trust the counsel He gives. And, when we invite God into our hearts and live according to His commandments, we are blessed today, and tomorrow, and forever.

Believe and do what God says. The life-changing consequences will be limitless, and the results will be confidence and peace of mind.

Franklin Graham

A LESSON FOR THE HEART AND SOUL

God rewards obedience and punishes disobedience. It's not enough to understand God's rules; you must also live by them.

THE POWER OF PERSEVERANCE

I do not consider myself yet to have taken hold of it.
But one thing I do: Forgetting what is behind and straining toward
what is ahead, I press on toward the goal to win the prize for which
God has called me heavenward in Christ Jesus.

Philippians 3:13–14 NIV

A well-lived life calls for preparation, determination, and, of course, lots of perseverance. As an example of perfect perseverance, we Christians need look no further than our Savior, Jesus Christ. Jesus finished what He began. Despite His suffering, despite the shame of the cross, Jesus was steadfast in His faithfulness to God. We, too, must remain faithful, especially during times of hardship. Sometimes, God may answer our prayers with silence, and when He does, we must patiently persevere.

Are you facing a tough situation? If so, remember this: whatever your problem, God can handle it. Your job is to keep persevering until He does.

Only the man who follows the command of Jesus single-mindedly and unresistingly lets his yoke rest upon him, finds his burden easy, and under its gentle pressure receives the power to persevere in the right way.

Dietrich Bonhoeffer

BUILDING A BETTER YOU

Life is an exercise in perseverance. If you persevere, you win.

DOING IT NOW

*We can't afford to waste a minute, must not squander these
precious daylight hours in frivolity and indulgence . . . .
Don't loiter and linger, waiting until the very last minute.
Dress yourselves in Christ, and be up and about!*
Romans 13:13–14 MSG

The habit of procrastination takes a two-fold toll on its victims. First, important work goes unfinished; second (and more importantly), valuable energy is wasted in the process of putting off the things that remain undone. Procrastination results from an individual's short-sighted attempt to postpone temporary discomfort. What results is a senseless cycle of (1) delay, followed by; (2) worry followed by; (3) a panicky and often futile attempt to "catch up." Procrastination is, at its core, a struggle against oneself; the only antidote is action.

Once you acquire the habit of doing what needs to be done when it needs to be done, you will avoid untold trouble, worry, and stress. So learn to defeat procrastination by paying less attention to your fears and more attention to your responsibilities. God has created a world that punishes procrastinators and rewards people who "do it now." Life doesn't procrastinate—neither should you.

Not now becomes never.

Martin Luther

BUILDING A BETTER YOU

It's easy to put off unpleasant tasks until "later." A far better strategy is this: Do the unpleasant work first so you can enjoy the rest of the day.

THE SIMPLE LIFE

Whoever becomes simple and elemental again,
like this child, will rank high in God's kingdom.
Matthew 18:4 MSG

You live in a world where simplicity is in short supply. Think for a moment about the complexity of your everyday life and compare it to the lives of your ancestors. Certainly, you are the beneficiary of many technological innovations, but those innovations have a price: In all likelihood, your world is highly complex.

Unless you take firm control of your time and your life, you may be overwhelmed by an ever-increasing tidal wave of complexity that threatens your happiness. But your Heavenly Father understands the joy of living simply, and so should you. So do yourself a favor: Keep your life as simple as possible. Simplicity is, indeed, genius. By simplifying your life, you are destined to improve it.

The most powerful life is the most simple life. The most powerful life is the life that knows where it's going, that knows where the source of strength is; it is the life that stays free of clutter and happenstance and hurriedness.

Max Lucado

A LESSON FOR THE HEART AND SOUL
Simplicity and peace are two concepts that are closely related. Complexity and peace are not.

ACCEPTING GOD'S GIFTS

For God so loved the world that He gave His only begotten Son,
that whoever believes in Him should not perish
but have everlasting life.
John 3:16 NKJV

God loves you—His love for you is deeper and more profound than you can imagine. God's love for you is so great that He sent His only Son to this earth to die for your sins and to offer you the priceless gift of eternal life.

You must decide whether or not to accept God's gift. Will you ignore it or embrace it? Will you return it or neglect it? Will you invite Christ to dwell in the center of your heart, or will you relegate Him to a position of lesser importance? The decision is yours, and so are the consequences. So choose wisely . . . and choose today.

The most profound essence of my nature is that I am capable of receiving God.

St. Augustine

Ask Christ to come into your heart to forgive you and help you. When you do, Christ will take up residence in your life by His Holy Spirit, and when you face temptations and trials, you will no longer face them alone.

Billy Graham

BUILDING A BETTER YOU

The ultimate choice for you is the choice to invite God's Son into your heart. Choose wisely . . . and immediately.

HOPE IS CONTAGIOUS

Finally, all of you be of one mind, having compassion for one another; love as brothers, be tenderhearted, be courteous.
1 Peter 3:8 NKJV

One of the reasons that God placed you here on earth is so that you might become a beacon of encouragement to the world. As a faithful follower of the One from Galilee, you have every reason to be hopeful, and you have every reason to share your hopes with others. When you do, you will discover that hope, like other human emotions, is contagious.

As a follower of Christ, you are instructed to choose your words carefully so as to build others up through wholesome, honest encouragement (Ephesians 4:29). So look for the good in others and celebrate the good that you find. As the old saying goes, "When someone does something good, applaud—you'll make two people happy."

He who becomes a brother to the bruised, a doctor to the despairing, and a comforter to the crushed may not actually say much. What he has to offer is often beyond the power of speech to convey. But, the weary sense it, and it is a balm of Gilead to their souls.

Vance Havner

BUILDING A BETTER YOU

Today, challenge your faith by finding at least three people who need your encouragement, and then give them as much encouragement as you can. Be generous with your words, with pats on the back, and with your prayers. And remember: Encouragement is contagious. You can't lift other people up without lifting yourself up, too.

EXCUSES AND MORE EXCUSES

And now, children, stay with Christ. Live deeply in Christ.
Then we'll be ready for him when he appears,
ready to receive him with open arms, with no cause for
red-faced guilt or lame excuses when he arrives.
1 John 2:28–29 MSG

We live in a world where excuses are everywhere. And it's precisely because excuses are so numerous that they are also so ineffective. When we hear the words, "I'm sorry but . . . ," most of us know exactly what is to follow: the excuse. The dog ate the homework. Traffic was terrible. It's the company's fault. The boss is to blame. The equipment is broken. We're out of that. And so forth, and so on.

Because we humans are such creative excuse-makers, all of the really good excuses have already been taken. In fact, the high-quality excuses have been used, re-used, over-used, and ab-used. That's why excuses don't work—we've heard them all before.

So, if you're wasting your time trying to concoct a new and improved excuse, don't bother. It's impossible. A far better strategy is this: do the work. Now. And let your excellent work speak loudly and convincingly for itself.

An excuse is only the skin of a reason stuffed with a lie.

Vance Havner

BUILDING A BETTER YOU

If you've acquired the unfortunate habit of making excuses . . . you'd better break that habit before that habit breaks you!

QUALITY TIME

So teach us to number our days,
that we may gain a heart of wisdom.
Psalm 90:12 NKJV

Make no mistake, caring for your family requires time—lots of time. You've probably heard about "quality time" and "quantity time." Your family needs both. So, as a responsible Christian, you should willingly invest large quantities of your time and energy in the care and nurturing of your clan.

While caring for your family, you should do your best to ensure that God remains squarely at the center of your household. When you do, God will bless you and yours in ways that you could have scarcely imagined.

Never give your family the leftovers and crumbs of your time.

Charles Swindoll

There is always room for more loving forgiveness within our homes.

James Dobson

BUILDING A BETTER YOU

Put God first in every aspect of your life. And while you're at it, put Him first in every aspect of your family's life, too.

YOUR BODY, GOD'S TEMPLE

*Don't you know that you are God's temple
and that God's Spirit lives in you?*
1 Corinthians 3:16 NCV

Are you shaping up or spreading out? Do you eat sensibly and exercise regularly, or do you spend most of your time on the couch with a high-calorie snack in one hand and a clicker in the other? Are you choosing to treat your body like a temple or a trash heap? How you answer these questions will help determine how long you live and how well you live.

Physical fitness is a choice, a choice that requires discipline—it's as simple as that. So, do yourself this favor: treat your body like a one-of-a-kind gift from God . . . because that's precisely what your body is.

Maximum physical health happens when the body—with all its chemicals, parts, and systems—is functioning as closely to the way God designed it to function.

Dr. Walt Larimore

If you desire to improve your physical well-being and your emotional outlook, increasing your faith can help you.

John Maxwell

BUILDING A BETTER YOU

If you seek an improved level of fitness—or if you seek any other worthy goal—ask God (and keep asking Him) until He answers your prayers.

INFINITE FORGIVENESS

*And forgive us our sins, for we ourselves
also forgive everyone in debt to us.*
Luke 11:4 NKJV

God's power to forgive, like His love, is infinite. Despite your shortcomings, despite your sins, God offers you immediate forgiveness and eternal life when you accept Christ as your Savior.

As a believer who is the recipient of God's forgiveness, how should you behave toward others? Should you forgive them (just as God has forgiven you), or should you remain embittered and resentful? The answer, of course, is found in God's Word: You are instructed to forgive others. When you do, you not only obey God's command, you also free yourself from a prison of your own making.

Only the truly forgiven are truly forgiving.

C. S. Lewis

The love of God is revealed in that He laid down His life for His enemies.

Oswald Chambers

BUILDING A BETTER YOU

God's Word instructs you to forgive others . . . no exceptions.

YOU ARE BLESSED

I will give you a new heart and put a new spirit within you.
Ezekiel 36:26 NKJV

If you sat down and began counting your blessings, how long would it take? A very, very long time! Your blessings include life, freedom, family, friends, talents, and possessions, for starters. But, your greatest blessing—a gift that is yours for the asking—is God's gift of salvation through Christ Jesus.

Today, begin making a list of your blessings. You most certainly will not be able to make a complete list, but take a few moments and jot down as many blessings as you can. Then give thanks to the giver of all good things: God. His love for you is eternal, as are His gifts. And it's never too soon—or too late—to offer Him thanks.

Blessings can either humble us and draw us closer to God or allow us to become full of pride and self-sufficiency.

Jim Cymbala

Jesus intended for us to be overwhelmed by the blessings of regular days. He said it was the reason he had come: "I am come that they might have life, and that they might have it more abundantly."

Gloria Gaither

A LESSON FOR THE HEART AND SOUL

If you need a little cheering up, start counting your blessings. In truth, you really have too many blessings to count, but it never hurts to try.

CHEERFULNESS 101

For the happy heart, life is a continual feast.
Proverbs 15:15 NLT

Few things in life are more sad, or, for that matter, more absurd, than a grumpy Christian. Christ promises us lives of abundance and joy, but He does not force His joy upon us. We must claim His joy for ourselves, and when we do, Jesus, in turn, fills our spirits with His power and His love.

How can we receive from Christ the joy that is rightfully ours? By giving Him what is rightfully His: our hearts and our souls.

When we earnestly commit ourselves to the Savior of mankind, when we place Jesus at the center of our lives and trust Him as our personal Savior, He will transform us, not just for today, but for all eternity. Then we, as God's children, can share Christ's joy and His message with a world that needs both.

Sour godliness is the devil's religion.

John Wesley

If his presence does not cheer you, surely heaven itself would not make you glad; for what is heaven but the full enjoyment of his love?

C. H. Spurgeon

A LESSON FOR THE HEART AND SOUL

Cheerfulness is an attitude that is highly contagious. And, remember that cheerfulness starts at the top. A cheerful household usually begins with cheerful adults.

A GROWING RELATIONSHIP WITH GOD

*But grow in the grace and knowledge of our Lord and
Savior Jesus Christ. To Him be the glory,
both now and to the day of eternity.*
2 Peter 3:18 NASB

Your relationship with God is ongoing; it unfolds day by day, and it offers countless opportunities to grow closer to Him . . . or not. As each new day unfolds, you are confronted with a wide range of decisions: how you will behave, where you will direct your thoughts, with whom you will associate, and what you will choose to worship. These choices, along with many others like them, are yours and yours alone. How you choose determines how your relationship with God will unfold.

Are you continuing to grow in your love and knowledge of the Lord, or are you "satisfied" with the current state of your spiritual health? Hopefully, you're determined to make yourself a growing Christian. Your Savior deserves no less, and neither, by the way, do you.

When it comes to walking with God, there is no such thing as instant maturity. God doesn't mass produce His saints. He hand tools each one, and it always takes longer than we expected.

Charles Swindoll

BUILDING A BETTER YOU

When Jesus endured His sacrifice on the cross, He paid a terrible price for you. What price are you willing to pay for Him?

INFINITE LOVE

For I am persuaded that neither death nor life, nor angels nor principalities nor powers, nor things present nor things to come, nor height nor depth, nor any other created thing, shall be able to separate us from the love of God which is in Christ Jesus our Lord.

Romans 8:38–39 NKJV

Christ's love for you is personal. He loves you so much that He gave His life in order that you might spend all eternity with Him. Christ loves you individually and intimately; His is a love unbounded by time or circumstance. Are you willing to experience an intimate relationship with Him? Your Savior is waiting patiently; don't make Him wait a single minute longer. Embrace His love today.

Christ is like a river that is continually flowing. There are always fresh supplies of water coming from the fountain-head, so that a man may live by it and be supplied with water all his life. So Christ is an ever-flowing fountain; he is continually supplying his people, and the fountain is not spent. They who live upon Christ may have fresh supplies from him for all eternity; they may have an increase of blessedness that is new, and new still, and which never will come to an end.

Jonathan Edwards

BUILDING A BETTER YOU

Jesus loves you. His love can—and should—be the cornerstone and the touchstone of your life.

NO COMPLAINTS

Do everything without complaining or arguing.
Then you will be innocent and without any wrong.
Philippians 2:14–15 NCV

Because we are imperfect human beings, we often lose sight of our blessings. Ironically, most of us have more blessings than we can count, but we may still find reasons to complain about the minor frustrations of everyday life. To do so, of course, is not only wrong; it is also the pinnacle of shortsightedness and a serious roadblock on the path to spiritual abundance.

Are you tempted to complain about the inevitable minor frustrations of everyday living? Don't do it! Today and every day, make it a practice to count your blessings, not your hardships. It's the truly decent way to live.

Jesus wept, but he never complained.

C. H. Spurgeon

I am sure it is never sadness—a proper, straight, natural response to loss—that does people harm, but all the other things, all the resentment, dismay, doubt and self-pity with which it is usually complicated.

C. S. Lewis

BUILDING A BETTER YOU

If you're wise, you'll fill your heart with gratitude. When you do, there's simply no room left for complaints.

SEEKING GOD AND FINDING HAPPINESS

Happy is he who has the God of Jacob for his help,
whose hope is in the Lord his God.
Psalm 146:5 NKJV

Happiness depends less upon our circumstances than upon our thoughts. When we turn our thoughts to God, to His gifts, and to His glorious creation, we experience the joy that God intends for His children. But, when we focus on the negative aspects of life, we suffer needlessly.

Do you sincerely want to be a happy Christian? Then set your mind and your heart upon God's love and His grace. The fullness of life in Christ is available to all who seek it and claim it. Count yourself among that number. Seek first the salvation that is available through a personal relationship with Jesus Christ, and then claim the joy, the peace, and the spiritual abundance that the Shepherd offers His sheep.

The happiness which brings enduring worth to life is not the superficial happiness that is dependent on circumstances. It is the happiness and contentment that fills the soul in the midst of the most distressing of circumstances.

Billy Graham

A LESSON FOR THE HEART AND SOUL

Happiness is a positive interpretation of the world and its events. Happiness requires that you train yourself to see the good in everything, no matter what happens.

THE SELF-FULFILLING PROPHECY

May He grant you according to your heart's desire,
and fulfill all your purpose.
Psalm 20:4 NKJV

The self-fulfilling prophecy is alive, well, and living at your house. If you trust God and have faith for the future, your optimistic beliefs will give you direction and motivation. That's one reason that you should never lose hope, but certainly not the only reason. The primary reason that you, as a believer, should never lose hope, is because of God's unfailing promises.

Make no mistake about it: thoughts are powerful things. Your thoughts have the power to lift you up or to hold you down. When you acquire the habit of hopeful thinking, you will have acquired a powerful tool for improving your life. So if you fall into the habit of negative thinking, think again. After all, God's Word teaches us that Christ can overcome every difficulty (John 16:33). And when God makes a promise, He keeps it.

The most profane word we use is "hopeless." When you say a situation or person is hopeless, you are slamming the door in the face of God.

Kathy Troccoli

BUILDING A BETTER YOU

As you plan for your future, be aware that attitudes have a way of transforming themselves into reality. In other words, how you think will help determine what you become. So think realistically about yourself and your situation while making a conscious effort to focus on hopes, not fears. When you do, you'll put the self-fulfilling prophecy to work for you.

COMPASSIONATE CHRISTIANITY

So, as those who have been chosen of God,
holy and beloved, put on a heart of compassion, kindness,
humility, gentleness and patience.
Colossians 3:12 NASB

The instructions of Colossians 3:12 are unambiguous: As Christians, we are to be compassionate, humble, gentle, and kind. But sometimes, we fall short. In the busyness and confusion of daily life, we may neglect to share a kind word or a kind deed. This oversight hurts others, but it hurts us most of all.

Today, slow yourself down and be alert for those who need your smile, your kind words, or your helping hand. Make kindness a centerpiece of your dealings with others. They will be blessed, and you will be too. Today, honor Christ by following His Golden Rule. He deserves no less, and neither, for that matter, do your friends.

When you extend hospitality to others, you're not trying to impress people, you're trying to reflect God to them.

Max Lucado

Be so preoccupied with good will that you haven't room for ill will.

E. Stanley Jones

A LESSON FOR THE HEART AND SOUL
Kindness is contagious—make sure that your family and friends catch it from you!

SPIRITUAL WEALTH

*Don't you realize that friendship with this world makes you
an enemy of God? I say it again, that if your aim is to
enjoy this world, you can't be a friend of God.*
James 4:4 NLT

Sometimes it's hard being a Christian, especially when the world keeps pumping out messages that are contrary to your faith.

The media is working around the clock in an attempt to rearrange your priorities. The media says that your appearance is all-important, that your clothes are all-important, that your relationships with the opposite sex are all-important, and that partying is all-important. But guess what? Those messages are lies. The "all-important" things in your life have little to do with parties and appearances. The all-important things in life have to do with your faith, your family, and your future. Period.

Are you willing to stand up for your faith? Are you willing to stand up and be counted, not just in church, where it's relatively easy to be a Christian, but also out there in the "real" world, where it's hard? Hopefully so, because you owe it to God and you owe it to yourself.

All those who look to draw their satisfaction from the wells of the world will soon be thirsty again!

Anne Graham Lotz

A LESSON FOR THE HEART AND SOUL

The media is sending out messages that are dangerous to your physical, emotional, and spiritual health. If you choose to believe those messages, you're setting yourself up for lots of trouble.

BELIEVING MAKES A DIFFERENCE

You have not seen Christ, but still you love him.
You cannot see him now, but you believe in him. So you are filled
with a joy that cannot be explained, a joy full of glory. And you are
receiving the goal of your faith—the salvation of your souls.
1 Peter 1:8–9 NCV

If you'd like to partake in the peace that only God can give, make certain that your actions are guided by His Word. And while you're at it, pay careful attention to the conscience that God, in His infinite wisdom, has placed in your heart. Don't treat your faith as if it were separate from your everyday life. Weave your beliefs into the very fabric of your day. When you do, God will honor your good works, and your good works will honor God.

If you seek to be a responsible believer, you must realize that it is never enough to hear the instructions of God; you must also live by them. And it is never enough to wait idly by while others do God's work here on earth; you, too, must act. Doing God's work is a responsibility that every Christian (including you) should bear. And when you do, your loving Heavenly Father will reward your efforts with a bountiful harvest.

Faith is to believe what you do not see; the reward of this faith is to see what you believe.

St. Augustine

A LESSON FOR THE HEART AND SOUL

When you stand up for your beliefs—and when you follow your conscience—you'll feel better about yourself. When you don't, you won't.

THE FUTILITY OF BLAMING OTHERS

Walking down the street, Jesus saw a man blind from birth.
His disciples asked, "Rabbi, who sinned: this man or his parents,
causing him to be born blind?" Jesus said, "You're asking the wrong
question. You're looking for someone to blame. There is no such
cause-effect here. Look instead for what God can do."
John 9:1–3 MSG

To blame others for our own problems is the height of futility. Yet blaming others is a favorite human pastime. Why? Because blaming is much easier than fixing, and criticizing others is so much easier than improving ourselves. So instead of solving our problems legitimately (by doing the work required to solve them) we are inclined to fret, to blame, and to criticize, while doing precious little else. When we do, our problems, quite predictably, remain unsolved.

So, instead of looking for someone to blame, look for something to fix, and then get busy fixing it. And as you consider your own situation, remember this: God has a way of helping those who help themselves, but He doesn't spend much time helping those who don't.

Bitterness only makes suffering worse and closes the spiritual channels through which God can pour His grace.

Warren Wiersbe

BUILDING A BETTER YOU

If you take responsibility for your actions, you're headed in the right direction. If you try to blame others, you're headed down a dead-end street.

CHARACTER COUNTS

But also for this very reason, giving all diligence,
add to your faith virtue, to virtue knowledge.
2 Peter 1:5 NKJV

Character is built slowly over a lifetime. It is the sum of every right decision, every honest word, every noble thought, and every heartfelt prayer. It is forged on the anvil of honorable work and polished by the twin virtues of generosity and humility. Character is a precious thing—difficult to build but easy to tear down. As believers in Christ, we must seek to live each day with discipline, honesty, and faith. When we do, integrity becomes a habit. And God smiles.

God cannot build character without our cooperation. If we resist Him, then He chastens us into submission. But, if we submit to Him, then He can accomplish His work. He is not satisfied with a halfway job. God wants a perfect work; He wants a finished product that is mature and complete.

Warren Wiersbe

BUILDING A BETTER YOU

Take time to think about your own character, both your strong points and your weaknesses. Then list three aspects of your character—longstanding habits or troublesome behaviors—that you would like to change. Finally, ask God to be your partner as you take steps to improve yourself and your life.

CHOOSING WISELY

But the wisdom that is from above is first pure, then peaceable,
gentle, willing to yield, full of mercy and good fruits,
without partiality and without hypocrisy.
James 3:17 NKJV

Because we are creatures of free will, we make choices—lots of them. When we make choices that are pleasing to our Heavenly Father, we are blessed. When we make choices that cause us to walk in the footsteps of God's Son, we enjoy the abundance that Christ has promised to those who follow Him. But when we make choices that are displeasing to God, we sow seeds that have the potential to bring forth a bitter harvest.

Today, as you encounter the challenges of everyday living, you will make hundreds of choices. Choose wisely. Make your thoughts and your actions pleasing to God. And remember: every choice that is displeasing to Him is the wrong choice—no exceptions.

We are either the masters or the victims of our attitudes. It is a matter of personal choice. Who we are today is the result of choices we made yesterday. Tomorrow, we will become what we choose today. To change means to choose to change.

John Maxwell

BUILDING A BETTER YOU

Every step of your life's journey is a choice . . . and the quality of those choices determines the quality of the journey.

NEW BEGINNINGS AND MID-COURSE CORRECTIONS

The prudent see danger and take refuge,
but the simple keep going and suffer from it.
Proverbs 27:12 NIV

In our fast-paced world, everyday life has become an exercise in managing change. Our circumstances change; our relationships change; our bodies change. We grow older every day, as does our world. Thankfully, God does not change. He is eternal, as are the truths that are found in His Holy Word.

Are you facing one of life's inevitable "mid-course corrections"? If so, you must place your faith, your trust, and your life in the hands of the One who does not change: your Heavenly Father. He is the unmoving rock upon which you must construct this day and every day. When you do, you are secure.

Sometimes your medicine bottle says, "Shake well before using." That is what God has to do with some of his people. He has to shake them well before they are usable.

Vance Havner

BUILDING A BETTER YOU

As you face uncertain times, make sure to build your future on a firm foundation: the unshakable foundation of God's eternal promises.

CHOOSING TO PLEASE GOD

I have set before you life and death, blessings and curses.
Now choose life, so that you and your children may live and
that you may love the LORD your God,
listen to his voice, and hold fast to him.
Deuteronomy 30:19–20 NIV

Sometimes, because you're an imperfect human being, you may become so wrapped up in meeting society's expectations that you fail to focus on God's expectations. To do so is a mistake of major proportions—don't make it. Instead, seek God's guidance as you focus your energies on becoming the best "you" that you can possibly be. And, when it comes to matters of conscience, seek approval not from your peers, but from your Creator.

Whom will you try to please today: God or man? Your primary obligation is not to please imperfect men and women. Your obligation is to strive diligently to meet the expectations of an all-knowing and perfect God. Trust Him always. Love Him always. Praise Him always. And make choices that please Him. Always.

No matter how many books you read, no matter how many schools you attend, you're never really wise until you start making wise choices.

Marie T. Freeman

BUILDING A BETTER YOU

Little decisions, when taken together over a long period of time, can have big consequences. So remember that when it comes to matters of health, fitness, stress, and spirituality, there are no small decisions.

HUMBLED BY HIS SACRIFICE

But God forbid that I should boast except in the cross of our Lord Jesus Christ, by whom the world has been crucified to me, and I to the world.
Galatians 6:14 NKJV

As we consider Christ's sacrifice on the cross, we should be profoundly humbled. And today, as we come to Christ in prayer, we should do so in a spirit of humble devotion.

Christ humbled Himself on a cross—for you. He shed His blood—for you. He has offered to walk with you through this life and throughout all eternity. As you approach Him today in prayer, think about His sacrifice and His grace. And be humble.

He came all the way from the comfort and beauty of heaven to the blood-stained cross of Palestine, not just for someone like me in the theoretical, but for precisely me in the personal and practical.
Bill Bright

The sacrifice of the Lamb is absolutely sufficient in itself to take away our sin and reconcile us to God.
Anne Graham Lotz

BUILDING A BETTER YOU

Christ made incredible sacrifices for mankind. What sacrifices will you make today for Him?

GOD'S ASSURANCE

I've told you all this so that trusting me, you will be unshakable and assured, deeply at peace. In this godless world you will continue to experience difficulties. But take heart! I've conquered the world.
John 16:33 MSG

Are you a confident believer, or do you live under a cloud of uncertainty and doubt? As a Christian, you have many reasons to be confident. After all, God is in His Heaven; Christ has risen; and you are the recipient of God's grace. Despite these blessings, you may, from time to time, find yourself being tormented by negative emotions—and you are certainly not alone.

Even the most faithful Christians are overcome by occasional bouts of fear and doubt. You are no different.

But even when you feel very distant from God, remember that God is never distant from you. When you sincerely seek His presence, He will touch your heart, calm your fears, and restore your confidence.

Believe and do what God says. The life-changing consequences will be limitless, and the results will be confidence and peace of mind.

Franklin Graham

Jesus gives us the ultimate rest, the confidence we need, to escape the frustration and chaos of the world around us.

Billy Graham

BUILDING A BETTER YOU

The more you trust God, the more confident you will become.

THE COURAGE TO LIVE BOLDLY

For God hath not given us the spirit of fear;
but of power, and of love, and of a sound mind.
2 Timothy 1:7 KJV

Do you prefer to face your fears rather than run from them? If so, you will be blessed because of your willingness to live courageously.

When Paul wrote Timothy, he reminded his young protégé that the God they served was a bold God, and God's spirit empowered His children with boldness also. Like Timothy, we face times of uncertainty and fear. God's message is the same to us, today, as it was to Timothy: We can live boldly because the spirit of God resides in us.

So today, as you face the challenges of everyday living, remember that God is with you . . . and you are protected.

The Holy Spirit is no skeptic, and the things he has written in our hearts are not doubts or opinions, but assertions—surer and more certain than sense or life itself.

Martin Luther

BUILDING A BETTER YOU

Attitudes are contagious, so it's important to associate with people who are upbeat, optimistic, and encouraging.

HIS POWER AND YOURS

*When we were baptized, we were buried with Christ and
shared his death. So, just as Christ was raised from the dead
by the wonderful power of the Father, we also can live a new life.*

Romans 6:4 NCV

When you invite Christ to rule over your heart, you avail yourself of His power. And make no mistake about it: You and Christ, working together, can do miraculous things. In fact, miraculous things are exactly what Christ intends for you to do, but He won't force you to do great things on His behalf. The decision to become a full-fledged participant in His power is a decision that you must make for yourself.

The words of John 14:12 make this promise: when you put absolute faith in Christ, you can share in His power. Today, trust the Savior's promise and expect a miracle in His name.

The amount of power you experience to live a victorious, triumphant Christian life is directly proportional to the freedom you give the Spirit to be Lord of your life!

Anne Graham Lotz

I now know the power of the risen Lord! He lives! The dawn of Easter has broken in my own soul! My night is gone!

Mrs. Charles E. Cowman

BUILDING A BETTER YOU

When you form a genuine partnership with God, you can do amazing things. So make God your partner in every aspect of your life.

CONFIDENT CHRISTIANITY

You are my hope; O Lord GOD, You are my confidence.
Psalm 71:5 NASB

We Christians have many reasons to be confident. God is in His Heaven; Christ has risen, and we are the sheep of His flock. Yet sometimes, even the most devout Christians can become discouraged. Discouragement, however, is not God's way; He is a God of possibility not negativity.

Are you a confident Christian? You should be. God's grace is eternal and His promises are unambiguous. So count your blessings, not your hardships. And live courageously. God is the Giver of all things good, and He watches over you today and forever.

If we indulge in any confidence that is not grounded on the Rock of Ages, our confidence is worse than a dream, it will fall on us and cover us with its ruins, causing sorrow and confusion.

C. H. Spurgeon

Believe and do what God says. The life-changing consequences will be limitless, and the results will be confidence and peace of mind.

Franklin Graham

BUILDING A BETTER YOU

Increase your confidence by living in God's will for your life.

TAKING TIME TO ASK

He heeded their prayer, because they put their trust in him.
1 Chronicles 5:20 NKJV

Amid the demands and the frustrations of everyday life, we can forget to slow ourselves down long enough to talk with God. Instead of turning our thoughts and prayers to Him, we rely upon our own resources. Instead of praying for strength and courage, we seek to manufacture it within ourselves. Instead of asking God for guidance, we depend only upon our own limited wisdom. The results of such behaviors are unfortunate and, on occasion, tragic.

Are you in need? Ask God to sustain you. Are you troubled? Take your worries to Him in prayer. Are you weary? Seek God's strength. In all things great and small, seek God's wisdom and His grace. He hears your prayers, and He will answer. All you must do is ask.

God makes prayer as easy as possible for us. He's completely approachable and available, and He'll never mock or upbraid us for bringing our needs before Him.

Shirley Dobson

God's help is near and always available, but it is only given to those who seek it.

Max Lucado

BUILDING A BETTER YOU

If you're searching for peace and abundance, ask for God's help—and keep asking—until He answers your prayers.

A BOOK UNLIKE ANY OTHER

For I am not ashamed of the gospel of Christ,
for it is the power of God to salvation for everyone who believes.
Romans 1:16 NKJV

God's Word is unlike any other book. A. W. Tozer wrote, "The purpose of the Bible is to bring men to Christ, to make them holy and prepare them for Heaven. In this it is unique among books, and it always fulfills its purpose."

George Mueller observed, "The vigor of our spiritual lives will be in exact proportion to the place held by the Bible in our lives and in our thoughts." As Christians, we are called upon to study God's Holy Word and then to share it with the world.

The Bible is a priceless gift, a tool for Christians to use as they share the Good News of their Savior, Christ Jesus. Too many Christians, however, keep their spiritual tool kits tightly closed and out of sight. Jonathan Edwards advised, "Be assiduous in reading the Holy Scriptures. This is the fountain whence all knowledge in divinity must be derived. Therefore let not this treasure lie by you neglected." God's Holy Word is, indeed, a priceless, one-of-a-kind treasure. Handle it with care, but, more importantly, handle it every day.

If we neglect the Bible, we cannot expect to benefit from the wisdom and direction that result from knowing God's Word.

Vonette Bright

BUILDING A BETTER YOU

Take a Bible with you wherever you go. You never know when you may need a midday spiritual pick-me-up.

ACKNOWLEDGING YOUR BLESSINGS

The Lord bless you and keep you; the Lord make His face shine upon you, and be gracious to you.
Numbers 6:24–25 NKJV

When the demands of life leave us rushing from place to place with scarcely a moment to spare, we may fail to pause and thank our Creator for His gifts. But, whenever we neglect to give proper thanks to the Father, we suffer because of our misplaced priorities.

Today, begin making a list of your blessings. You most certainly will not be able to make a complete list, but take a few moments and jot down as many blessings as you can. Then, give thanks to the Giver of all good things: God. His love for you is eternal, as are His gifts. And it's never too soon—or too late—to offer Him thanks.

Think of the blessings we so easily take for granted: Life itself; preservation from danger; every bit of health we enjoy; every hour of liberty; the ability to see, to hear, to speak, to think, and to imagine all this comes from the hand of God.

Billy Graham

BUILDING A BETTER YOU

Don't overlook God's gifts. Every sunrise represents yet another beautifully wrapped gift from God. Unwrap it; treasure it; use it; and give thanks to the Giver.

GOD KNOWS . . . AND CARES

*But with me it is a very small thing that I should be judged
by you or by a human court. In fact, I do not even judge myself.
For I know nothing against myself, yet I am not justified by this;
but He who judges me is the Lord.*

1 Corinthians 4:3–4 NKJV

If you're like most people, you seek the admiration of your neighbors, your coworkers, and your family members. But the eagerness to please others should never overshadow your eagerness to please God. If you seek to fulfill the purposes that God has in store for you, then you must be a "doer of the word." And how can you do so? By putting God first.

Martin Luther issued this stern warning: "You may as well quit reading and hearing the Word of God and give it to the devil if you do not desire to live according to it." Luther understood that obedience leads to abundance just as surely as disobedience leads to disaster; you should understand it, too.

Would you like a time-tested formula for successful living? Here it is: Don't just listen to God's Word, live by it. Does this sound too simple? Perhaps it is simple, but it is also the only way to reap the marvelous riches that God has in store for you.

The best evidence of our having the truth is our walking in the truth.

Matthew Henry

BUILDING A BETTER YOU

When it comes to doing the right thing, don't put it off. If you're not willing to do the right thing today, why should you (or anybody else, for that matter) expect you to change tomorrow?

HEEDING GOD'S CALL

*One thing I do, forgetting those things which are behind and
reaching forward to those things which are ahead, I press toward
the goal for the prize of the upward call of God in Christ Jesus.*
Philippians 3:13–14 NKJV

It is vitally important that you heed God's call. In John 15:16, Jesus says, "You did not choose me, but I chose you and appointed you to go and bear fruit—fruit that will last" (NIV). In other words, you have been called by Christ, and now, it is up to you to decide precisely how you will answer.

Have you already found your special calling? If so, you're a very lucky person. If not, keep searching and keep praying until you discover it. And remember this: God has important work for you to do—work that no one else on earth can accomplish but you.

When you become consumed by God's call on your life, everything will take on new meaning and significance. You will begin to see every facet of your life, including your pain, as a means through which God can work to bring others to Himself.

Charles Stanley

God never calls without enabling us. In other words, if he calls you to do something, he makes it possible for you to do it.

Luci Swindoll

BUILDING A BETTER YOU

God has a plan for your life, a divine calling that you can either answer or ignore. How you choose to respond to God's calling will determine the direction you take and the contributions you make.

STRENGTH FOR THE DAY

I can do all things through Christ which strengtheneth me.
Philippians 4:13 KJV

Have you made God the cornerstone of your life, or is He relegated to a few hours on Sunday morning? Have you genuinely allowed God to reign over every corner of your heart, or have you attempted to place Him in a spiritual compartment? The answer to these questions will determine the direction of your day and your life.

God loves you. In times of trouble, He will comfort you; in times of sorrow, He will dry your tears. When you are weak or sorrowful, God is as near as your next breath. He stands at the door of your heart and waits. Welcome Him in and allow Him to rule. And then, accept the peace, and the strength, and the protection, and the abundance that only God can give.

The God we seek is a God who is intrinsically righteous and who will be so forever. With His example and His strength, we can share in that righteousness.

Bill Hybels

The knowledge that we are never alone calms the troubled sea of our lives and speaks peace to our souls.

A. W. Tozer

A LESSON FOR THE HEART AND SOUL

God can handle it. Corrie ten Boom advised, "God's all-sufficiency is a major. Your inability is a minor. Major in majors, not in minors." Enough said.

PERFECT WISDOM

Therefore everyone who hears these words of mine and puts them into practice is like a wise man who built his house on the rock.
Matthew 7:24–25 NIV

Where will you place your trust today? Will you trust in the wisdom of fallible men and women, or will you place your faith in God's perfect wisdom? Where you choose to place your trust will determine the direction and quality of your life.

Are you tired? Discouraged? Fearful? Be comforted and trust God. Are you worried or anxious? Be confident in God's power and trust His Holy Word. Are you confused? Listen to the quiet voice of your Heavenly Father. He is not a God of confusion. Talk with Him; listen to Him; trust Him. He is steadfast, and He is your protector . . . forever.

If you lack knowledge, go to school. If you lack wisdom, get on your knees.

Vance Havner

The Scriptures were not given for our information, but for our transformation.

D. L. Moody

BUILDING A BETTER YOU

God's wisdom is perfect, and it's available to you. So if you want to become wise, become a student of God's Word and a follower of His Son.

HEALTHY CHOICES

*I shall yet praise him, who is the health of
my countenance, and my God.*
Psalm 42:11 KJV

The journey toward improved health is not only a common-sense exercise in personal discipline, it is also a spiritual journey ordained by our Creator. God does not intend that we abuse our bodies by giving in to our excessive appetites or to slothful behavior. To the contrary, God has instructed us to protect our physical bodies to the greatest extent we can. To do otherwise is to disobey Him.

God's plan for you includes provisions for your spiritual, physical, and emotional health. But, He expects you to do your fair share of the work! In a world that is chock-full of tasty temptations, you may find it all too easy to make unhealthy choices. Your challenge, of course, is to resist those unhealthy temptations by every means you can, including prayer. And rest assured: when you ask for God's help, He will give it.

If you desire to improve your physical well-being and your emotional outlook, increasing your faith can help you.

John Maxwell

A LESSON FOR THE HEART AND SOUL

Life is a gift—health must be earned. We earn good health by cultivating healthy habits.

TO GOD BE THE GLORY

Likewise you younger people, submit yourselves to your elders.
1 Peter 5:5 NKJV

As Christians, we have a profound reason to be humble: We have been refashioned and saved by Jesus Christ, and that salvation came not because of our own good works but because of God's grace. Thus, we are not "self-made"; we are "God-made"; and "Christ-saved." How, then, can we be boastful?

Dietrich Bonhoeffer observed, "It is very easy to overestimate the importance of our own achievements in comparison with what we owe others." In other words, reality breeds humility. So, instead of puffing out your chest and saying, "Look at me!" give credit where credit is due, starting with God. And, rest assured: There is no such thing as a self-made man. All of us are made by God . . . and He deserves the glory, not us.

A humble heart is like a magnet that draws the favor of God toward us.

Jim Cymbala

A LESSON FOR THE HEART AND SOUL

Humility leads to happiness; pride doesn't. Max Lucado writes, "God exalts humility. When God works in our lives, helping us to become humble, he gives us a permanent joy. Humility gives us a joy that cannot be taken away." Enough said.

A DOSE OF LAUGHTER

A joyful heart is good medicine, but a broken spirit dries up the bones.
Proverbs 17:22 NASB

Laughter is medicine for the soul, but sometimes, amid the stresses of the day, we forget to take our medicine. Instead of viewing our world with a mixture of optimism and humor, we allow worries and distractions to rob us of the joy that God intends for our lives. Today, as you go about your daily activities, approach life with a smile and a chuckle. After all, God created laughter for a reason . . . and Father indeed knows best. So laugh!

When you have good, healthy relationships with your family and friends you're more prompted to laugh and not to take yourself so seriously.

Dennis Swanberg

A keen sense of humor helps us to overlook the unbecoming, understand the unconventional, tolerate the unpleasant, overcome the unexpected, and outlast the unbearable.

Billy Graham

BUILDING A BETTER YOU

If you can't see the joy and humor in everyday life, you're not paying attention to the right things. Remember the donut-maker's creed: "As you travel through life brother, whatever be your goal, keep your eye upon the donut, and not upon the hole."

CONTENTMENT THAT LASTS

*But godliness with contentment is great gain. For we brought
nothing into the world, and we can take nothing out of it.
But if we have food and clothing, we will be content with that.*
1 Timothy 6:6–8 NIV

The preoccupation with happiness and contentment is an ever-present theme in the modern world. We are bombarded with messages that tell us where to find peace and pleasure in a world that worships materialism and wealth. But, lasting contentment is not found in material possessions; genuine contentment is a spiritual gift from God to those who trust in Him and follow His commandments. When God dwells at the center of our lives, peace and contentment will belong to us just as surely as we belong to God.

He is truly happy who has all that he wishes to have, and wishes to have nothing that he ought not to have.

St. Augustine

The happiness which brings enduring worth to life is not the superficial happiness that is dependent on circumstances. It is the happiness and contentment that fills the soul in the midst of the most distressing of circumstances.

Billy Graham

A LESSON FOR THE HEART AND SOUL

God offers you His peace, His protection, and His promises. If you accept these gifts, you will be content.

NEW AND APPROVED

*Now we look inside, and what we see is that anyone united
with the Messiah gets a fresh start, is created new.
The old life is gone; a new life burgeons! Look at it!*
2 Corinthians 5:17 MSG

Think, for a moment, about the "old" you, the person you were before you invited Christ to reign over your heart. Now, think about the "new" you, the person you have become since then. Is there a difference between the "old" you and the "new and improved" version? There should be! And that difference should be noticeable not only to you but also to others.

The Bible clearly teaches that when we welcome Christ into our hearts, we become new creations through Him. Our challenge, of course, is to behave ourselves like new creations. When we do, God fills our hearts, He blesses our endeavors, and He transforms our lives . . . forever.

The transforming love of God has repositioned me for eternity. I am now a new man, forgiven, basking in the warm love of our living God, trusting His promises and provision, and enjoying life to the fullest.

Bill Bright

BUILDING A BETTER YOU

All of your talents and opportunities come from God. Give Him thanks, and give Him the glory.

ABOVE AND BEYOND OUR CIRCUMSTANCES

*Should we accept only good things from
the hand of God and never anything bad?*
Job 2:10 NLT

All of us face difficult days. Sometimes even the most devout Christians become discouraged, and you are no exception. After all, you live in a world where expectations can be high and demands can be even higher.

If you find yourself enduring difficult circumstances, remember that God remains in His Heaven. If you become discouraged with the direction of your day or your life, turn your thoughts and prayers to Him. He is a God of possibility, not negativity. He will guide you through your difficulties and beyond them.

When you realize that your circumstances, no matter how overwhelming or pressing, are ruled by a King who seeks your highest good, you can truly "consider it all joy . . . when you encounter various trials, knowing that the testing of your faith produces endurance . . . that you may be perfect and complete, lacking in nothing" (James 1:2-4).

Charles Swindoll

A LESSON FOR THE HEART AND SOUL

If it weren't for trouble, we might think we could handle our lives by ourselves. Jim Cymbala writes, "Trouble is one of God's great servants because it reminds us how much we continually need the Lord." We should thank the Lord for challenges that bring us closer to Him.

THE BEST POLICY

The godly are directed by their honesty.
Proverbs 11:5 NLT

From the time we are children, we are taught that honesty is the best policy, but sometimes, being honest is hard. So, we convince ourselves that it's alright to tell "little white lies." But there's a problem: Little white lies tend to grow up, and when they do, they cause havoc and pain in our lives.

For Christians, the issue of honesty is not a topic for debate. Honesty is not just the best policy, it is God's policy, pure and simple. And if we are to be servants worthy of our Savior, Jesus Christ, we must avoid all lies, white or otherwise. So, if you're tempted to sow the seeds of deception (perhaps in the form of a "harmless" white lie), resist that temptation. Truth is God's way, and a lie—of whatever color—is not.

Integrity is not a given factor in everyone's life. It is a result of self-discipline, inner trust, and a decision to be relentlessly honest in all situations in our lives.

John Maxwell

A LESSON FOR THE HEART AND SOUL

Beware of "white" lies. Sometimes, we're tempted to "shade" the truth. Unfortunately, little white lies have a tendency to turn black . . . and they grow. The best strategy is to avoid untruths of all sizes and colors.

GOD'S LESSONS

Get all the advice and instruction you can,
and be wise the rest of your life.
Proverbs 19:20 NLT

When it comes to learning life's lessons, we can either do things the easy way or the hard way. The easy way can be summed up as follows: when God teaches us a lesson, we learn it . . . the first time! Unfortunately, too many of us learn much more slowly than that.

When we resist God's instruction, He continues to teach, whether we like it or not. Our challenge, then, is to discern God's lessons from the experiences of everyday life. Hopefully, we learn those lessons sooner rather than later because the sooner we do, the sooner He can move on to the next lesson and the next, and the next.

Enjoy the adventure of receiving God's guidance. Taste it, revel in it, appreciate the fact that the journey is often a lot more exciting than arriving at the destination.

Bill Hybels

When you persevere through a trial, God gives you a special measure of insight.

Charles Swindoll

BUILDING A BETTER YOU

Never stop learning. Think of it like this: when you're through learning, you're through.

TOO MANY POSSESSIONS

Love not the world, neither the things that are in the world.
If any man love the world, the love of the Father is not in him.
1 John 2:15 KJV

On the grand stage of a well-lived life, material possessions should play a rather small role. Of course, we all need the basic necessities of life, but once we meet those needs for ourselves and for our families, the piling up of possessions creates more problems than it solves. Our real riches, of course, are not of this world. We are never really rich until we are rich in spirit.

How much stuff is too much stuff? Well, if your desire for stuff is getting in the way of your desire to know God, then you've got too much stuff—it's as simple as that. So, if you find yourself wrapped up in the concerns of the material world, it's time to reorder your priorities. And, it's time to begin storing up riches that will endure throughout eternity—the spiritual kind.

Greed is evil because it substitutes material things for the place of honor that the Creator ought to have in an individual's life.

Charles Stanley

A LESSON FOR THE HEART AND SOUL

The world wants you to believe that "money and stuff" can buy happiness. Don't believe it! Genuine happiness comes not from money, but from the things that money can't buy—starting, of course, with your relationship to God and His only begotten Son.

ON BEING AN OPTIMISTIC CHRISTIAN

*My cup runs over. Surely goodness and mercy shall follow me
all the days of my life; and I will dwell in the house of the Lord forever.*
Psalm 23:5–6 NKJV

To be a pessimistic Christian is a contradiction in terms, yet sometimes even the most devout Christians fall prey to fear, doubt, and discouragement. But, God has a different plan for our lives. The comforting words of the 23rd Psalm remind us of God's blessings. In response to His grace, we should strive to focus our thoughts on things that are pleasing to Him, not upon things that are evil, discouraging, or frustrating.

So, the next time you find yourself mired in the pit of pessimism, remember God's Word and redirect your thoughts. This world is God's creation; look for the best in it, and trust Him to take care of the rest.

Keep your feet on the ground, but let your heart soar as high as it will. Refuse to be average or to surrender to the chill of your spiritual environment.

A. W. Tozer

BUILDING A BETTER YOU

Be a realistic optimist. Your attitude toward the future will help create your future. So think realistically about yourself and your situation while making a conscious effort to focus on hopes, not fears. When you do, you'll put the self-fulfilling prophecy to work for you.

HOPE FOR THE JOURNEY

That is why we can say with confidence,
"The Lord is my helper, so I will not be afraid.
What can mere mortals do to me?"
Hebrews 13:6 NLT

Because we are saved by a risen Christ, we can have hope for the future, no matter how desperate our circumstances may seem. After all, God has promised that we are His throughout eternity. And, He has told us that we must place our hopes in Him.

Today, summon the courage to follow God. Even if the path seems difficult, even if your heart is fearful, trust your Heavenly Father and follow Him. Trust Him with your day and your life. Do His work, care for His children, and share His Good News. Let Him guide your steps. He will not lead you astray.

Why rely on yourself and fall? Cast yourself upon His arm. Be not afraid. He will not let you slip. Cast yourself in confidence. He will receive you and heal you.

St. Augustine

Faith is stronger than fear.

John Maxwell

BUILDING A BETTER YOU

Today, think about the rewards of living courageously. And remember: The best way to overcome stress is by taking your concerns to God . . . and leaving them there.

DURING DARK DAYS

I have heard your prayer, I have seen your tears; surely I will heal you.
2 Kings 20:5 NKJV

The sadness that accompanies any significant loss is an inevitable fact of life. In time, sadness runs its course and gradually abates. Depression, on the other hand, is a physical and emotional condition that is highly treatable.

If you find yourself feeling "blue," perhaps it's a logical reaction to the ups and downs of daily life. But if you or someone close to you have become dangerously depressed, it's time to seek professional help.

Some days are light and happy, and some days are not. When we face the inevitable dark days of life, we must choose how we will respond. Will we allow ourselves to sink even more deeply into our own sadness, or will we do the difficult work of pulling ourselves out? We bring light to the dark days of life by turning first to God, and then to trusted family members, friends, and medical professionals. When we do, the clouds will eventually part, and the sun will shine once more upon our souls.

Feelings of uselessness and hopelessness are not from God, but from the evil one, the devil, who wants to discourage you and thwart your effectiveness for the Lord.

Bill Bright

BUILDING A BETTER YOU

Depression is serious business, and it's a highly treatable disease . . . treat it that way.

BEING GENTLE
WITH YOURSELF

You're blessed when you're content with just who you are—
no more, no less. That's the moment you find yourselves
proud owners of everything that can't be bought.
Matthew 5:5 MSG

Being patient with other people can be difficult. But sometimes, we find it even more difficult to be patient with ourselves. We have high expectations and lofty goals. We want to receive God's blessings now, not later. And, of course, we want our lives to unfold according to our own wishes and our own timetables—not God's. Yet throughout the Bible, we are instructed that patience is the companion of wisdom. Proverbs 16:32 teaches us that "Patience is better than strength" (NCV). God's message, then, is clear: We must be patient with all people, beginning with that particular person who stares back at us each time we gaze into the mirror.

The Bible affirms the importance of self-acceptance by exhorting believers to love others as they love themselves (Matthew 22:37-40). Furthermore, the Bible teaches that when we genuinely open our hearts to Him, God accepts us just as we are. And, if He accepts us—faults and all—then who are we to believe otherwise?

May God help us to express and define ourselves in our one-of-a-kind way.

Luci Swindoll

A LESSON FOR THE HEART AND SOUL
You were wonderfully made by a loving God who knew exactly what He was doing. Accept it.

OUR ULTIMATE SAVIOR

*And we have seen and testify that the Father
has seen sent the Son as Savior of the world.*
1 John 4:14 NKJV

Thomas Brooks spoke for believers of every generation when he observed, "Christ is the sun, and all the watches of our lives should be set by the dial of his motion." Christ, indeed, is the ultimate Savior of mankind and the personal Savior of those who believe in Him. As His servants, we should place Him at the very center of our lives. And, every day that God gives us breath, we should share Christ's love and His message with a world that needs both.

Christ is no Moses, no exactor, no giver of laws, but a giver of grace, a Savior; he is infinite mercy and goodness, freely and bountifully given to us.

Martin Luther

Look at yourself, or at others, and you will sink; look at Christ, and you can walk on anything.

E. Stanley Jones

BUILDING A BETTER YOU

Every life is built upon something. Let the foundation of your life be the love of God and the salvation of Christ.

A PLACE OF WORSHIP

For where two or three come together in my name,
there am I with them.
Matthew 18:20 NIV

The Bible teaches that we should worship God in our hearts and in our churches (Acts 20:28). We have clear instructions to "feed the church of God" and to worship our Creator in the presence of fellow believers.

We live in a world that is teeming with temptations and distractions—a world where good and evil struggle in a constant battle to win our minds, our hearts, and our souls. Our challenge, of course, is to ensure that we cast our lot on the side of God. One way that we remain faithful to Him is through the practice of regular, purposeful worship with our families. When we worship the Father faithfully and fervently, we are blessed.

The Church, as announced by Christ, seen in the book of Acts, and explained by Paul, is a thing of great simplicity and rare beauty. The church, as we see it today, is unsymmetrical, highly complex, and anything but beautiful.

A. W. Tozer

BUILDING A BETTER YOU

Make church a celebration, not an obligation. Your attitude toward church is important, in part, because it is contagious . . . so celebrate accordingly!

THE SON OF ENCOURAGEMENT

A cheerful look brings joy to the heart,
and good news gives health to the bones.
Proverbs 15:30 NIV

Barnabas, a man whose name meant "Son of Encouragement," was a leader in the early Christian church. He was known for his kindness and for his ability to encourage others. Because of Barnabas, many people were introduced to Christ. And today, as believers living in a difficult world, we must seek to imitate the "Son of Encouragement."

We imitate Barnabas when we speak kind words to our families and to our friends. We imitate Barnabas when our actions give credence to our beliefs. We imitate Barnabas when we are generous with our possessions and with our praise. We imitate Barnabas when we give hope to the hopeless and encouragement to the downtrodden.

Today, be like Barnabas: become a source of encouragement to those who cross your path. When you do so, you will quite literally change the world, one person—and one moment—at a time.

God is still in the process of dispensing gifts, and He uses ordinary individuals like us to develop those gifts in other people.

Howard Hendricks

BUILDING A BETTER YOU

Encouragement is contagious. You can't lift other people up without lifting yourself up, too.

LOST IN THE CROWD

The fear of human opinion disables;
trusting in God protects you from that.
Proverbs 29:25 MSG

Rick Warren observed, "Those who follow the crowd usually get lost in it." We know these words to be true, but oftentimes we fail to live by them. Instead of trusting God for guidance, we imitate our neighbors and suffer the consequences. Instead of seeking to please our Father in Heaven, we strive to please our peers, with decidedly mixed results.

Whom will you try to please today: Your God or your associates? Your obligation is most certainly not to neighbors, to friends, or even to family members. Your obligation is to an all-knowing, all-powerful God. You must seek to please Him first and always. No exceptions.

People who constantly, and fervently, seek the approval of others live with an identity crisis. They don't know who they are, and they are defined by what others think of them.

Charles Stanley

Do you want to be wise? Choose wise friends.

Charles Swindoll

BUILDING A BETTER YOU

If you are burdened with a "people-pleasing" personality, outgrow it. Realize that you can't please all of the people all of the time, nor should you attempt to.

FOOLISH PRIDE

Do nothing from selfishness or empty conceit,
but with humility of mind regard one another
as more important than yourselves.
Philippians 2:3 NASB

Sometimes our faith is tested more by prosperity than by adversity. Why? Because in times of plenty, we are tempted to stick out our chests and say, "I did that." But nothing could be further from the truth. All of our blessings start and end with God, and whatever "it" is, He did it. And He deserves the credit.

Who are the greatest among us? Are they the proud and the powerful? Hardly. The greatest among us are the humble servants who care less for their own glory and more for God's glory. If we seek greatness in God's eyes, we must forever praise God's good works, not our own.

The Bible never says that God resists a drunkard, a thief, or even a murderer, but he does resist the proud. Every kind of sin can be cleansed and forgiven if we humble ourselves and confess it to the Lord.

Jim Cymbala

BUILDING A BETTER YOU

All of your talents and abilities come from God. Give Him thanks, and give Him the glory.

SEEKING AND FINDING

Ask, and God will give to you. Search, and you will find.
Knock, and the door will open for you. Yes, everyone who
asks will receive. Everyone who searches will find.
And everyone who knocks will have the door opened.

Matthew 7:7–8 NCV

Where is God? He is everywhere you have ever been and everywhere you will ever go. He is with you night and day; He knows your every thought; He hears your every heartbeat.

Sometimes, in the crush of your daily duties, God may seem far away. Or sometimes, when the disappointments and sorrows of life leave you brokenhearted, God may seem distant, but He is not. When you earnestly seek God, you will find Him because He is here, waiting patiently for you to reach out to Him . . . right here . . . right now.

Mark it down. God never turns away the honest seeker. Go to God with your questions. You may not find all the answers, but in finding God, you know the One who does.

Max Lucado

O God. You are always the same. Let me know myself and know You.

St. Augustine

A LESSON FOR THE HEART AND SOUL

God is everywhere you have ever been and everywhere you will ever be. If you seek Him sincerely and often, you will find Him.

THE WISDOM TO CELEBRATE

A miserable heart means a miserable life;
a cheerful heart fills the day with a song.
Proverbs 15:15 MSG

The Christian life is a cause for celebration, but sometimes we don't feel much like celebrating. In fact, when the weight of the world seems to bear down upon our shoulders, celebration may be the last thing on our minds . . . but it shouldn't be. As God's children, we are all blessed beyond measure on good days and bad. This day is a non-renewable resource—once it's gone, it's gone forever. We should give thanks for this day while using it for the glory of God.

What will your attitude be today? Will you be fearful, angry, bored, or worried? Will you be cynical, bitter, or pessimistic? If so, God wants to have a little talk with you.

God created you in His own image, and He wants you to experience joy and abundance. But, God will not force His joy upon you; you must claim it for yourself. So today, and every day thereafter, celebrate the life that God has given you. Think optimistically about yourself and your future. Give thanks to the One who has given you everything, and trust in your heart that He wants to give you so much more.

The things we think are the things that feed our souls. If we think on pure and lovely things, we shall grow pure and lovely like them; and the converse is equally true.

Hannah Whitall Smith

BUILDING A BETTER YOU

If you want to improve the quality of your thoughts, ask God to help you.

A PROMISE TO COUNT ON

*God blesses the people who patiently endure testing.
Afterward they will receive the crown of life that God
has promised to those who love him.*

James 1:12 NLT

Throughout the seasons of life, we must all endure life-altering personal losses that leave us breathless. When we do, we may be overwhelmed by fear, by doubt, or by both. Thankfully, God has promised that He will never desert us. And God keeps His promises.

Life is often challenging, but as Christians, we must trust the promises of our Heavenly Father. God loves us, and He will protect us. In times of hardship, He will comfort us; in times of sorrow, He will dry our tears. When we are troubled, or weak, or sorrowful, God is with us. His love endures, not only for today, but also for all of eternity.

Teach us to set our hopes on heaven, to hold firmly to the promise of eternal life, so that we can withstand the struggles and storms of this world.

Max Lucado

A LESSON FOR THE HEART AND SOUL

Sometimes our losses mean that we must start over. From scratch. As believers, we can find comfort in the knowledge that wherever we find ourselves, whether on the mountaintops of life or in the deepest valleys of despair, God is there with us.

ULTIMATE ACCOUNTABILITY

Walk in a manner worthy of the God who calls you into
His own kingdom and glory.
1 Thessalonians 2:12 NASB

For most of us, it is a daunting thought: one day, perhaps soon, we'll come face-to-face with our Heavenly Father, and we'll be called to account for our actions here on earth. Our personal histories will certainly not be surprising to God; He already knows everything about us. But the full scope of our activities may be surprising to us. Some of us will be pleasantly surprised; others will not be.

Today, do whatever you can to ensure that your thoughts and your deeds are pleasing to your Creator. Because you will, at some point in the future, be called to account for your actions. And the future may be sooner than you think.

Our walk counts far more than our talk, always!

George Mueller

The measure of a man is not what he does on Sunday, but rather who he is Monday through Saturday.

Anonymous

A LESSON FOR THE HEART AND SOUL

How can you guard your steps? By walking with Jesus every day of your life.

GOD'S ALLY

Be self-controlled and alert. Your enemy the devil prowls
around like a roaring lion looking for someone to devour.
Resist him, standing firm in the faith....
1 Peter 5:8–9 NIV

Nineteenth-century clergyman Edwin Hubbel Chapin warned, "Neutral men are the devil's allies." His words were true then, and they're true now. Neutrality in the face of evil is a sin. Yet all too often, we fail to fight evil, not because we are neutral, but because we are shortsighted: We don't fight the devil because we don't recognize his handiwork.

If we are to recognize evil and fight it, we must pay careful attention. We must pay attention to God's Word, and we must pay attention to the realities of everyday life. When we observe life objectively, and when we do so with eyes and hearts that are attuned to God's Holy Word, we can no longer be neutral believers. And when we are no longer neutral, God rejoices while the devil despairs.

Christianity isn't a religion about going to Sunday school, potluck suppers, being nice, holding car washes, sending your secondhand clothes off to Mexico—as good as those things might be. This is a world at war.

John Eldredge

A LESSON FOR THE HEART AND SOUL

Evil exists, and it exists someplace not too far from you. You must guard your steps and your heart accordingly.

FAITH THAT WORKS

*I can already hear one of you agreeing by saying, "Sounds good.
You take care of the faith department, I'll handle the works
department." Not so fast. You can no more show me your works
apart from your faith than I can show you my faith
apart from my works. Faith and works,
works and faith, fit together hand in glove.*

James 2:18 MSG

It is important to remember that the work required to build and sustain our faith is an ongoing process. Corrie ten Boom advised, "Be filled with the Holy Spirit; join a church where the members believe the Bible and know the Lord; seek the fellowship of other Christians; learn and be nourished by God's Word and His many promises. Conversion is not the end of your journey—it is only the beginning."

The work of nourishing your faith can and should be joyful work. The hours that you invest in Bible study, prayer, meditation, and worship should be times of enrichment and celebration. And, as you continue to build your life upon a foundation of faith, you will discover that the journey toward spiritual maturity lasts a lifetime. As a child of God, you are never fully "grown": instead, you can continue "growing up" every day of your life. And that's exactly what God wants you to do.

A LESSON FOR THE HEART AND SOUL

Faith should be practiced more than studied. Vance Havner said, "Nothing is more disastrous than to study faith, analyze faith, make noble resolves of faith, but never actually to make the leap of faith." How true!

FINANCIAL SECURITY

Honor the Lord with your wealth and the firstfruits from all your crops. Then your barns will be full, and your wine barrels will overflow with new wine.

Proverbs 3:9–10 NCV

The quest for financial security is a journey that leads us across many peaks and through a few unexpected valleys. When we reach the mountaintops, we find it easy to praise God and to give thanks. But, when we face disappointment or financial hardship, it seems so much more difficult to trust God's perfect plan. But, trust Him we must.

As you strive to achieve financial security for your family, remember this: The next time you find your courage tested to the limit (and it will be), lean upon God's promises. Trust His Son. Remember that God is always near and that He is your protector and your deliverer. Always.

One of the dangers of having a lot of money is that you may be quite satisfied with the kinds of happiness money can give and so fail to realize your need for God. If everything seems to come simply by signing checks, you may forget that you are at every moment totally dependent on God.

C. S. Lewis

BUILDING A BETTER YOU

It pays to be frugal. If you spend more than you make, you're sending Old Man Trouble an engraved invitation to become an integral part of your life—and that's a very big mistake.

NOW IS THE TIME

So, my son, throw yourself into this work for Christ.
2 Timothy 1:1 MSG

God's love for you is deeper and more profound than you can imagine. God's love for you is so great that He sent His only Son to this earth to die for your sins and to offer you the priceless gift of eternal life. Now, you must decide whether or not to accept God's gift. Will you ignore it or embrace it? Will you return it or neglect it? Will you accept Christ's love and build a lifelong relationship with Him, or will you turn away from Him and take a different path?

Your decision to allow Christ to reign over your heart is the pivotal decision of your life. It is a decision that you cannot ignore. It is a decision that is yours and yours alone. Accept God's gift now. Allow His Son to preside over your heart, your thoughts, and your life, starting this very instant.

If we seek salvation, we are taught by the very name of Jesus that it is "of him." If we seek any other gifts of the Spirit, they will be found in his anointing. If we seek strength, it lies in his dominion; if purity, in his conception; if gentleness, it appears in his birth.

John Calvin

BUILDING A BETTER YOU

Think about ways that you can follow Christ—and think about ways you can encourage others to do the same.

A LIFE OF FULFILLMENT

For You, O God, have tested us; You have refined us
as silver is refined . . . we went through fire and through water;
but You brought us out to rich fulfillment.
Psalm 66:10–12 NKJV

Everywhere we turn, or so it seems, the world promises fulfillment, contentment, and happiness. But the contentment that the world offers is fleeting and incomplete. Thankfully, the fulfillment that God offers is all encompassing and everlasting.

Sometimes, amid the inevitable busyness of life, we can forfeit—albeit temporarily—the joy of Christ as we wrestle with the challenges of daily living. Yet God's Word is clear: Fulfillment through Christ is available to all who seek it and claim it. Count yourself among that number. Seek first a personal, transforming relationship with Jesus, and then claim the joy, the fulfillment, and the spiritual abundance that the Shepherd offers His sheep.

Find satisfaction in him who made you, and only then find satisfaction in yourself as part of his creation.

St. Augustine

We are never more fulfilled than when our longing for God is met by His presence in our lives.

Billy Graham

BUILDING A BETTER YOU

Want to increase your sense of fulfillment? Then strive to find God's path for your life . . . and follow it.

FRIENDS AND FAMILY

As iron sharpens iron, a friend sharpens a friend.
Proverbs 27:17 NLT

A loving family is a treasure from God; so is a trustworthy friend. If you are a member of a close knit, supportive family, offer a word of thanks to your Creator. And if you have a close circle of trustworthy friends, consider yourself richly blessed.

Today, let us praise God for our family and for our friends. God has placed these people along our paths. Let us love them and care for them. And, let us give thanks to the Father for all the people who enrich our lives. These people are, in a very real sense, gifts from God; we should treat them as such.

God often keeps us on the path by guiding us through the counsel of friends and trusted spiritual advisors.

Bill Hybels

Do you want to be wise? Choose wise friends.

Charles Swindoll

BUILDING A BETTER YOU

Thank your Creator God for the family and friends He has placed along your path. Cherish those relationships, and do your best to make them flourish.

WHY HE SENT HIS SON

For all have sinned and fall short of the glory of God.
Romans 3:23 NKJV

Despite our shortcomings, God sent His Son so that we might be redeemed from our sins. In doing so, our Heavenly Father demonstrated His infinite mercy and His infinite love. We have received countless gifts from God, but none can compare with the gift of salvation. God's grace is the ultimate gift, and we owe Him the ultimate in thanksgiving.

Christ sacrificed His life on the cross so that we might have eternal life. This gift, freely given from God's only begotten Son, is the priceless possession of everyone who accepts Him as Lord and Savior. We return our Savior's love by welcoming Him into our hearts and sharing His message and His love. When we do so, we are blessed here on earth and throughout all eternity.

The grace of God is infinite and eternal. As it had no beginning, so it can have no end, and being an attribute of God, it is as boundless as infinitude.

A. W. Tozer

The most amazing thing about grace to the suffering heart and soul is its utter sufficiency.

Bill Bright

A LESSON FOR THE HEART AND SOUL

God's grace isn't earned, but freely given—what an amazing, humbling gift.

A WORTHY DISCIPLE

He has showed you, O man, what is good.
And what does the LORD require of you? To act justly and to
love mercy and to walk humbly with your God.
Micah 6:8 NIV

When Jesus addressed His disciples, He warned that each one must, "take up his cross and follow Me." The disciples must have known exactly what the Master meant. In Jesus' day, prisoners were forced to carry their own crosses to the location where they would be put to death. Thus, Christ's message was clear: In order to follow Him, Christ's disciples must deny themselves and, instead, trust Him completely. Nothing has changed since then.

If we are to be disciples of Christ, we must trust Him and place Him at the very center of our beings. Jesus never comes "next." He is always first.

Do you seek to be a worthy disciple of Christ? Then pick up His cross today and every day that you live. When you do, He will bless you now and forever.

He cannot bless us unless He has us. When we try to keep within us an area that is our own, we try to keep an area of death. Therefore, in love, He claims all. There's no bargaining with Him.

C. S. Lewis

A LESSON FOR THE HEART AND SOUL

If you want to be a disciple of Christ . . . follow in His footsteps, obey His commandments, and share His never-ending love.

HIS STRENGTH

Now I take limitations in stride, and with good cheer,
these limitations that cut me down to size—abuse, accidents,
opposition, bad breaks. I just let Christ take over!
And so the weaker I get, the stronger I become.
2 Corinthians 12:10 MSG

Life is a tapestry of good days and difficult days, with good days predominating. During the good days, we are tempted to take our blessings for granted (a temptation that we must resist with all our might). But, during life's difficult days, we discover precisely what we're made of. And more importantly, we discover what our faith is made of.

Has your faith been put to the test yet? If so, then you know that with God's help, you can endure life's darker days. But if you have not yet faced the inevitable trials and tragedies of life, don't worry: you will. And when your faith is put to the test, rest assured that God is perfectly willing—and always ready—to give you strength for the struggle.

God is the only one who can make the valley of trouble a door of hope.

Catherine Marshall

BUILDING A BETTER YOU

If you're going through difficult times, consider it an opportunity for spiritual growth. Elisabeth Elliot correctly observes, "God's curriculum will always include lessons we wish we could skip. With an intimate understanding of our deepest needs and individual capacities, He chooses our curriculum." So ask yourself this question: "What is God trying to teach me today?"

NEIGHBORS IN NEED

*Each one of us needs to look after the good of the people around us,
asking ourselves, "How can I help?" That's exactly what Jesus did.*
Romans 15:2–3 MSG

Neighbors. We know that we are instructed to love them, and yet there's so little time . . . and we're so busy. No matter. As Christians, we are commanded by our Lord and Savior Jesus Christ to love our neighbors just as we love ourselves. Period.

This very day, you will encounter someone who needs a word of encouragement, or a pat on the back, or a helping hand, or a heartfelt prayer. And, if you don't reach out to your friend, who will? If you don't take the time to understand the needs of your neighbors, who will? If you don't love your brothers and sisters, who will? So, today, look for a neighbor in need . . . and then do something to help. Father's orders.

Encouraging others means helping people, looking for the best in them, and trying to bring out their positive qualities.

John Maxwell

A LESSON FOR THE HEART AND SOUL

It's good to feel compassion for others . . . but it's better to do something to ease their suffering. Martin Luther wrote, "Faith never asks whether good works are to be done, but has done them before there is time to ask the question, and it is always doing them." So when in doubt, do something good!

BORN AGAIN

You have been born again, and this new life did not come from
something that dies, but from something that cannot die. You were
born again through God's living message that continues forever.
1 Peter 1:23 NCV

Why did Christ die on the cross? Christ sacrificed His life so that we might be born again. This gift, freely given from God's only begotten Son, is the priceless possession of everyone who accepts Him as Lord and Savior.

Let us claim Christ's gift today. Let us walk with the Savior, let us love Him, let us praise Him, and let us share His message of salvation with all those who cross our paths.

The comforting words of Ephesians 2:8 make God's promise clear: "For by grace you have been saved through faith, and that not of yourselves; it is the gift of God" (NKJV). Thus, we are saved not because of our good deeds but because of our faith in Christ. May we, who have been given so much, praise our Savior for the gift of salvation, and may we share the joyous news of our Master's limitless love with our families, with our friends, and with the world.

Jesus divided people—everyone—into two classes—the once-born and the twice-born, the unconverted and the converted. No other distinction mattered.

E. Stanley Jones

A LESSON FOR THE HEART AND SOUL

A true conversion experience results in a life transformed by Christ and a commitment to following in His footsteps.

DEFEATING DISCOURAGEMENT

And the Lord, He is the one who goes before you.
He will be with you, He will not leave you nor forsake you;
do not fear nor be dismayed.

Deuteronomy 31:8 NKJV

When we fail to meet the expectations of others (or, for that matter, the expectations that we have set for ourselves), we may be tempted to abandon hope. Thankfully, on those cloudy days when our strength is sapped and our faith is shaken, there exists a source from which we can draw courage and wisdom. That source is God.

When we seek to form a more intimate and dynamic relationship with our Creator, He renews our spirits and restores our souls. God's promise is made clear in Isaiah 40:31: "But those who wait on the Lord shall renew their strength; they shall mount up with wings like eagles, they shall run and not be weary, they shall walk and not faint" (NKJV). And upon this promise we can—and should—depend.

What is the cure for disillusionment? Putting our complete hope and trust in the living Lord.

Charles Swindoll

BUILDING A BETTER YOU

If you're feeling discouraged, try to redirect your thoughts away from the troubles that plague you—focus, instead, upon the opportunities that surround you.

ENTHUSIASM FOR CHRIST

*So roll up your sleeves, put your mind in gear, be totally ready to
receive the gift that's coming when Jesus arrives. Don't lazily slip back
into those old grooves of evil, doing just what you feel like doing.
You didn't know any better then; you do now. As obedient children,
let yourselves be pulled into a way of life shaped by God's life,
a life energetic and blazing with holiness.*

1 Peter 1:13–15 MSG

John Wesley advised, "Catch on fire with enthusiasm and people
will come for miles to watch you burn." His words still ring true.
When we fan the flames of enthusiasm for Christ, our faith serves
as a beacon to others.

Our world desperately needs faithful believers who share the
Good News of Jesus with joyful exuberance. Be such a believer.
The world desperately needs your enthusiasm—now!

We act as though comfort and luxury were the chief requirements
of life, when all we need to make us really happy is something to
be enthusiastic about.

Charles Kingsley

Enthusiasm, like the flu, is contagious—we get it from one another.

Barbara Johnson

A LESSON FOR THE HEART AND SOUL

When you become genuinely enthused about your life and your
faith, you'll guard your heart and improve your life.

WHAT KIND OF EXAMPLE?

In everything set them an example by doing what is good.
Titus 2:7 NIV

What kind of example are you? Are you the kind of person whose life serves as a powerful example of decency and morality? Are you a man or woman whose behavior serves as a positive role model for others? Are you the kind of person whose actions, day in and day out, are based upon integrity, fidelity, and a love for the Lord? If so, you are not only blessed by God, you are also a powerful force for good in a world that desperately needs positive influences such as yours.

Phillips Brooks advised, "Be such a man, and live such a life, that if every man were such as you, and every life a life like yours, this earth would be God's Paradise." And that's sound advice because our families and friends are watching . . . and so, for that matter, is God.

A holy life will produce the deepest impression. Lighthouses blow no horns; they only shine.

D. L. Moody

A LESSON FOR THE HEART AND SOUL

Your life is a sermon. What kind of sermon will you preach? The words you choose to speak may have some impact on others, but not nearly as much impact as the life you choose to live. Today, pause to consider the tone, the theme, and the context of your particular sermon, and ask yourself if it's a message that you're proud to deliver.

SHOUTING THE GOOD NEWS

As you go, preach this message: "The kingdom of heaven is near."
Matthew 10:7 NIV

The Good News of Jesus Christ should be shouted from the rooftops by believers the world over. But all too often, it is not. For a variety of reasons, many Christians keep their beliefs to themselves, and when they do, the world suffers because of their failure to speak up.

As believers, we are called to share the transforming message of Jesus with our families, with our neighbors, and with the world. Jesus commands us to become fishers of men. And, the time to go fishing is now. We must share the Good News of Jesus Christ today—tomorrow may indeed be too late.

The evangelistic harvest is always urgent. The destiny of men and of nations is always being decided. Every generation is strategic. We are not responsible for the past generation, and we cannot bear the full responsibility for the next one, but we do have our generation. God will hold us responsible as to how well we fulfill our responsibilities to this age and take advantage of our opportunities.

Billy Graham

A LESSON FOR THE HEART AND SOUL

God's Word clearly instructs you to share His Good News with the world. If you're willing, God will empower you to share your faith.

THE WISDOM TO OBEY

And this world is fading away, along with everything it craves.
But if you do the will of God, you will live forever.
1 John 2:17 NLT

Since God created Adam and Eve, we human beings have been rebelling against our Creator. Why? Because we are unwilling to trust God's Word, and we are unwilling to follow His commandments. God has given us a guidebook for righteous living called the Holy Bible. It contains thorough instructions which, if followed, lead to fulfillment, righteousness, and salvation. But, if we choose to ignore God's commandments, the results are as predictable as they are tragic.

Talking about God is easy; living by His commandments is considerably harder. But, unless we are willing to abide by God's laws, all of our righteous proclamations ring hollow. How can we best proclaim our love for the Lord? By obeying Him. And, for further instructions, read the manual.

God will never reveal more truth about Himself until you have obeyed what you know already.

Oswald Chambers

BUILDING A BETTER YOU

If you're trying to mold your relationship with Jesus into something that fits comfortably into your own schedule and your own personal theology, you may be headed for trouble. A far better strategy is to conform yourself to Jesus, not vice versa.

GOOD PRESSURES, BAD PRESSURES

Obviously, I'm not trying to be a people pleaser!
No, I am trying to please God. If I were still trying to please people,
I would not be Christ's servant.
Galatians 1:10 NLT

Our world is filled with pressures: some good, some bad. The pressures that we feel to follow God's will and obey His commandments are positive pressures. God places them on our hearts, and He intends that we act in accordance with His leadings. But we also face different pressures, ones that are definitely not from God. When we feel pressured to do things—or even to think thoughts—that lead us away from God, we must beware.

Society seeks to mold us into more worldly beings; God seeks to mold us into new beings that are most certainly not conformed to this world. If we are to please God, we must resist the pressures that society seeks to impose upon us, and we must conform ourselves, instead, to God's will, to His path, and to His Son.

Ambition! We must be careful what we mean by it. If it means the desire to get ahead of other people—which is what I think it does mean—then it is bad. If it simply means wanting to do a thing well, then it is good. It isn't wrong for an actor to want to act his part as well as it can possibly be acted, but the wish to have his name in bigger type than the other actors is a bad one.

C. S. Lewis

A LESSON FOR THE HEART AND SOUL

Peer pressure can be good or bad. God wants you to seek out the good and flee from the bad.

NO IS AN ANSWER

He granted their request because they trusted in Him.
1 Chronicles 5:20 HCSB

God answers our prayers. What God does not do is this: He does not always answer our prayers as soon as we might like, and He does not always answer our prayers by saying "Yes." God isn't an order-taker, and He's not some sort of cosmic vending machine. Sometimes—even when we want something very badly—our loving Heavenly Father responds to our requests by saying "No," and we must accept His answer, even if we don't understand it.

God answers prayers not only according to our wishes but also according to His master plan. We cannot know that plan, but we can know the Planner . . . and we must trust His wisdom, His righteousness, and His love. Always.

Let's never forget that some of God's greatest mercies are His refusals. He says no in order that He may, in some way we cannot imagine, say yes. All His ways with us are merciful. His meaning is always love.

Elisabeth Elliot

A LESSON FOR THE HEART AND SOUL

When God says "No," that's good! Why? Because God knows what's best; God wants what's best; and God is trying to lead you to a place that is best for you. So trust Him . . . especially when He says "No."

TAKING RISKS

Is anything too hard for the Lord?
Genesis 18:14 NKJV

As we consider the uncertainties of the future, we are confronted with a powerful temptation: the temptation to "play it safe." Unwilling to move mountains, we fret over molehills. Unwilling to entertain great hopes for the tomorrow, we focus on the unfairness of the today. Unwilling to trust God completely, we take timid half-steps when God intends that we make giant leaps.

Today, ask God for the courage to step beyond the boundaries of your doubts. Ask Him to guide you to a place where you can realize your full potential—a place where you are freed from the fear of failure. Ask Him to do His part, and promise Him that you will do your part. Don't ask Him to lead you to a "safe" place; ask Him to lead you to the "right" place . . . and remember: those two places are seldom the same.

The really committed leave the safety of the harbor, accept the risk of the open seas of faith, and set their compasses for the place of total devotion to God and whatever life adventures He plans for them.

Bill Hybels

BUILDING A BETTER YOU

If you're about to make a big decision or take a significant risk, always pray about it first. And the bigger the decision, the more you should pray about it.

ABUNDANT PEACE

The peace of God, which surpasses all understanding,
will guard your hearts and minds through Christ Jesus.
Philippians 4:7 NKJV

If you are a thoughtful believer, you will open yourself to the spiritual abundance that your Savior offers by following Him completely and without reservation. Do you sincerely seek the riches that our Savior offers to those who give themselves to Him? Then follow Him. When you do, you will receive the love, the peace, and the joy that He has promised. Seek first the salvation that is available through a personal, passionate relationship with Christ, and then claim the joy, the peace, and the spiritual abundance that the Shepherd offers His sheep.

God's riches are beyond anything we could ask or even dare to imagine! If my life gets gooey and stale, I have no excuse.

Barbara Johnson

God loves you and wants you to experience peace and life—abundant and eternal.

Billy Graham

A LESSON FOR THE HEART AND SOUL

Abundance and obedience go hand-in-hand. Obey God first and expect to receive His abundance second, not vice versa.

GOD AND FAMILY

Let the Word of Christ—the Message—have the run of the house.
Give it plenty of room in your lives.
Colossians 3:16 MSG

These are difficult days for our nation and for our families. But, thankfully, God is bigger than all of our challenges. God loves us and protects us. In times of trouble, He comforts us; in times of sorrow, He dries our tears. When we are troubled, or weak, or sorrowful, God is as near as our next breath.

Are you concerned for the well-being of your family? You are not alone. We live in a world where temptation and danger seem to lurk on every street corner. Parents and children alike have good reason to be watchful. But, despite the evils of our time, God remains steadfast. Even in these difficult days, no problem is too big for God.

The first essential for a happy home is love.

Billy Graham

Living life with a consistent spiritual walk deeply influences those we love most.

Vonette Bright

A LESSON FOR THE HEART AND SOUL

If you're lucky enough to be a member of a loving, supportive family, then you owe it to yourself—and to them—to share your thoughts, your hopes, your encouragement, and your love.

THE LAST WORD

For God has not given us a spirit of timidity,
but of power and love and discipline.
Therefore do not be ashamed of the testimony of our Lord....
2 Timothy 1:7–8 NASB

All of us may find our courage tested by the inevitable disappointments and tragedies of life. After all, ours is a world filled with uncertainty, hardship, sickness, and danger. Old Man Trouble, it seems, is never too far from the front door.

When we focus upon our fears and our doubts, we may find many reasons to lie awake at night and fret about the uncertainties of the coming day. A better strategy, of course, is to focus not upon our fears, but instead upon our God.

God is your shield and your strength; you are His forever. So don't focus your thoughts upon the fears of the day. Instead, trust God's plan and His eternal love for you. And remember: God is good, and He has the last word.

You needn't worry about not feeling brave. Our Lord didn't—see the scene in Gethsemane. How thankful I am that when God became man He did not choose to become a man of iron nerves; that would not have helped weaklings like you and me nearly so much.

C. S. Lewis

BUILDING A BETTER YOU

Are you feeling anxious or fearful? If so, trust God more. Entrust the future—your future—to God.

THE WISDOM TO FORGIVE

*Therefore, God's chosen ones, holy and loved, put on heartfelt
compassion, kindness, humility, gentleness, and patience,
accepting one another and forgiving one another if anyone
has a complaint against another. Just as the Lord has forgiven you,
so also you must forgive.*
Colossians 3:12–13 HCSB

When people behave badly, it's hard to forgive them. How hard? Sometimes, it's very hard! But God tells us that we must forgive other people, even when we'd rather not. So, if you're angry with anybody (or if you're upset by something you yourself have done) it's now time to forgive.

God instructs you to treat other people exactly as you wish to be treated. And since you want to be forgiven for the mistakes that you make, you must be willing to extend forgiveness to other people for the mistakes that they have made. If you can't seem to forgive someone, you should keep asking God to help you until you do. And you can be sure of this: if you keep asking for God's help, He will give it.

Miracles broke the physical laws of the universe; forgiveness broke the moral rules.

Philip Yancey

BUILDING A BETTER YOU

Forgiveness is its own reward. Bitterness is its own punishment. Guard your words and your thoughts accordingly.

CONDUCT AND CHARACTER

Lead a quiet and peaceable life in all godliness and honesty.
1 Timothy 2:2 KJV

Charles Stanley said, "The Bible teaches that we are accountable to one another for our conduct and character." Christians agree. As believers in Christ, we must seek to live each day with discipline, honesty, and faith. When we do, at least two things happen: integrity becomes a habit, and God blesses us because of our obedience to Him. Living a life of integrity isn't always the easiest way, but it is always the right way . . . and God clearly intends that it should be our way, too.

Character isn't built overnight; it is built slowly over a lifetime. It is the sum of every right decision and every honest word. It is forged on the anvil of honorable work and polished by the twin virtues of honesty and fairness. Character is a precious thing—difficult to build and wonderful to behold.

Learning God's truth and getting it into our heads is one thing, but living God's truth and getting it into our characters is quite something else.

Warren Wiersbe

The single most important element in any human relationship is honesty—with oneself, with God, and with others.

Catherine Marshall

A LESSON FOR THE HEART AND SOUL

Remember: Character is more important than popularity.

READY. SET. GO!

Do not neglect the gift that is in you.
1 Timothy 4:14 NKJV

God has given you talents and opportunities that are uniquely yours. Are you willing to use your gifts in the way that God intends? And are you willing to summon the discipline that is required to develop your talents and to hone your skills? That's precisely what God wants you to do, and that's precisely what you should desire for yourself.

As you seek to expand your talents, you will undoubtedly encounter stumbling blocks along the way, such as the fear of rejection or the fear of failure. When you do, don't stumble! Just continue to refine your skills, and offer your services to God. And when the time is right, He will use you—but it's up to you to be thoroughly prepared when He does.

Let us use the gifts of God lest they be extinguished by our slothfulness.

John Calvin

There's a unique sense of fulfillment that comes when we submit our gifts to God's use and ask him to energize them in a supernatural way—and then step back to watch what he does.

Lee Strobel

BUILDING A BETTER YOU

You are the sole owner of your own set of talents and opportunities. God has given you your own particular gifts—the rest is up to you.

GREAT IS THY FAITHFULNESS

God is faithful, by whom you were called into the fellowship of His Son, Jesus Christ our Lord.
1 Corinthians 1:9 NKJV

God is faithful to us even when we are not faithful to Him. God keeps His promises to us even when we stray far from His will. He continues to love us even when we disobey His commandments. But God does not force His blessings upon us. If we are to experience His love and His grace, we must claim them for ourselves.

Are you tired, discouraged or fearful? Be comforted: God is with you. Are you confused? Listen to the quiet voice of your Heavenly Father. Are you bitter? Talk with God and seek His guidance. Are you celebrating a great victory? Thank God and praise Him. He is the Giver of all things good. In whatever condition you find yourself, trust God and be comforted. The Father is with you now and forever.

God's faithfulness has never depended on the faithfulness of his children . . . . God is greater than our weakness. In fact, I think, it is our weakness that reveals how great God is.

Max Lucado

A LESSON FOR THE HEART AND SOUL

Of this you can be sure: God's faithfulness is steadfast, unwavering, and eternal.

WITH YOU ALWAYS

You will teach me how to live a holy life. Being with you will fill me
with joy; at your right hand I will find pleasure forever.
Psalm 16:11 NCV

Do you ever wonder if God is really here? If so, you're not the first person to think such thoughts. In fact, some of the biggest heroes in the Bible had their doubts—and so, perhaps, will you. But when questions arise and doubts begin to creep into your mind, remember this: You can talk with God any time. In fact, He's right here, right now, listening to your thoughts and prayers, watching over your every move.

Sometimes, you will allow yourself to become very busy, and that's when you may be tempted to ignore God. But, when you quiet yourself long enough to acknowledge His presence, God will touch your heart and restore your spirit. By the way, He's ready to talk right now. Are you?

When we are in the presence of God, removed from distractions, we are able to hear him more clearly, and a secure environment has been established for the young and broken places in our hearts to surface.

John Eldredge

BUILDING A BETTER YOU

Perhaps you have become wrapped up in the world's problems or your own problems. If so, it's time to open yourself up to God. When you do, God will bless you and comfort you.

LOVE THAT FORGIVES

*But when you are praying, first forgive anyone you are
holding a grudge against, so that your
Father in heaven will forgive your sins, too.*

Mark 11:25 NLT

Genuine love is an exercise in forgiveness. If we wish to build lasting relationships, we must learn how to forgive. Why? Because our loved ones are imperfect (as are we). How often must we forgive our family and friends? More times than we can count. Why? Because that's what God wants us to do.

Perhaps granting forgiveness is hard for you. If so, you are not alone. Genuine, lasting forgiveness is often difficult to achieve—difficult but not impossible. Thankfully, with God's help, all things are possible, and that includes forgiveness. But, even though God is willing to help, He expects you to do some of the work. And make no mistake: forgiveness is work, which is okay with God. He knows that the payoffs are worth the effort.

I firmly believe a great many prayers are not answered because we are not willing to forgive someone.

D. L. Moody

BUILDING A BETTER YOU

Holding a grudge? Drop it. Never expect other people to be more forgiving than you are. And remember: the best time to forgive is now.

A HELPING HAND

The greatest among you will be your servant.
For whoever exalts himself will be humbled,
and whoever humbles himself will be exalted.
Matthew 23:11–12 NIV

Jesus has much to teach us about generosity. He teaches that the most esteemed men and women are not the self-congratulatory leaders of society but are, instead, the humblest of servants. If you were being graded on generosity, how would you score? Would you earn "A"s in philanthropy and humility? Hopefully so. But if your grades could stand a little improvement, this is the perfect day to begin.

Today, you may feel the urge to hoard your blessings. Don't do it. Instead, give generously to your neighbors, and do so without fanfare. Find a need and fill it . . . humbly. Lend a helping hand and share a word of kindness . . . anonymously. This is God's way.

The mark of a Christian is that he will walk the second mile and turn the other cheek. A wise man or woman gives the extra effort, all for the glory of the Lord Jesus Christ.

John Maxwell

BUILDING A BETTER YOU

Today, challenge your faith by thinking of at least one small, practical step you can take to help someone in need.

THE SHEPHERD'S CARE

For Your righteousness, O God, reaches to the heavens,
You who have done great things.
Psalm 71:19 NASB

It's a promise that is made over and over again in the Bible: Whatever "it" is, God can handle it.

Life isn't always easy. Far from it! Sometimes, life can be very, very difficult. But even then, even during our darkest moments, we're protected by a loving Heavenly Father. When we're worried, God can reassure us; when we're sad, God can comfort us. When our hearts are broken, God is not just near, He is here. So we must lift our thoughts and prayers to Him. When we do, He will answer our prayers. Why? Because He is our Shepherd, and He has promised to protect us now and forever.

God is great and God is powerful, but we must invite him to be powerful in our lives. His strength is always there, but it's up to us to provide a channel through which that power can flow.

Bill Hybels

He is always thinking about us. We are before his eyes. The Lord's eye never sleeps, but is always watching out for our welfare. We are continually on his heart.

C. H. Spurgeon

A LESSON FOR THE HEART AND SOUL

God wants to provide for you and your loved ones. When you trust your life and your future to God, He will provide for your needs.

BLESSED BEYOND MEASURE

May the Lord bless you and keep you.
May the Lord show you his kindness and have mercy on you.
Numbers 6:24–25 NCV

Have you counted your blessings lately? You should. Of course, God's gifts are too numerous to count, but as a grateful Christian, you should attempt to count them nonetheless. Your blessings include life, family, friends, talents, and possessions, for starters. And your greatest gift—a treasure that was paid for on the cross and is yours for the asking—is God's gift of salvation through Christ Jesus.

As believing Christians, we have all been blessed beyond measure. Thus, thanksgiving should become a habit, a regular part of our daily routines. Today, let us pause and thank our Creator for His blessings. And let us demonstrate our gratitude to the Giver of all things good by using His gifts for the glory of His kingdom.

God's love for His children is unconditional, no strings attached. But, God's blessings on our lives do come with a condition—obedience.

Jim Gallery

A LESSON FOR THE HEART AND SOUL

God wants to bless you abundantly and eternally. When you trust God completely and obey Him faithfully, you will be blessed.

TRUST HIM TO GUIDE YOU

*Trust the Lord your God with all your heart and lean
not on your own understanding; in all your ways acknowledge him,
and he will make your paths straight.*

Proverbs 3:5–6 NIV

As Christians whose salvation has been purchased by the blood of Christ, we have every reason to live joyously and courageously. After all, Christ has already fought and won our battle for us—He did so on the cross at Calvary. But despite Christ's sacrifice, and despite God's promises, we may become confused or disoriented by the endless complications and countless distractions of life.

If you're unsure of your next step, lean upon God's promises and lift your prayers to Him. Remember that God is your protector. Open yourself to His heart, and trust Him to guide you. When you do, God will direct your steps, and you will receive His blessings today, tomorrow, and throughout eternity.

God's guidance is even more important than common sense. I can declare that the deepest darkness is outshone by the light of Jesus.

Corrie ten Boom

BUILDING A BETTER YOU

If you want God's guidance, ask for it. When you pray for guidance, God will give it.

ULTIMATE PROTECTION

Do not be afraid or discouraged,
for the LORD is the one who goes before you.
He will be with you; he will neither fail you nor forsake you.
Deuteronomy 31:8 NLT

God has promised to protect us, and He intends to fulfill His promise. In a world filled with dangers and temptations, God is the ultimate armor. In a world filled with misleading messages, God's Word is the ultimate truth. In a world filled with more frustrations than we can count, God's Son offers the ultimate peace.

Will you accept God's peace and wear God's armor against the dangers of our world? Hopefully so, because when you do, you can live courageously, knowing that you possess the ultimate protection: God's unfailing love for you.

The promises of God's Word sustain us in our suffering, and we know Jesus sympathizes and empathizes with us in our darkest hour.

Bill Bright

We are never out of reach of Satan's devices, so we must never be without the whole armor of God.

Warren Wiersbe

A LESSON FOR THE HEART AND SOUL

You are protected by God . . . now and always. The only security that lasts is the security that flows from the loving heart of God.

HOW TO TREAT OTHERS: A SIMPLE RULE OF THUMB

Therefore, whatever you want men to do to you, do also to them,
for this is the Law and the Prophets.
Matthew 7:12 NKJV

Would you like to make the world a better place? If so, you can start by practicing the Golden Rule.

Is the Golden Rule your rule, or is it just another Bible verse that goes in one ear and out the other? Jesus made Himself perfectly clear: He instructed you to treat other people in the same way that you want to be treated. But sometimes, especially when you're feeling the pressures of everyday living, obeying the Golden Rule can seem like an impossible task—but it's not. So if you want to know how to treat other people, ask the person you see every time you look into the mirror. The answer you receive will tell you exactly what to do.

Faith never asks whether good works are to be done, but has done them before there is time to ask the question, and it is always doing them.

Martin Luther

BUILDING A BETTER YOU

When you become a living, breathing example of the Golden Rule in action, other people will notice, and the results will be better than gold.

HIS HEALING TOUCH

I am the Lord that healeth thee.
Exodus 15:26 KJV

Are you concerned about your spiritual, physical, or emotional health? If so, there is a timeless source of comfort and assurance that is as near as your bookshelf. That source is the Holy Bible.

God's Word has much to say about every aspect of your life, including your health. And, when you face concerns of any sort—including health-related challenges—God is with you. So trust your medical doctor to do his or her part, but place your ultimate trust in your benevolent Heavenly Father. His healing touch, like His love, endures forever.

Jesus Christ is the One by Whom, for Whom, through Whom everything was made. Therefore, He knows what's wrong in your life and how to fix it.

Anne Graham Lotz

Ultimate healing and the glorification of the body are certainly among the blessings of Calvary for the believing Christian. Immediate healing is not guaranteed.

Warren Wiersbe

BUILDING A BETTER YOU

God has given you a body, and He's placed you in charge of caring for it. Your body is a temple that should be treated with respect. So be proactive about your health: Don't sit around and wait for things to get worse; seek the best help you can find for your health problems.

THE ULTIMATE INSTRUCTION MANUAL

He who despises the word will be destroyed,
but he who fears the commandment will be rewarded.
Proverbs 13:13 NKJV

The Holy Bible contains thorough instructions which, if followed, lead to fulfillment, righteousness, and salvation. But, if we choose to ignore God's commandments, the results are as predictable as they are tragic.

A righteous life has many components: faith, honesty, generosity, love, kindness, humility, gratitude, and worship, to name but a few. If we seek to follow the steps of our Savior, Jesus Christ, we must seek to live according to His commandments. Let us follow God's commandments, and let us conduct our lives in such a way that we might be shining examples for those who have not yet found Christ.

God meant that we adjust to the Gospel—not the other way around.

Vance Havner

Bible history is filled with people who began the race with great success but failed at the end because they disregarded God's rules.

Warren Wiersbe

BUILDING A BETTER YOU

If you're wise, you'll allow God to guide you today and every day of your life. When you pray for guidance, God will give it.

ADDITIONAL RESPONSIBILITIES

*So he who had received five talents came and brought five other talents,
saying, "Lord, you delivered to me five talents; look,
I have gained five more talents besides them." His lord said to him,
"Well done, good and faithful servant; you were faithful
over a few things, I will make you ruler over many things.
Enter into the joy of your lord."*
Matthew 25:20–21 NKJV

God has promised us this: when we do our duties in small matters, He will give us additional responsibilities. Sometimes, those responsibilities come when God changes the course of our lives so we may better serve Him. Sometimes, our rewards come in the form of temporary setbacks that lead, in turn, to greater victories. Sometimes, God rewards us by answering "no" to our prayers so that He can say "yes" to a far grander request that we, with our limited understanding, would never have thought to ask for.

If you seek to be God's servant in great matters, be faithful, be patient, and be dutiful in smaller matters. Then step back and watch as God surprises you with the spectacular creativity of His infinite wisdom and His perfect plan.

A LESSON FOR THE HEART AND SOUL

Sometimes, waiting faithfully for God's plan to unfold is more important than understanding God's plan. Ruth Bell Graham once said, "When I am dealing with an all-powerful, all-knowing God, I, as a mere mortal, must offer my petitions not only with persistence, but also with patience. Someday I'll know why." So even when you can't understand God's plans, you must trust Him and never lose faith!

UP FOR THE CHALLENGE

I will be your God throughout your lifetime—
until your hair is white with age. I made you, and I will care for you.
I will carry you along and save you.
Isaiah 46:4 NLT

God has promised to lift you up and guide your steps if you let Him do so. God has promised that when you entrust your life to Him completely and without reservation, He will give you the strength to meet any challenge, the courage to face any trial, and the wisdom to live in His righteousness.

God's hand uplifts those who turn their hearts and prayers to Him. Will you count yourself among that number? Will you accept God's peace and wear God's armor against the temptations and distractions of our dangerous world? If you do, you can live courageously and optimistically, knowing that you have been forever touched by the loving, unfailing, uplifting hand of God.

He can accomplish anything He chooses to do. If He ever asks you to do something, He Himself will enable you to do it.

Henry Blackaby

Our valleys may be filled with foes and tears, but we can lift our eyes to the hills to see God and the angels.

Billy Graham

A LESSON FOR THE HEART AND SOUL

God wants to provide for you and your loved ones. When you trust your life and your future to God, He will provide for your needs.

BUILDING SELF-ESTEEM

And let us not grow weary while doing good,
for in due season we shall reap if we do not lose heart.
Galatians 6:9 NKJV

Would you like to make the world a better place and feel better about yourself at the same time? If so, you can start by practicing the Golden Rule.

The Bible teaches us to treat other people with respect, kindness, courtesy, and love. When we do, we make other people happy, we make God happy, and we feel better about ourselves.

So if you're wondering how to make the world—and your world—a better place, here's a great place to start: Let the Golden Rule be your rule. And if you want to know how to treat other people, ask the person you see every time you glance in the mirror.

When you launch an act of kindness out into the crosswinds of life, it will blow kindness back to you.

Dennis Swanberg

Holy service in constant fellowship with God is heaven below.

C. H. Spurgeon

A LESSON FOR THE HEART AND SOUL

The more you help others, the better you'll feel about yourself. So don't delay: somebody needs your help today.

FILLED WITH THE SPIRIT

Don't be drunk with wine, because that will ruin your life.
Instead, let the Holy Spirit fill and control you.
Ephesians 5:18 NLT

When you are filled with the Holy Spirit, your words and deeds will reflect a love and devotion to Christ. When you are filled with the Holy Spirit, the steps of your life's journey are guided by the Lord. When you allow God's Spirit to work in you and through you, you will be energized and transformed.

Today, allow yourself to be filled with the Spirit of God. And then stand back in amazement as God begins to work miracles in your own life and in the lives of those you love.

God cannot reveal anything to us if we have not His spirit.

Oswald Chambers

The Holy Spirit is like a living and continually flowing fountain in believers. We have the boundless privilege of tapping into that fountain every time we pray.

Shirley Dobson

A LESSON FOR THE HEART AND SOUL

The Holy Spirit is God in us, providing us with all we need to be effective Christians.

HOPE FOR TODAY

*You have already heard about this hope in the message of truth,
the gospel that has come to you. It is bearing fruit and growing
all over the world, just as it has among you since the day
you heard it and recognized God's grace in the truth.*
Colossians 1:5–6 HCSB

Despite God's promises, despite Christ's love, and despite our countless blessings, we frail human beings can still lose hope from time to time. When we do, we need the encouragement of Christian friends, the life-changing power of prayer, and the healing truth of God's Holy Word. If we find ourselves falling into the spiritual traps of worry and discouragement, we should seek the healing touch of Jesus and the encouraging words of fellow Christians. Even though this world can be a place of trials and struggles, God has promised us peace, joy, and eternal life if we give ourselves to Him. And, of course, God keeps His promises today, tomorrow, and forever.

Teach us to set our hopes on heaven, to hold firmly to the promise of eternal life, so that we can withstand the struggles and storms of this world.

Max Lucado

Our hope in Christ for the future is the mainstream of our joy.

C. H. Spurgeon

A LESSON FOR THE HEART AND SOUL

Never be afraid to hope—or to ask—for a miracle.

A SHINING LIGHT

While ye have light, believe in the light,
that ye may be the children of light.
John 12:36 KJV

The Bible says that you are "the light that gives light to the world." What kind of light have you been giving off? Hopefully, you've been a good example for everybody to see. Why? Because the world needs all the light it can get, and that includes your light, too!

Christ showed enduring love for you by willingly sacrificing His own life so that you might have eternal life. As a response to His sacrifice, you should love Him, praise Him, and share His message of salvation with your neighbors and with the world. So let your light shine today and every day. When you do, God will bless you now and forever.

You can't light another's path without casting light on your own.

John Maxwell

If Jesus is the preeminent One in our lives, then we will love each other, submit to each other, and treat one another fairly in the Lord.

Warren Wiersbe

BUILDING A BETTER YOU

Leadership is a responsibility that must not be taken lightly. If you choose to lead others, you should first choose to follow Jesus.

THE PRINCE OF PEACE

Peace I leave with you; My peace I give to you;
not as the world gives do I give to you.
Do not let your heart be troubled, nor let it be fearful.
John 14:27 NASB

Have you found the genuine peace that can be yours through Jesus Christ? Or are you still rushing after the illusion of "peace and happiness" that the world promises but cannot deliver? The beautiful words of John 14:27 remind us that Jesus offers us peace, not as the world gives, but as He alone gives. Our challenge is to accept Christ's peace into our hearts and then, as best we can, to share His peace with our neighbors.

Today, as a gift to yourself, to your family, and to your friends, claim the inner peace that is your spiritual birthright: the peace of Jesus Christ. It is offered freely; it has been paid for in full; it is yours for the asking. So ask. And then share.

A great many people are trying to make peace, but that has already been done. God has not left it for us to do; all we have to do is to enter into it.

D. L. Moody

A LESSON FOR THE HEART AND SOUL

God offers peace that passes human understanding . . . and He wants you to make His peace your peace.

ENTHUSIASTIC DISCIPLESHIP

Do your work with enthusiasm. Work as if you were serving the Lord, not as if you were serving only men and women.

Ephesians 6:7 NCV

With whom will you choose to walk today? Will you walk with shortsighted people who honor the ways of the world, or will you walk with the Son of God? Jesus walks with you. Are you walking with Him? Hopefully, you will choose to walk with Him today and every day of your life.

Jesus has called upon believers of every generation (and that includes you) to follow in His footsteps. And God's Word promises that when you follow in Christ's footsteps, you will learn how to live freely and lightly (Matthew 11:28-30).

Jesus doesn't want you to be a run-of-the-mill, follow-the-crowd kind of person. Jesus wants you to be a "new creation" through Him. And that's exactly what you should want for yourself, too. Jesus deserves your extreme enthusiasm; the world deserves it; and you deserve the experience of sharing it.

A disciple is a follower of Christ. That means you take on His priorities as your own. His agenda becomes your agenda. His mission becomes your mission.

Charles Stanley

A LESSON FOR THE HEART AND SOUL

Talk is cheap. Real ministry has legs. When it comes to being a disciple, make sure that you back up your words with deeds.

THE POWER OF WORDS

*Watch the way you talk. Let nothing foul or dirty
come out of your mouth. Say only what helps, each word a gift.*
Ephesians 4:29 MSG

The words that we speak have the power to do great good or great harm. If we speak words of encouragement and hope, we can lift others up. And that's exactly what God commands us to do!

Sometimes, when we feel uplifted and secure, it easy to speak kind words. Other times, when we are discouraged or tired, we can scarcely summon the energy to uplift ourselves, much less anyone else. God intends that we speak words of kindness, wisdom, and truth, no matter our circumstances, no matter our emotions. When we do, we share a priceless gift with the world, and we give glory to the One who gave His life for us. As believers, we must do no less.

We urgently need people who encourage and inspire us to move toward God and away from the world's enticing pleasures.

Jim Cymbala

People who inspire others are those who see invisible bridges at the end of dead-end streets.

Charles Swindoll

A LESSON FOR THE HEART AND SOUL

When you help other people feel better about themselves, you'll feel better about yourself, too.

A PASSION FOR LIFE

But those who wait on the Lord shall renew their strength;
they shall mount up with wings like eagles,
they shall run and not be weary, they shall walk and not faint.
Isaiah 40:31 NKJV

Are you enthusiastic about your life and your faith? Hopefully so. But if your zest for life has waned, it is now time to redirect your efforts and recharge your spiritual batteries. And that means refocusing your priorities (by putting God first) and counting your blessings (instead of your troubles).

Nothing is more important than your wholehearted commitment to your Creator and to His only begotten Son. Your faith must never be an afterthought; it must be your ultimate priority, your ultimate possession, and your ultimate passion. When you become passionate about your faith, you'll become passionate about your life, too. And God will smile.

If your heart has grown cold, it is because you have moved away from the fire of His presence.

Beth Moore

BUILDING A BETTER YOU

Don't wait for enthusiasm to find you . . . go looking for it. Look at your life and your relationships as exciting adventures. Don't wait for life to spice itself; spice things up yourself.

TEMPORARY SETBACKS

A time to weep, and a time to laugh;
a time to mourn, and a time to dance....
Ecclesiastes 3:4 KJV

The occasional disappointments and failures of life are inevitable. Such setbacks are simply the price that we must occasionally pay for our willingness to take risks as we follow our dreams. But even when we encounter bitter disappointments, we must never lose faith.

When we encounter the inevitable difficulties of life-here-on-earth, God stands ready to protect us. Our responsibility, of course, is to ask Him for protection. When we call upon Him in heartfelt prayer, He will answer—in His own time and according to His own plan—and He will heal us. And, while we are waiting for God's plans to unfold and for His healing touch to restore us, we can be comforted in the knowledge that our Creator can overcome any obstacle, even if we cannot.

Our problem isn't that we've failed. Our problem is that we haven't failed enough. We haven't been brought low enough to learn what God wants us to learn.

Charles Swindoll

BUILDING A BETTER YOU

Use your experiences—both good and bad—to learn, to grow, to share, and to teach.

AN AWESOME GOD

Respect for the Lord gives life.
It is like a fountain that can save people from death.
Proverbs 14:27 NCV

God's hand shapes the universe, and it shapes our lives. God maintains absolute sovereignty over His creation, and His power is beyond comprehension. As believers, we must cultivate a sincere respect for God's awesome power. God has dominion over all things, and until we acknowledge His sovereignty, we lack the humility we need to live righteously, and we lack the humility we need to become wise.

The fear of the Lord is, indeed, the beginning of knowledge. So today, as you face the realities of everyday life, remember this: until you acquire a healthy, respectful fear of God's power, your education is incomplete, and so is your faith.

When true believers are awed by the greatness of God and by the privilege of becoming His children, then they become sincerely motivated, effective evangelists.

Bill Hybels

A healthy fear of God will do much to deter us from sin.

Charles Swindoll

A LESSON FOR THE HEART AND SOUL

When you possess a healthy fear of God, He will guide your steps and guard your heart.

RECOUPING YOUR LOSSES

Trouble chases sinners, while blessings chase the righteous!
Proverbs 13:21 NLT

Have you ever made a financial blunder? If so, welcome to a very large club! Almost everyone experiences financial pressures from time to time, and so, perhaps, will you.

When we commit the inevitable missteps of life, we must correct them, learn from them, and pray for the wisdom not to repeat them. When we do, our mistakes become lessons, and our lives become adventures in growth, not stagnation.

So here's the big question: Have you used your mistakes as stumbling blocks or stepping stones? The answer to that question will determine how quickly you gain financial security and peace of mind.

If you work hard and maintain an attitude of gratitude, you'll find it easier to manage your finances every day.

John Maxwell

Sadly, family problems and even financial problems are seldom the real problem, but often the symptom of a weak or nonexistent value system.

Dave Ramsey

BUILDING A BETTER YOU

Live within your means and save money from every paycheck. Never spend more than you make.

SUFFICIENT FOR YOUR NEEDS

And God is able to make all grace abound toward you,
that you, always having all sufficiency in all things,
may have an abundance for every good work.
2 Corinthians 9:8 NKJV

Of this you can be sure: the love of God is sufficient to meet your needs. Whatever dangers you may face, whatever heartbreaks you must endure, God is with you, and He stands ready to comfort you and to heal you.

The Psalmist writes, "Weeping may endure for a night, but joy comes in the morning" (Psalm 30:5 NKJV). But when we are suffering, the morning may seem very far away. It is not. God promises that He is "near to those who have a broken heart" (Psalm 34:18 NKJV).

If you are experiencing the intense pain of a recent loss, or if you are still mourning a loss from long ago, perhaps you are now ready to begin the next stage of your journey with God. If so, be mindful of this fact: the loving heart of God is sufficient to meet any challenge, including yours.

An infinite God can give all of Himself to each of His children. He does not distribute Himself that each may have a part, but to each one He gives all of Himself as fully as if there were no others.

A. W. Tozer

A LESSON FOR THE HEART AND SOUL

Whatever you need, God can provide. He is always sufficient to meet your needs.

THE MORNING WATCH

Morning by morning he wakens me and opens
my understanding to his will.
The Sovereign Lord has spoken to me, and I have listened.
Isaiah 50:4–5 NLT

Each new day is a gift from God, and if you are wise, you will spend a few quiet moments each morning thanking the Giver.

Warren Wiersbe writes, "Surrender your mind to the Lord at the beginning of each day." And that's sound advice. When you begin each day with your head bowed and your heart lifted, you are reminded of God's love, His protection, and His commandments. Then, you can align your priorities for the coming day with the teachings and commandments that God has placed upon your heart.

So, if you've acquired the unfortunate habit of trying to "squeeze" God into the corners of your life, it's time to reshuffle the items on your to-do list by placing God first. And if you haven't already done so, form the habit of spending quality time with your Father in Heaven. He deserves it . . . and so do you.

Meditating upon His Word will inevitably bring peace of mind, strength of purpose, and power for living.

Bill Bright

BUILDING A BETTER YOU

Decide how much of your time God deserves, and then give it to Him. Don't organize your day so that God gets "what's left." Give Him what you honestly believe He deserves.

A SACRIFICIAL LOVE

I am the good shepherd.
The good shepherd gives His life for the sheep.
John 10:11 NKJV

How much does Christ love us? More than we, as mere mortals, can comprehend. His love is perfect and steadfast. Even though we are fallible and wayward, the Shepherd cares for us still. Even though we have fallen far short of the Father's commandments, Christ loves us with a power and depth that is beyond our understanding. The sacrifice that Jesus made upon the cross was made for each of us, and His love endures to the edge of eternity and beyond.

Christ's love changes everything. When you accept His gift of grace, you are transformed, not only for today, but also for all eternity. If you haven't already done so, accept Jesus Christ as your Savior. He's waiting patiently for you to invite Him into your heart. Please don't make Him wait a single minute longer.

If it is maintained that anything so small as the Earth must, in any event, be too unimportant to merit the love of the Creator, we reply that no Christian ever supposed we did merit it. Christ did not die for men because they were intrinsically worth dying for, but because He is intrinsically love, and therefore loves infinitely.

C. S. Lewis

A LESSON FOR THE HEART AND SOUL

Jesus is the light of the world. Make sure that you are capturing and reflecting His light.

A CLEAR CONSCIENCE

If then you were raised with Christ, seek those things which are above,
where Christ is, sitting at the right hand of God.
Set your mind on things above, not on things on the earth.
Colossians 3:1–2 NKJV

Few things in life torment us more than a guilty conscience. And, few things in life provide more contentment than the knowledge that we are obeying God's commandments.

A clear conscience is one of the rewards we earn when we obey God's Word and follow His will. When we follow God's will and accept His gift of salvation, our earthly rewards are never-ceasing, and our Heavenly rewards are everlasting.

Guilt is a gift that leads us to grace.

Franklin Graham

One of the ways God has revealed Himself to us is in the conscience. Conscience is God's lamp within the human breast.

Billy Graham

A LESSON FOR THE HEART AND SOUL

If you're not sure what to do, slow down and listen to your conscience. That little voice inside your head is remarkably dependable, but you can't depend upon it if you never listen to it. So stop, listen, and learn—your conscience is almost always right!

CONSIDERING THE CROSS

*But God forbid that I should boast except in the cross
of our Lord Jesus Christ, by whom the world has been
crucified to me, and I to the world.*
Galatians 6:14 NKJV

As we consider Christ's sacrifice on the cross, we should be profoundly humbled and profoundly grateful. And today, as we come to Christ in prayer, we should do so in a spirit of quiet, heartfelt devotion to the One who gave His life so that we might have life eternal.

He was the Son of God, but He wore a crown of thorns. He was the Savior of mankind, yet He was put to death on a rough-hewn cross made of wood. He offered His healing touch to an unsaved world, and yet the same hands that had healed the sick and raised the dead were pierced with nails.

Christ humbled Himself on a cross—for you. As you approach Him today in prayer, think about His love and His sacrifice. And be grateful.

No man understands the Scriptures unless he is acquainted with the cross.

Martin Luther

The heaviest end of the cross lies ever on His shoulders. If He bids us carry a burden, He carries it also.

C. H. Spurgeon

A LESSON FOR THE HEART AND SOUL

The salvation that Jesus provided on the cross is free to us, but it cost Him so much. We must never take His sacrifice for granted.

PROBLEMS IN PERSPECTIVE

It is important to look at things from God's point of view.
1 Corinthians 4:6 MSG

If a temporary loss of perspective has left you worried, exhausted, or both, it's time to readjust your thought patterns. Negative thoughts are habit-forming; thankfully, so are positive ones. With practice, you can form the habit of focusing on God's priorities and your possibilities. When you do, you'll soon discover that you will spend less time fretting about your challenges and more time praising God for His gifts.

When you call upon the Lord and prayerfully seek His will, He will give you wisdom and perspective. When you make God's priorities your priorities, He will direct your steps and calm your fears. So today and every day hereafter, pray for a sense of balance and perspective. And remember: no problems are too big for God—and that includes yours.

Earthly fears are no fears at all. Answer the big question of eternity, and the little questions of life fall into perspective.

Max Lucado

Stand still and refuse to retreat. Look at it as God looks at it and draw upon his power to hold up under the blast.

Charles Swindoll

A LESSON FOR THE HEART AND SOUL

When you focus on the world, you lose perspective. When you focus on God's promises, you gain clearer perspective.

GOD WANTS TO USE YOU

To everything there is a season,
a time for every purpose under heaven.
Ecclesiastes 3:1 NKJV

God has things He wants you to do and places He wants you to go. The most important decision of your life is your commitment to accept Jesus Christ as your personal Lord and Savior. And, once your eternal destiny is secured, you will undoubtedly ask yourself the question "What's next?" If you earnestly seek God's will for your life, you will find it . . . in time.

You may be certain that God is planning to use you in surprising, wonderful ways. And you may be certain that He intends to lead you along a path of His choosing. Your task is to watch for His signs, to listen to His words, to obey His commandments, and to follow where He leads.

Their distress is due entirely to their deliberate determination to use themselves for a purpose other than God's.

Oswald Chambers

It is important to set goals because if you do not have a plan, a goal, a direction, a purpose, and a focus, you are not going to accomplish anything for the glory of God.

Bill Bright

BUILDING A BETTER YOU

God has a plan for you, a definite purpose that only you can accomplish. Your job is to pray for wisdom and listen quietly for God's guidance.

A PASSIONATE LIFE

Never be lacking in zeal,
but keep your spiritual fervor, serving the Lord.
Romans 12:11 NIV

Are you passionate about your life, your loved ones, your work, and your faith? As a believer who has been saved by a risen Christ, you should be.

As a thoughtful Christian, you have every reason to be enthusiastic about life, but sometimes the inevitable struggles of life may cause you to feel decidedly unenthusiastic. If you feel that your enthusiasm is slowly fading away, it's time to slow down, to rest, to count your blessings, and to pray. When you feel worried or weary, you must pray fervently for God to renew your sense of wonderment and excitement.

Life with God is a glorious adventure; revel in it. When you do, God will most certainly smile upon your work and your life.

This is Christianity as God intended it—a passionate, willful, and fully emotional relationship.

Bill Hybels

People who work for money only are usually miserable, because there is no fulfillment and no meaning to what they do.

Dave Ramsey

BUILDING A BETTER YOU

Involve yourself in activities that you can support wholeheartedly and enthusiastically. It's easier to celebrate life when you're passionately involved in life.

THE POWER OF WORDS

Wise men store up knowledge, but the mouth of a fool invites ruin.
Proverbs 10:14 NIV

All too often, in the rush to have ourselves heard, we speak first and think next . . . with unfortunate results. God's Word reminds us that, "Reckless words pierce like a sword, but the tongue of the wise brings healing" (Proverbs 12:18 NIV). If we seek to be a source of encouragement to friends and family, then we must measure our words carefully. Words are important: They can hurt or heal. Words can uplift us or discourage us, and reckless words, spoken in haste, cannot be erased.

Today, measure your words carefully. Use words of kindness and praise, not words of anger or derision. Remember that you have the power to heal others or to injure them, to lift others up or to hold them back. When you lift them up, your wisdom will bring healing and comfort to a world that needs both.

Like dynamite, God's power is only latent power until it is released. You can release God's dynamite power into people's lives and the world through faith, your words, and prayer.

Bill Bright

When you talk, choose the very same words that you would use if Jesus were looking over your shoulder. Because He is.

Marie T. Freeman

BUILDING A BETTER YOU

God understands the importance of the words you speak . . . and so must you.

DOERS OF THE WORD

But prove yourselves doers of the word, and not merely hearers.
James 1:22 NASB

The old saying is both familiar and true: Actions speak louder than words. And as believers, we must beware: our actions should always give credence to the changes that Christ can make in the lives of those who walk with Him.

God calls upon each of us to act in accordance with His will and with respect for His commandments. If we are to be responsible believers, we must realize that it is never enough simply to hear the instructions of God; we must also live by them. And it is never enough to wait idly by while others do God's work here on earth; we, too, must act. Doing God's work is a responsibility that each of us must bear, and when we do, our loving Heavenly Father rewards our efforts with a bountiful harvest.

Our Lord is searching for people who will make a difference. Christians dare not dissolve into the background or blend into the neutral scenery of the world.

Charles Swindoll

BUILDING A BETTER YOU

Pick out one important obligation that you've been putting off. Then, take at least one specific step toward the completion of the task you've been avoiding. Even if you don't finish the job, you'll discover that it's easier to finish a job that you've already begun than to finish a job that you've never started.

CHOOSING THE GOOD LIFE

And in that day you will ask Me nothing. Most assuredly,
I say to you, whatever you ask the Father in My name
He will give you. Until now you have asked nothing in My name.
Ask, and you will receive, that your joy may be full.

John 16:23–24 NKJV

God offers us abundance through His Son, Jesus. Whether or not we accept God's abundance is, of course, up to each of us. When we entrust our hearts and our days to the One who created us, we experience abundance through the grace and sacrifice of His Son, Jesus. But, when we turn our thoughts and our energies away from God's commandments, we inevitably forfeit the spiritual abundance that might otherwise be ours.

What is your focus today? Are you focused on God's Word and His will for your life? Or are you focused on the distractions and temptations of a difficult world? The answer to this question will, to a surprising extent, determine the quality and the direction of your day.

If you sincerely seek the spiritual abundance that your Savior offers, then follow Him completely and without reservation. When you do, you will receive the love, the life, and the abundance that He has promised.

It would be wrong to have a "poverty complex," for to think ourselves paupers is to deny either the King's riches or to deny our being His children.

Catherine Marshall

A LESSON FOR THE HEART AND SOUL

Abundant living may or may not include material wealth, but abundant living always includes the spiritual riches that you receive when you obey God's Word.

SERENITY NOW

Do not remember the former things, nor consider the things of old.
Behold, I will do a new thing.
Isaiah 43:18–19 NKJV

The American theologian Reinhold Niebuhr composed a profoundly simple verse that came to be known as the Serenity Prayer: "God, grant me the serenity to accept the things I cannot change, the courage to change the things I can, and the wisdom to know the difference." Niebuhr's words are far easier to recite than they are to live by. Why? Because most of us want life to unfold in accordance with our own wishes and timetables. But sometimes God has other plans.

If you've encountered unfortunate circumstances that are beyond your power to control, accept those circumstances . . . and trust God. When you do, you can be comforted in the knowledge that your Creator is both loving and wise, and that He understands His plans perfectly, even when you do not.

Acceptance is taking from God's hand absolutely anything He gives, looking into His face in trust and thanksgiving, knowing that the confinement of the situation we're in is good and for His glory.

Charles Swindoll

BUILDING A BETTER YOU

Acceptance means learning to trust God more. Today, think of at least one aspect of your life that you've been reluctant to accept, and then prayerfully ask God to help you trust Him more by accepting the past.

A PRICELESS TREASURE

Man shall not live by bread alone,
but by every word that proceeds from the mouth of God.
Matthew 4:4 NKJV

The Bible is a roadmap for life here on earth and for life eternal; it should be the map for you. The Bible is a priceless gift, a tool for Christians to use as they share the Good News of their Savior, Christ Jesus. Too many Christians, however, keep their spiritual tool kits tightly closed and out of sight.

Jonathan Edwards advised, "Be assiduous in reading the Holy Scriptures. This is the fountain whence all knowledge in divinity must be derived. Therefore let not this treasure lie by you neglected."

God's Holy Word is, indeed, a priceless, one-of-a-kind treasure. Handle it with care, but more importantly, handle it every day . . . starting today.

The vigor of our spiritual lives will be in exact proportion to the place held by the Bible in our lives and in our thoughts.

George Mueller

BUILDING A BETTER YOU

How you choose to use your Bible is, of course, up to you . . . and so are the consequences. So today, challenge your faith by making sure that you're spending quality time each day studying God's Word.

BEYOND TODAY'S WORRY

Whoever gives heed to instruction prospers,
and blessed is he that trusts in the Lord.
Proverbs 16:20 NIV

Because we are imperfect beings, we worry. Even though we are Christians who have been given the assurance of salvation—even though we are Christians who have received the promise of God's love and protection—we find ourselves fretting over the countless details of everyday life. Jesus understood our concerns when He spoke the reassuring words found in Matthew 6: "Therefore I tell you, do not worry about your life . . ."

As you consider the promises of Jesus, remember that God still sits in His Heaven and you are His beloved child. Then, perhaps, you will worry a little less and trust God a little more, and that's as it should be because God is trustworthy . . . and you are protected.

The secret of Christian quietness is not indifference, but the knowledge that God is my Father, He loves me, and that I shall never think of anything He will forget. Then, worry becomes an impossibility.

Oswald Chambers

BUILDING A BETTER YOU

If you're worried about the future . . . stop worrying and start working. The more time you spend working, the less time you'll have to spend worrying. Don't fret about your problems; fix them!

FEEDING THE CHURCH

The church, you see, is not peripheral to the world; the world is
peripheral to the church. The church is Christ's body, in which he
speaks and acts, by which he fills everything with his presence.
Ephesians 1:23 MSG

One way that we come to know God is by involving ourselves in His church.

In the Book of Acts, Luke reminds us to "feed the church of God" (20:28). As Christians who have been saved by a loving, compassionate Creator, we are compelled not only to worship Him in our hearts but also to worship Him in the presence of fellow believers.

Do you feed the church of God? Do you attend regularly, and are you an active participant? The answer to these questions will have a profound impact on the quality and direction of your spiritual journey.

So do yourself a favor: Become actively involved in your church. Don't just go to church out of habit. Go to church out of a sincere desire to know and worship God. When you do, you'll be blessed by the One who sent His Son to die so that you might have everlasting life.

What the church needs is not better machinery nor new organizations, but instead it needs men whom the Holy Spirit can use—men of prayer, men mighty in prayer.

E. M. Bounds

A LESSON FOR THE HEART AND SOUL

Jesus promised that the church would be triumphant. So, you simply can't go wrong investing your life in His church. The church is eternal.

A MAN OF PRAYER

Rejoice always, pray without ceasing, in everything give thanks;
for this is the will of God in Christ Jesus for you.
1 Thessalonians 5:16–18 NKJV

Is prayer an integral part of your daily life, or is it a hit-or-miss habit? Do you "pray without ceasing," or is your prayer life an afterthought? Do you regularly pray in the solitude of the early morning darkness, or do you lower your head only when others are watching? The answer to these questions will determine the direction of your day—and your life.

So here's your challenge: pray early and often. Begin your prayers early in the morning and continue them throughout the day. And remember this: God does answer your prayers, but He's not likely to answer those prayers until you've prayed them.

Prayer is the most important tool for your mission to the world. People may refuse our love or reject our message, but they are defenseless against our prayers.

Rick Warren

BUILDING A BETTER YOU

Today, ask yourself if your prayer life is all that it should be. If the answer is yes, keep up the good work. But if the answer is no, set aside a specific time each morning to talk to God. And then, when you've set aside a time for prayer, don't allow yourself to become sidetracked.

AN ATTITUDE OF GRATITUDE

And let the peace of God rule in your hearts . . . and be ye thankful.
Colossians 3:15 KJV

For most of us, life is busy and complicated. We have countless responsibilities, some of which begin before sunrise and many of which end long after sunset. Amid the rush and crush of the daily grind, it is easy to lose sight of God and His blessings. But, when we forget to slow down and say "Thank You" to our Maker, we rob ourselves of His presence, His peace, and His joy.

Our task, as believing Christians, is to praise God many times each day. Then, with gratitude in our hearts, we can face our daily duties with the perspective and power that only He can provide.

Nobody who gets enough food and clothing in a world where most are hungry and cold has any business to talk about "misery."

C. S. Lewis

A spirit of thankfulness makes all the difference.

Billy Graham

BUILDING A BETTER YOU

Developing an attitude of gratitude is key to a joyful and satisfying life. So ask yourself this question: "Am I grateful enough?"

BECOMING WISE

Whoever walks with the wise will become wise;
whoever walks with fools will suffer harm.
Proverbs 13:20 NLT

Wisdom does not spring up overnight—it takes time. To become wise, we must seek God's wisdom and live according to His Word. And, we must not only learn the lessons of the Christian life, we must also live by them.

Do you seek to live a life of righteousness and wisdom? If so, you must study the ultimate source of wisdom: the Word of God. You must seek out worthy mentors and listen carefully to their advice. You must associate, day in and day out, with godly men and women. And, you must act in accordance with your beliefs. When you do these things, you will become wise . . . and you will be a blessing to your friends, to your family, and to the world.

Having a doctrine pass before the mind is not what the Bible means by knowing the truth. It's only when it reaches down deep into the heart that the truth begins to set us free, just as a key must penetrate a lock to turn it, or as rainfall must saturate the earth down to the roots in order for your garden to grow.

John Eldredge

BUILDING A BETTER YOU

Need wisdom? God's got it. If you want it, then study God's Word and associate with godly people.

A FOUNDATION OF HONESTY

The honest person will live in safety, but the dishonest will be caught.
Proverbs 10:9 NCV

Lasting relationships are built upon a foundation of honesty and trust. It has been said on many occasions that honesty is the best policy. For believers, it is far more important to note that honesty is God's policy. And if we are to be servants worthy of our Savior, Jesus Christ, we must be honest and forthright in all our communications with others.

Sometimes, honesty is difficult; sometimes, honesty is painful; sometimes, honesty makes us feel uncomfortable. Despite these temporary feelings of discomfort, we must make honesty the hallmark of all our relationships; otherwise, we invite needless suffering into our own lives and into the lives of those we love.

The commandment of absolute truthfulness is really only another name for the fullness of discipleship.

Dietrich Bonhoeffer

We can teach our children that being honest protects from guilt and provides for a clear conscience.

Josh McDowell

A LESSON FOR THE HEART AND SOUL

One of your greatest possessions is integrity. Don't lose it. Billy Graham was right when he said, "Integrity is the glue that holds our way of life together. We must constantly strive to keep our integrity intact. When wealth is lost, nothing is lost; when health is lost, something is lost; when character is lost, all is lost."

A WING AND A PRAYER

Be cheerful. Keep things in good repair. Keep your spirits up.
Think in harmony. Be agreeable. Do all that,
and the God of love and peace will be with you for sure.
2 Corinthians 13:11 MSG

Mrs. Charles E. Cowman, the author of the classic devotional text *Streams in the Desert*, wrote, "Two wings are necessary to lift our souls toward God: prayer and praise. Prayer asks. Praise accepts the answer." That's why we should find the time to lift our concerns to God in prayer, and to praise Him for all that He has done.

John Wesley correctly observed, "Sour godliness is the devil's religion." These words remind us that pessimism and doubt are some of the most important tools that Satan uses to achieve his objectives. Our challenge, of course, is to ensure that Satan cannot use these tools on us.

Are you a cheerful Christian? You should be! And what is the best way to attain the joy that is rightfully yours? By giving Christ what is rightfully His: your heart, your soul, and your life.

Christ can put a spring in your step and a thrill in your heart. Optimism and cheerfulness are products of knowing Christ.

Billy Graham

How changed our lives would be if we could only fly through the days on wings of surrender and trust!

Hannah Whitall Smith

A LESSON FOR THE HEART AND SOUL

Cheerfulness is its own reward—but not its only reward.

TERMINATING THE TANTRUM

Make no friendship with an angry man, and with a furious man do not go, lest you learn his ways and set a snare for your soul.
Proverbs 22:24–25 NKJV

Temper tantrums are usually unproductive, unattractive, unforgettable, and unnecessary. Perhaps that's why Proverbs 16:32 states that, "Controlling your temper is better than capturing a city" (NCV).

If you've allowed anger to become a regular visitor at your house, today you must pray for wisdom, for patience, and for a heart that is so filled with love and forgiveness that it contains no room for bitterness. God will help you terminate your tantrums if you ask Him to. And God can help you perfect your ability to be patient if you ask Him to. So ask Him, and then wait patiently for the ever-more-patient you to arrive.

Anger is the noise of the soul; the unseen irritant of the heart; the relentless invader of silence.

Max Lucado

Anger is the fluid that love bleeds when you cut it.

C. S. Lewis

A LESSON FOR THE HEART AND SOUL

If you think you're about to explode in anger, slow down, catch your breath, and walk away if you must. It's better to walk away—and keep walking—than it is to blurt out angry words that can't be un-blurted.

LIVING IN AN ANXIOUS WORLD

Cast all your anxiety on him because he cares for you.
1 Peter 5:7 NIV

We live in a world that often breeds anxiety and fear. When we come face-to-face with tough times, we may fall prey to discouragement, doubt, or depression. But our Father in Heaven has other plans. God has promised that we may lead lives of abundance, not anxiety. In fact, His Word instructs us to "be anxious for nothing" (Philippians 4:6). But how can we put our fears to rest? By taking those fears to God and leaving them there.

As you face the challenges of daily life, you may find yourself becoming anxious, troubled, discouraged, or fearful. If so, turn every one of your concerns over to your Heavenly Father. The same God who created the universe will comfort you if you ask Him . . . so ask Him and trust Him. And then watch in amazement as your anxieties melt into the warmth of His loving hands.

One of the main missions of God is to free us from the debilitating bonds of fear and anxiety. God's heart is broken when He sees us so demoralized and weighed down by fear.

Bill Hybels

A LESSON FOR THE HEART AND SOUL

You have worries, but God has solutions. Your challenge is to trust Him to solve the problems that you can't.

COUNTING YOUR BLESSINGS

*And now, dear brothers and sisters, let me say one more thing as
I close this letter. Fix your thoughts on what is true and honorable
and right. Think about things that are pure and lovely and admirable.
Think about things that are excellent and worthy of praise.*

Philippians 4:8 NLT

How will you direct your thoughts today? Will you obey the words of Philippians 4:8 by dwelling upon those things that are honorable, just, and commendable? Or will you allow your thoughts to be hijacked by the negativity that seems to dominate our troubled world? Are you fearful, angry, bored, or worried? Are you so preoccupied with the concerns of this day that you fail to thank God for the promise of eternity? Are you confused, bitter, or pessimistic? If so, God wants to have a little talk with you.

God intends for you to experience joy and abundance. So, today and every day hereafter, celebrate the life that God has given you by focusing your thoughts upon those things that are worthy of praise. Today, count your blessings instead of your hardships. And thank the Giver of all things good for gifts that are simply too numerous to count.

Attitude is more important than the past, than education, than money, than circumstances, than what people do or say. It is more important than appearance, giftedness, or skill.

Charles Swindoll

BUILDING A BETTER YOU

A positive attitude leads to positive results; a negative attitude leads elsewhere.

SMILES AND MORE SMILES

Jacob said, "For what a relief it is to see your friendly smile.
It is like seeing the smile of God!"
Genesis 33:10 NLT

Life should never be taken for granted. Each day is a priceless gift from God and should be treated as such.

Hannah Whitall Smith observed, "How changed our lives would be if we could only fly through the days on wings of surrender and trust!" And Clement of Alexandria noted, "All our life is a celebration for us; we are convinced, in fact, that God is always everywhere. We sing while we work . . . we pray while we carry out all life's other occupations." These words remind us that this day is God's creation, a gift to be treasured and savored.

Today, let us celebrate life with smiles on our faces and kind words on our lips. After all, this is God's day, and He has given us clear instructions for its use. We are commanded to rejoice and be glad. So, with no further ado, let the celebration begin.

The people whom I have seen succeed best in life have always been cheerful and hopeful people who went about their business with smiles on their faces.

Charles Kingsley

BUILDING A BETTER YOU

If you're too stressed out to celebrate life today, start thanking God for the gifts He has given you. Try counting those gifts one-by-one. When you do, you won't stay stressed for long.

A QUIET PLACE

Now in the morning, having risen a long while before daylight,
He went out and departed to a solitary place; and there He prayed.
Mark 1:35 NKJV

In the first chapter of Mark, we read that in the darkness of the early morning hours, Jesus went to a solitary place and prayed. So, too, should we. But sometimes, finding quiet moments of solitude is difficult indeed. We live in a noisy world, a world filled with distractions, frustrations, and complications. But if we allow the distractions of a clamorous world to separate us from God's peace, we do ourselves a profound disservice. Are you one of those busy people who rush through the day with scarcely a single moment for quiet contemplation and prayer? If so, it's time to reorder your priorities. Nothing is more important than the time you spend with your Savior. So be still and claim the inner peace that is your spiritual birthright: the peace of Jesus Christ.

The more complicated life becomes, the more we need to quiet our souls before God.

Elisabeth Elliot

In the center of a hurricane there is absolute quiet and peace. There is no safer place than in the center of the will of God.

Corrie ten Boom

BUILDING A BETTER YOU

Be still and listen to God. He has something important to say to you.

LIVING IN CHRIST'S LOVE

Yes, my dear children, live in him so that when Christ comes back,
we can be without fear and not be ashamed in his presence.
If you know that Christ is all that is right,
you know that all who do right are God's children.

1 John 2:28–29 NCV

Even though we are imperfect, fallible human beings, even though we have fallen far short of God's commandments, Christ loves us still. His love is perfect and steadfast; it does not waver—it does not change. Our task, as believers, is to accept Christ's love and to encourage others to do likewise.

In today's troubled world, we all need the love and the peace that is found through the Son of God. Thankfully, Christ's love has no limits; it can encircle all of us. And it's up to each of us to ensure that it does.

We shall find in Christ enough of everything we need—for the body, for the mind, and for the spirit—to do what He wants us to do as long as He wants us to do it.

Vance Havner

If you come to Christ, you will always have the option of an ever-present friend. You don't have to dial long-distance. He'll be with you every step of the way.

Bill Hybels

A LESSON FOR THE HEART AND SOUL

Today and every day, give thanks for Christ's sacrifice. It is the ultimate expression of His love for you.

GOD IS HERE

Draw close to God, and God will draw close to you.
James 4:8 NLT

God is constantly making Himself available to you; therefore, when you approach Him obediently and sincerely, You will most certainly find Him: God is always available to you. Whenever it seems to you that God is distant, disinterested, or altogether absent, you may rest assured that your feelings are a reflection of your own emotional state, not an indication of God's absence.

If, during life's darker days, you seek to establish a closer relationship with Him, you can do so because God is not just near, He is here.

Christianity says we were created by a righteous God to flourish and be exhilarated in a righteous environment. God has "wired" us in such a way that the more righteous we are, the more we'll actually enjoy life.

Bill Hybels

We look for visions of heaven, but we never dream that, all the time, God is in the commonplace things and people around us.

Oswald Chambers

BUILDING A BETTER YOU

Where is your focus today? Remember that it's important to focus your thoughts on Jesus first.

UNDERSTAND YOU ARE GOD-MADE

By humility and the fear of the Lord are riches and honor and life.
Proverbs 22:4 NKJV

We have heard the phrase on countless occasions: "He's a self-made man." In truth, none of us are self-made. We all owe countless debts that we can never repay. Our first debt, of course, is to our Father in Heaven—Who has given us everything that we are and will ever be—and to His Son Who sacrificed His own life so that we might live eternally. We are also indebted to ancestors, parents, teachers, friends, spouses, family members, coworkers, fellow believers . . . and the list, of course, goes on.

Most of us, it seems, are more than willing to stick out our chests and say, "Look at me; I did that!" But in our better moments, in the quiet moments when we search the depths of our own hearts, we know better. Whatever "it" is, God did that. And He deserves the credit.

We can never have more of true faith than we have of true humility.
Andrew Murray

The preoccupation with self is the enemy of humility.
Franklin Graham

A LESSON FOR THE HEART AND SOUL

God favors the humble just as surely as He disciplines the proud.

THE BREAD OF LIFE

And Jesus said to them, "I am the bread of life.
He who comes to Me shall never hunger,
and he who believes in Me shall never thirst."
John 6:35 NKJV

He was the Son of God, but He wore a crown of thorns. He was the Savior of mankind, yet He was put to death on a roughhewn cross made of wood. He offered His healing touch to an unsaved world, and yet the same hands that had healed the sick and raised the dead were pierced with nails.

Jesus Christ, the Son of God, was born into humble circumstances. He walked this earth, not as a ruler of men, but as the Savior of mankind. His crucifixion, a torturous punishment that was intended to end His life and His reign, instead became the pivotal event in the history of all humanity.

Jesus is the bread of life. Accept His grace. Share His love. And follow in His footsteps.

Our Lord is the Bread of Life. His proportions are perfect. There never was too much or too little of anything about Him. Feed on Him for a well-balanced ration. All the vitamins and calories are there.

Vance Havner

BUILDING A BETTER YOU

Today, think about your relationship with Jesus: what it is, what it should be, and what it will be today, tomorrow, and throughout all eternity.

THE VOICE OF GOD

Listen in silence before me....
Isaiah 41:1 NLT

Sometimes God speaks loudly and clearly. More often, He speaks in a quiet voice—and if you are wise, you will be listening carefully when He does. To do so, you must carve out quiet moments each day to study His Word and sense His direction.

Can you quiet yourself long enough to listen to your conscience? Are you attuned to the subtle guidance of your intuition? Are you willing to pray sincerely and then to wait quietly for God's response. Hopefully so. Usually God refrains from sending His messages on stone tablets or city billboards. More often, He communicates in subtler ways. If you sincerely desire to hear His voice, you must listen carefully, and you must do so in the silent corners of your quiet, willing heart.

When we come to Jesus stripped of pretensions, with a needy spirit, ready to listen, He meets us at the point of need.

Catherine Marshall

In the soul-searching of our lives, we are to stay quiet so we can hear Him say all that He wants to say to us in our hearts.

Charles Swindoll

BUILDING A BETTER YOU

Prayer is two-way communication with God. Talking to God isn't enough; you should also listen to Him.

MANKIND'S TREASURE HUNT

For where your treasure is, there your heart will be also.
Luke 12:34 NKJV

All of mankind is engaged in a colossal, worldwide treasure hunt. Some people seek treasure from earthly sources, treasures such as material wealth or public acclaim; others seek God's treasures by making Him the cornerstone of their lives.

What kind of treasure hunter are you? Are you so caught up in the demands of everyday living that you sometimes allow the search for worldly treasures to become your primary focus? If so, it's time to think long and hard about what you value, and why. All the items on your daily to-do list are not created equal. That's why you must put first things first by placing God in His rightful place: first place. The world's treasures are difficult to find and difficult to keep; God's treasures are ever-present and everlasting. Which treasures, then, will you claim as your own?

There is absolutely no evidence that complexity and materialism lead to happiness. On the contrary, there is plenty of evidence that simplicity and spirituality lead to joy, a blessedness that is better than happiness.

Dennis Swanberg

BUILDING A BETTER YOU

Today, think long and hard about the priorities and values that guide your decision-making. And then, when you finally put all that material stuff in perspective, begin storing up riches that will endure throughout eternity—the spiritual kind.

WISDOM IN A DONUT SHOP

My cup runs over. Surely goodness and mercy
shall follow me all the days of my life;
and I will dwell in the house of the Lord Forever.
Psalm 23:5–6 NKJV

Many years ago, this rhyme was posted on the wall of a small donut shop:

As you travel through life brother,
Whatever be your goal,
Keep your eye upon the donut,
And not upon the hole.

These simple words remind us of a profound truth: We should spend more time looking at the things we have, not worrying about the things we don't have.

When you think about it, you've got more blessings than you can count. So make it a habit to thank God for the gifts He's given you, not the gifts you wish He'd given you.

The essence of optimism is that it takes no account of the present, but it is a source of inspiration, of vitality, and of hope. Where others have resigned, it enables a man to hold his head high, to claim the future for himself, and not abandon it to his enemy.

Dietrich Bonhoeffer

A LESSON FOR THE HEART AND SOUL

Today (and every day), it's time to count your blessings and to think optimistically about your future.

PLEASING GOD

But neither exile nor homecoming is the main thing.
Cheerfully pleasing God is the main thing,
and that's what we aim to do, regardless of our conditions.
2 Corinthians 5:9 MSG

When God made you, He equipped you with an array of talents and abilities that are uniquely yours. It's up to you to discover those talents and to use them, but sometimes the world will encourage you to do otherwise. At times, society will attempt to cubbyhole you, to standardize you, and to make you fit into particular, preformed mold. Sometimes, because you're an imperfect human being, you may become so wrapped up in meeting society's expectations that you fail to focus on God's expectations. To do so is a mistake of major proportions—don't make it.

Who will you try to please today: God or man? Your primary obligation is not to please imperfect men and women. Your obligation is to strive diligently to meet the expectations of an all-knowing and perfect God. Trust Him always. Love Him always. Praise Him always. And seek to please Him. Always.

All our offerings, whether music or martyrdom, are like the intrinsically worthless present of a child, which a father values indeed, but values only for the intention.

C. S. Lewis

BUILDING A BETTER YOU

First, focus on your relationship with God. Then, you'll find that every other relationship and every other aspect of your life will be more fulfilling.

COMMUNITY LIFE

Regarding life together and getting along with each other,
you don't need me to tell you what to do.
You're God-taught in these matters. Just love one another!
1 Thessalonians 4:9 MSG

As we travel along life's road, we build lifelong relationships with a small, dear circle of family and friends. And how best do we build and maintain these relationships? By following the Word of God. Healthy relationships are built upon honesty, compassion, responsible behavior, trust, and optimism. Healthy relationships are built upon the Golden Rule. Healthy relationships are built upon sharing and caring. All of these principles are found time and time again in God's Holy Word. When we read God's Word and follow His commandments, we enrich our own lives and the lives of those who are closest to us.

We discover our role in life through our relationships with others.

Rick Warren

Horizontal relationships—relationships between people—are crippled at the outset unless the vertical relationship—the relationship between each person and God—is in place.

Ed Young

A LESSON FOR THE HEART AND SOUL

When you understand that Christianity is about servanthood, other people become your focus and your ministry.

KEEP POSSESSIONS IN PERSPECTIVE

A man's life does not consist in the abundance of his possessions.
Luke 12:15 NIV

All too often, we focus our thoughts and energies on the accumulation of earthly treasures, leaving precious little time to accumulate the only treasures that really matter: the spiritual kind. Our material possessions have the potential to do great good or terrible harm, depending upon how we choose to use them. As believers, our instructions are clear: We must use our possessions in accordance with God's commandments, and we must be faithful stewards of the gifts He has seen fit to bestow upon us.

Today, let us honor God by placing no other gods before Him. God comes first; everything else comes next—and "everything else" most certainly includes all of our earthly possessions.

If you want to be truly happy, you won't find it on an endless quest for more stuff. You'll find it in receiving God's generosity and in passing that generosity along.

Bill Hybels

A LESSON FOR THE HEART AND SOUL

Everything we have is on loan from God. Holocaust survivor Corrie ten Boom writes, "I have held many things in my hands, and I have lost them all; but whatever I have placed in God's hands, that I still possess." Remember: your real riches are in Heaven, so conduct yourself accordingly.

HE RENEWS
OUR STRENGTH

Have you not known? Have you not heard? The everlasting God,
the Lord, the Creator of the ends of the earth,
neither faints nor is weary. His understanding is unsearchable.
He gives power to the weak, and to those who have
no might He increases strength.
Isaiah 40:28–29 NKJV

When we genuinely lift our hearts and prayers to God, He renews our strength. Are you almost too weary to lift your head? Then bow it. Offer your concerns and your fears to your Father in Heaven. He is always at your side, offering His love and His strength.

Are you troubled or anxious? Take your anxieties to God in prayer. Are you weak or worried? Delve deeply into God's Holy Word and sense His presence in the quiet moments of the day. Are you spiritually exhausted? Call upon fellow believers to support you, and call upon Christ to renew your spirit and your life. Your Savior will never let you down. To the contrary, He will always lift you up if you ask Him to. So what, dear friend, are you waiting for?

God is not running an antique shop! He is making all things new!

Vance Havner

BUILDING A BETTER YOU

God wants to give you peace, and He wants to renew your spirit. It's up to you to slow down and give Him a chance to do so.

SHARING THE GOOD NEWS

For Christ did not send me to baptize, but to preach the gospel,
not with wisdom of words, lest the cross of Christ
should be made of no effect.
1 Corinthians 1:17 NKJV

In his second letter to Timothy, Paul offers a message to believers of every generation when he writes, "God has not given us a spirit of timidity" (1:7 NASB). Paul's meaning is crystal clear: When sharing our testimonies, we, as Christians, must be courageous, forthright, and unashamed.

We live in a world that desperately needs the healing message of Christ Jesus. Every believer, each in his or her own way, bears a personal responsibility for sharing that message. If you are a believer in Christ, you know how He has touched your heart and changed your life. Now it's your turn to share the Good News with others. And remember: today is the perfect time to share your testimony because tomorrow may quite simply be too late.

If I can love folks the way they are we have greater chance of winning them to the kingdom.

Dennis Swanberg

How many people have you made homesick for God?

Oswald Chambers

A LESSON FOR THE HEART AND SOUL

Whether you realize it or not, you have a profound responsibility to tell as many people as you can about the eternal life that Christ offers to those who believe in Him.

THE TRAP OF ADDICTION

Therefore submit to God. Resist the devil and he will flee from you.
Draw near to God and He will draw near to you. Cleanse your hands,
you sinners; and purify your hearts, you double-minded.
James 4:7–8 NKJV

The dictionary defines *addiction* as "the compulsive need for a habit-forming substance; the condition of being habitually and compulsively occupied with something." That definition is accurate, but incomplete. For Christians, addiction has an additional meaning: It means compulsively worshipping something other than God.

Unless you're living on a deserted island, you know people who are full-blown addicts—probably lots of people. If you, or someone you love, is suffering from the blight of addiction, remember that help is available.

And if you're one of those fortunate people who has never experimented with addictive substances, congratulations. You have just spared yourself a lifetime of headaches and heartaches.

Addiction is the most powerful psychic enemy of humanity's desire for God.

Gerald May

BUILDING A BETTER YOU

Ultimately, you and you alone are responsible for controlling your appetites. Others may warn you, help you, or encourage you, but in the end, the habits that rule your life are the very same habits that you yourself have formed. Thankfully, since you formed these habits, you can also break them—if you decide to do so.

FORGIVENESS AT HOME

Let all bitterness, wrath, anger, clamor, and evil speaking be put away from you, with all malice. And be kind to one another, tenderhearted, forgiving one another, just as God in Christ forgave you.
Ephesians 4:31–32 NKJV

Sometimes, it's easy to become angry with the people we love most, and sometimes it's hard to forgive them. After all, we know that our family will still love us no matter how angry we become. But while it's easy to become angry at home, it's usually wrong.

The next time you're tempted to lose your temper or to remain angry at a close family member, ask God to help you find the wisdom to forgive. And while you're at it, do your best to calm down sooner rather than later because peace is always beautiful, especially when it's peace at your house.

Get rid of the poison of built-up anger and the acid of long-term resentment.

Charles Swindoll

When something robs you of your peace of mind, ask yourself if it is worth the energy you are expending on it. If not, then put it out of your mind in an act of discipline. Every time the thought of "it" returns, refuse it.

Kay Arthur

A LESSON FOR THE HEART AND SOUL
When you lose your temper . . . you lose.

CHRIST'S LOVE CHANGES EVERYTHING

Your old life is dead. Your new life, which is your real life—even though invisible to spectators—is with Christ in God. He is your life.
Colossians 3:3 MSG

What does the love of Christ mean to His believers? It changes everything. His love is perfect and steadfast. Even though we are fallible, and wayward, the Good Shepherd cares for us still. Even though we have fallen far short of the Father's commandments, Christ loves us with a power and depth that is beyond our understanding. And, as we accept Christ's love and walk in Christ's footsteps, our lives bear testimony to His power and to His grace. Yes, Christ's love changes everything; may we invite Him into our hearts so it can then change everything in us.

Has he taken over your heart? Perhaps He resides there, but does He preside there?

Vance Havner

It has been the faith of the Son of God who loves me and gave Himself for me that has held me in the darkest valley and the hottest fires and the deepest waters.

Elisabeth Elliot

A LESSON FOR THE HEART AND SOUL

Jesus loves you. Period. His love is amazing, it's wonderful, and it's meant for you.

SO MANY TEMPTATIONS

No temptation has overtaken you except such as is common to man;
but God is faithful, who will not allow you to be tempted
beyond what you are able, but with the temptation will also make
the way of escape, that you may be able to bear it.

1 Corinthians 10:13 NKJV

This world is filled to the brim with temptations. Some of these temptations are small; eating a second scoop of ice cream, for example, is tempting, but not very dangerous. Other temptations, however, are not nearly so harmless. The devil is working 24/7, and he's causing pain and heartache in more ways than ever before. Thankfully, in the battle against Satan, we are never alone. God is always with us, and He gives us the power to resist temptation whenever we ask Him for the strength to do so.

In a letter to believers, Peter offered a stern warning: "Your adversary, the devil, prowls around like a roaring lion, seeking someone to devour" (1 Peter 5:8 NASB). As Christians, we must take that warning seriously, and we must behave accordingly.

Man without God is always torn between two urges. His nature prompts him to do wrong, and his conscience urges him to do right. Christ can rid you of that inner conflict.

Billy Graham

A LESSON FOR THE HEART AND SOUL

Sometimes immorality is obvious and sometimes it's not. So beware: the most subtle forms of sin are often the most dangerous.

THE ANSWER TO ADVERSITY

I have heard your prayer, I have seen your tears; surely I will heal you.
2 Kings 20:5 NKJV

From time to time, all of us must endure discouragement and defeat. And, we sometimes experience life-changing personal losses that leave us reeling. When we do, God stands ready to protect us. When we are troubled, we must call upon God, and, in His own time and according to His own plan, He will heal us.

Are you anxious? Take those anxieties to God. Are you troubled? Take your troubles to Him. Does your world seem to be trembling beneath your feet? Seek protection from the One who cannot be moved. The same God who created the universe will protect you if you ask Him . . . so ask Him.

We should not be upset when unexpected and upsetting things happen. God, in his wisdom, means to make something of us which we have not yet attained, and He is dealing with us accordingly.

J. I. Packer

Teach us to set our hopes on heaven, to hold firmly to the promise of eternal life, so that we can withstand the struggles and storms of this world.

Max Lucado

BUILDING A BETTER YOU

In dealing with difficult situations, view God as your comfort and your strength. And remember: Tough times can also be times of intense personal growth.

WHAT DOESN'T CHANGE

Jesus Christ is the same yesterday, today, and forever.
Hebrews 13:8 NCV

Our world is in a state of constant change. God is not. At times, the world seems to be trembling beneath our feet. But we can be comforted in the knowledge that our Heavenly Father is the rock that cannot be shaken. His Word promises, "I am the Lord, I do not change" (Malachi 3:6 NKJV).

Every day that we live, we mortals encounter a multitude of changes—some good, some not so good, some downright disheartening. On those occasions when we must endure life-changing personal losses that leave us breathless, there is a place we can turn for comfort and assurance—we can turn to God. When we do, our loving Heavenly Father stands ready to protect us, to comfort us, to guide us, and, in time, to heal us.

Live for today, but hold your hands open to tomorrow. Anticipate the future and its changes with joy. There is a seed of God's love in every event, every circumstance, every unpleasant situation in which you may find yourself.

Barbara Johnson

BUILDING A BETTER YOU

When it comes to making big changes or big purchases, proceed slowly. Otherwise, you may find yourself uncomfortably perched atop a merry-go-round that is much easier to start than it is to stop.

LOVE IS A CHOICE

Beloved, if God so loved us, we also ought to love one another.
1 John 4:11 NKJV

Love is always a choice. Sometimes, of course, we may "fall in love," but it takes work to stay there. Sometimes, we may be "swept off our feet," but the "sweeping" is only temporary; sooner or later, if love is to endure, one must plant one's feet firmly on the ground. The decision to love another person for a lifetime is much more than the simple process of "falling in" or "being swept up." It requires "reaching out," "holding firm," and "lifting up." Love, then, becomes a decision to honor and care for the other person, come what may.

How do you spell love? When you reach the point where the happiness, security, and development of another person is as much of a driving force to you as your own happiness, security, and development, then you have a mature love. True love is spelled G-I-V-E.

Josh McDowell

Beware that you are not swallowed up in books! An ounce of love is worth a pound of knowledge.

John Wesley

A LESSON FOR THE HEART AND SOUL

God is love, and He expects us to share His love.

BEYOND MATERIALISM

*For what will it profit a man if he gains the whole world,
and loses his own soul?
Or what will a man give in exchange for his soul?*
Mark 8:36–37 NKJV

In our modern society, we need money to live. But as Christians, we must never make the acquisition of money the central focus of our lives. Money is a tool, but it should never overwhelm our sensibilities. The focus of life must be squarely on things spiritual, not things material.

Whenever we place our love for material possessions above our love for God—or when we yield to the countless other temptations of everyday living—we find ourselves engaged in a struggle between good and evil. Let us respond to this struggle by freeing ourselves from that subtle yet powerful temptation: the temptation to love the world more than we love God.

The cross is laid on every Christian. It begins with the call to abandon the attachments of this world.

Dietrich Bonhoeffer

A LESSON FOR THE HEART AND SOUL

God's Word warns against the spiritual trap of materialism. Material possessions may seem appealing at first, but they pale in comparison to the spiritual gifts that God gives to those who put Him first. Count yourself among that number.

GOD'S GUIDANCE FOR YOUR NEW BEGINNING

Trust in the LORD with all your heart;
do not depend on your own understanding.
Seek his will in all you do, and he will direct your paths.
Proverbs 3:5–6 NLT

Proverbs 3:5-6 makes this promise: if you acknowledge God's sovereignty over every aspect of your life, He will guide your path. And, as you prayerfully consider the path that God intends for you to take, here are things you should do: You should study His Word and be ever-watchful for His signs. You should associate with fellow believers who will encourage your spiritual growth. You should listen carefully to that inner voice that speaks to you in the quiet moments of your daily devotionals. And you should be patient. Your Heavenly Father may not always reveal Himself as quickly as you would like, but rest assured that God intends to use you in wonderful, unexpected ways. Your challenge is to watch, to listen, to learn . . . and to follow.

There's not much you can't achieve or endure if you know God is walking by your side. Just remember: Someone knows, and Someone cares.

Bill Hybels

BUILDING A BETTER YOU

Following Christ is a daily journey. When you decide to walk in the footsteps of the Master, that means you're agreeing to be a disciple seven days a week, not just on Sunday.

CARING FOR
THE DOWNTRODDEN

I tell you the truth, whatever you did for one of
the least of these brothers of mine, you did for me.
Matthew 25:40 NIV

How fortunate we are to live in a land of opportunities and possibilities. But, for many people around the world, opportunities are scarce at best. In too many corners of the globe, hardworking men and women struggle mightily to provide food and shelter for their families.

When we care for the downtrodden, we follow in the footsteps of Christ. And, when we show compassion for those who suffer, we abide by the commandments of the One who created us. May we, who have been given so much, hear the Word of God . . . and may we follow it.

If you want to be truly happy, you won't find it on an endless quest for more stuff. You'll find it in receiving God's generosity and then passing that generosity along.

Bill Hybels

It's not difficult to make an impact on your world. All you really have to do is put the needs of others ahead of your own. You can make a difference with a little time and a big heart.

James Dobson

BUILDING A BETTER YOU

Want to admire the person you see in the mirror? Try being a little more generous. The more generous you are, the better you'll feel about yourself.

HIS AWESOME CREATION

Then God saw everything that He had made,
and indeed it was very good.
Genesis 1:31 NKJV

When we consider God's glorious universe, we marvel at the miracle of nature. The smallest seedlings and grandest stars are all part of God's infinite creation. God has placed His handiwork on display for all to see, and if we are wise, we will make time each day to celebrate the world that surrounds us.

Today, as you fulfill the demands of everyday life, pause to consider the majesty of Heaven and earth. It is as miraculous as it is beautiful, as incomprehensible as it is breathtaking.

The Psalmist reminds us that the Heavens are a declaration of God's glory (Psalm 19:1). May we never cease to praise the Father for a universe that stands as an awesome testimony to His presence and His power.

God expresses His love through creation.

Charles Stanley

Today you will encounter God's creation. When you see the beauty around you, let each detail remind you to lift your head in praise.

Max Lucado

A LESSON FOR THE HEART AND SOUL

Every day can be a celebration of God's creation. And every day should be.

LIMITLESS POWER, LIMITLESS LOVE

*I pray also that you will have greater understanding in your heart
so you will know the hope to which he has called us
and that you will know how rich and glorious are the blessings
God has promised his holy people. And you will know that
God's power is very great for us who believe.*

Ephesians 1:18–19 NCV

Because God's power is limitless, it is far beyond the comprehension of mortal minds. Yet even though we cannot fully understand the awesome power of God, we can praise it. When we worship God with faith and assurance, when we place Him at the absolute center of our lives, we invite His love into our hearts. In turn, we grow to love Him more deeply as we sense His love for us. St. Augustine wrote, "I love you, Lord, not doubtingly, but with absolute certainty. Your Word beat upon my heart until I fell in love with you, and now the universe and everything in it tells me to love you."

Let us pray that we, too, will turn our hearts to the Creator, knowing with certainty that His heart has ample room for each of us, and that we, in turn, must make room in our hearts for Him.

We have a God who delights in impossibilities.

Andrew Murray

A LESSON FOR THE HEART AND SOUL

God is in control of His world and your world. Rely upon Him. Vance Havner writes, "When we get to a place where it can't be done unless God does it, God will do it!" So teach your children that God can handle anything.

WAITING FOR GOD

The Lord is good to those who wait for Him,
to the soul who seeks Him. It is good that one should hope
and wait quietly for the salvation of the Lord.
Lamentations 3:25–26 NKJV

We human beings are so impatient. We know what we want, and we know exactly when we want it: RIGHT NOW! But, God knows better. He has created a world that unfolds according to His own timetable, not ours.

As Christians, we must be patient as we wait for God to show us the wonderful plans that He has in store for us. And while we're waiting for God to make His plans clear, let's keep praying and keep giving thanks to the One who has given us more blessings than we can count.

Grass that is here today and gone tomorrow does not require much time to mature. A big oak tree that lasts for generations requires much more time to grow and mature. God is concerned about your life through eternity. Allow Him to take all the time He needs to shape you for His purposes. Larger assignments will require longer periods of preparation.

Henry Blackaby

BUILDING A BETTER YOU

God has very big plans in store for your life, so trust Him and wait patiently for those plans to unfold. And remember: God's timing is best, so don't allow yourself to become discouraged if things don't work out exactly as you wish. Instead of worrying about your future, entrust it to God.

THE DIRECTION OF YOUR THOUGHTS

My cup runs over. Surely goodness and mercy shall follow me all the days of my life; and I will dwell in the house of the Lord Forever.
Psalm 23:5–6 NKJV

God has given you free will, including the ability to influence the direction and the tone of your thoughts. And, here's how God wants you to direct those thoughts: "Finally brothers, whatever is true, whatever is honorable, whatever is just, whatever is pure, whatever is lovely, whatever is commendable—if there is any moral excellence and if there is any praise—dwell on these things" (Philippians 4:8 HCSB).

The quality of your attitude will help determine the quality of your life, so you must guard your thoughts accordingly. The next time you find yourself dwelling upon the negative aspects of your life, refocus your attention on things positive. And, the next time you're tempted to waste valuable time gossiping or complaining, resist those temptations with all your might. And remember: You'll never whine your way to the top . . . so don't waste your breath.

Outlook determines outcome and attitude determines action.

Warren Wiersbe

BUILDING A BETTER YOU

Take a few minutes to think about the last time you let a negative attitude take control of your day. Then, write down a detailed scouting report about what went wrong.

BEYOND ENVY

Therefore, laying aside all malice, all deceit, hypocrisy, envy,
and all evil speaking, as newborn babes, desire the pure milk
of the word, that you may grow thereby.
1 Peter 2:1–2 NKJV

Because we are frail, imperfect human beings, we are sometimes envious of others. But God's Word warns us that envy is sin. Thus, we must guard ourselves against the natural tendency to feel resentment and jealousy when other people experience good fortune. As believers, we have absolutely no reason to be envious of any people on earth. After all, as Christians we are already recipients of the greatest gift in all creation: God's grace. We have been promised the gift of eternal life through God's only begotten Son, and we must count that gift as our most precious possession.

So here's a simple suggestion that is guaranteed to bring you happiness: fill your heart with God's love, God's promises, and God's Son . . . and when you do so, leave no room for envy, hatred, bitterness, or regret.

How can you possess the miseries of envy when you possess in Christ the best of all portions?

C. H. Spurgeon

Discontent dries up the soul.

Elisabeth Elliot

A LESSON FOR THE HEART AND SOUL

Envy is a sin. And, it's a major waste of time and energy. So get over it.

WE ARE ALL ROLE MODELS

You are the light of the world. A city set on a hill cannot be hidden;
nor does anyone light a lamp and put it under a basket,
but on the lampstand, and it gives light to all who are in the house.
Let your light shine before men in such a way that they may see your
good works, and glorify your Father who is in heaven.
Matthew 5:14–16 NASB

Whether we like it or not, we are role models. Hopefully, the lives we lead and the choices we make will serve as enduring examples of the spiritual abundance that is available to all who worship God and obey His commandments.

Ask yourself this question: Are you the kind of role model that you would want to emulate? If so, congratulations. But if certain aspects of your behavior could stand improvement, the best day to begin your self-improvement regimen is this one. Because whether you realize it or not, people you love are watching your behavior, and they're learning how to live. You owe it to them—and to yourself—to live righteously and well.

There is nothing anybody else can do that can stop God from using us. We can turn everything into a testimony.

Corrie ten Boom

BUILDING A BETTER YOU

Today, ask yourself this: If every Christian followed your example, what kind of world would we live in? If you like the answer you receive from the person in the mirror, keep doing what you're doing. But if you find room for improvement, start making those improvements today.

MOVING ON

You have heard that the law of Moses says, "Love your neighbor"
and hate your enemy. But I say, love your enemies!
Pray for those who persecute you! In that way,
you will be acting as true children of your Father in heaven.
Matthew 5:43–45 NLT

Sometimes, people can be discourteous and cruel. Sometimes people can be unfair, unkind, and unappreciative. Sometimes people get angry and frustrated. So what's a Christian to do? God's answer is straightforward: forgive, forget, and move on. In Luke 6:37, Jesus instructs, "Do not judge, and you will not be judged. Do not condemn, and you will not be condemned. Forgive, and you will be forgiven" (HCSB).

Today and every day, make sure that you're quick to forgive others for their shortcomings. And when other people misbehave (as they most certainly will from time to time), don't pay too much attention. Just forgive those people as quickly as you can, and try to move on . . . as quickly as you can.

A keen sense of humor helps us to overlook the unbecoming, understand the unconventional, tolerate the unpleasant, overcome the unexpected, and outlast the unbearable.

Billy Graham

A LESSON FOR THE HEART AND SOUL

If you can't find it in your heart to forgive those who have hurt you, you're hurting yourself more than you're hurting anyone else.

THE NEED FOR
SELF-DISCIPLINE

Do you not know that those who run in a race all run,
but one receives the prize? Run in such a way that you may obtain it.
And everyone who competes for the prize is temperate in all things.
Now they do it to obtain a perishable crown,
but we for an imperishable crown.
1 Corinthians 9:24–25 NKJV

God is clear: we must exercise self-discipline in all matters. Self-discipline is not simply a proven way to get ahead, it's also an integral part of God's plan for our lives. If we genuinely seek to be faithful stewards of our time, our talents, and our resources, we must adopt a disciplined approach to life. Otherwise, our talents are wasted and our resources are squandered.

Our greatest rewards result from hard work and perseverance. May we, as disciplined believers, be willing to work for the rewards we so earnestly desire.

God is the perfect Parent to strong-willed children. We need to thank Him for His constant training. And learn from it.

Charles Stanley

BUILDING A BETTER YOU

If you choose to lead a disciplined lifestyle, your steps will be protected. If you choose to lead an undisciplined lifestyle, your steps will be misdirected.

FAITH VERSUS FEAR

Fear not, for I am with you;
Be not dismayed, for I am your God. I will strengthen you.
Isaiah 41:10 NKJV

A terrible storm rose quickly on the Sea of Galilee, and the disciples were afraid. Although they had witnessed many miracles, the disciples feared for their lives, so they turned to Jesus, and He calmed the waters and the wind.

The next time you find yourself facing a fear-provoking situation, remember that the One who calmed the wind and the waves is also your personal Savior. Then ask yourself which is stronger: your faith or your fear. The answer should be obvious. So, when the storm clouds form overhead and you find yourself being tossed on the stormy seas of life, remember that wherever you are, God is there, too. And, because He cares for you, you are protected.

The Lord Jesus by His Holy Spirit is with me, and the knowledge of His presence dispels the darkness and allays any fears.

Bill Bright

When we meditate on God and remember the promises He has given us in His Word, our faith grows, and our fears dissolve.

Charles Stanley

A LESSON FOR THE HEART AND SOUL

Everybody faces obstacles. Don't overestimate the size of yours.

THE CORNERSTONE

*Let us fix our eyes on Jesus, the author and perfecter of our faith,
who for the joy set before him endured the cross, scorning its shame,
and sat down at the right hand of the throne of God.*

Hebrews 12:2 NIV

Is Christ the focus of your life? Are you fired with enthusiasm for Him? Are you an energized Christian who allows God's Son to reign over every aspect of your day? Make no mistake; that's exactly what God intends for you to do.

God has given you the gift of eternal life through His Son. In response to God's priceless gift, you are instructed to focus your thoughts, your prayers, and your energies upon God and His only begotten Son. To do so, you must resist the subtle yet powerful temptation to become a "spiritual dabbler." A person who dabbles in the Christian faith is unwilling to place God above all other things. Resist that temptation; make God the cornerstone and the touchstone of your life. When you do, He will give you all the strength and wisdom you need to live victoriously for Him.

Give me the person who says, "This one thing I do, and not these fifty things I dabble in."

D. L. Moody

BUILDING A BETTER YOU

Whether you are talking to someone or working at your job, focus your attention on the task at hand. There is an important difference between "investing yourself" and "going through the motions."

LIFE ETERNAL

In a little while the world will not see me anymore,
but you will see me. Because I live, you will live, too.
John 14:19 NCV

How marvelous it is that God became a man and walked among us. Had He not chosen to do so, we might feel removed from a distant Creator. But ours is not a distant God. Ours is a God who understands—far better than we ever could—the essence of what it means to be human.

God understands our hopes, our fears, and our temptations. He understands what it means to be angry and what it costs to forgive. He knows the heart, the conscience, and the soul of every person who has ever lived, including you. And God has a plan of salvation that is intended for you. Accept it. Accept God's gift through the person of His Son Christ Jesus, and then rest assured: God walked among us so that you might have eternal life. Amazing though it may seem, He did it for you.

Let us see the victorious Jesus: the conqueror of the tomb, the one who defied death. And let us be reminded that we, too, will be granted the same victory!

Max Lucado

A LESSON FOR THE HEART AND SOUL

God offers you a priceless gift: the gift of eternal life. If you have not already done so, accept God's gift today—tomorrow may be too late.

HIS TRANSFORMING POWER

Your old life is dead. Your new life, which is your real life—even though invisible to spectators—is with Christ in God. He is your life.
Colossians 3:3 MSG

God's hand has the power to transform your day and your life. Your task is to accept Christ's grace with a humble, thankful heart as you receive the "new life" that can be yours through Him.

Righteous believers who fashion their days around Jesus see the world differently; they act differently, and they feel differently about themselves and their neighbors. Hopefully, you, too, will be such a believer.

Do you desire to improve some aspect of your life? If so, don't expect changing circumstances to miraculously transform you into the person you want to become. Transformation starts with God, and it starts in the quiet corners of a willing human heart—like yours.

There is not a single thing that Jesus cannot change, control, and conquer because He is the living Lord.

Franklin Graham

BUILDING A BETTER YOU

Jesus made radical sacrifices for you, and now He's asking you to make radical changes for Him. Are you willing to be a radical Christian? If so, you will be blessed for your willingness to serve God and to walk faithfully and closely in the footsteps of His only begotten Son.

HONORING GOD

Honor the Lord with your possessions, and with the firstfruits of all your increase; so your barns will be filled with plenty.
Proverbs 3:9–10 NKJV

Whom will you choose to honor today? If you honor God and place Him at the center of your life, every day is a cause for celebration. But if you fail to honor your Heavenly Father, you're asking for trouble, and lots of it.

At times, your life is probably hectic, demanding, and complicated. When the demands of life leave you rushing from place to place with scarcely a moment to spare, you may fail to pause and thank your Creator for the blessings He has bestowed upon you. But that's a big mistake. So honor God for who He is and for what He has done for you. And don't just honor Him on Sunday morning. Praise Him all day long, every day, for as long as you live . . . and then for all eternity.

Praise opens the window of our hearts, preparing us to walk more closely with God. Prayer raises the window of our spirit, enabling us to listen more clearly to the Father.

Max Lucado

God shows unbridled delight when He sees people acting in ways that honor Him.

Bill Hybels

A LESSON FOR THE HEART AND SOUL

God has given you everything. You must honor Him with your words, your actions, and your prayers.

COMMISSIONED TO WITNESS

Therefore go and make disciples of all nations, baptizing them in the name of the Father and of the Son and of the Holy Spirit, and teaching them to obey everything I have commanded you. And surely I am with you always, to the very end of the age.

Matthew 28:19–20 NIV

After His resurrection, Jesus Christ addressed His disciples. As recorded in the 28th chapter of Matthew, Christ instructed His followers to share His message with the world. This "Great Commission" applies to Christians of every generation, including our own.

As believers, we are called to share the Good News of Jesus with our families, with our neighbors, and with the world. Christ commanded His disciples to become fishers of men. We must do likewise, and we must do so today. Tomorrow may indeed be too late.

Witnessing is not something that we do for the Lord; it is something that He does through us if we are filled with the Holy Spirit.

Warren Wiersbe

We must, without apology, without fear, without ceasing, preach and practice our beliefs, carrying them out to the point of suffering.

R. G. Lee

A LESSON FOR THE HEART AND SOUL

The best day to respond to Christ's Great Commission is this day.

THINGS I NEED TO CHANGE THIS YEAR

☐

☐

☐

☐

☐

☐

☐

☐

THINGS I NEED TO CHANGE THIS YEAR

☐ _____
_____
_____

☐ _____
_____
_____

☐ _____
_____
_____

☐ _____
_____
_____

☐ _____
_____
_____

☐ _____
_____
_____

☐ _____
_____
_____

☐ _____
_____

THINGS I NEED TO CHANGE THIS YEAR

- [ ] _____
  _____
  _____

- [ ] _____
  _____
  _____

- [ ] _____
  _____
  _____

- [ ] _____
  _____
  _____

- [ ] _____
  _____
  _____

- [ ] _____
  _____
  _____

- [ ] _____
  _____
  _____

- [ ] _____
  _____

THINGS I NEED TO CHANGE THIS YEAR

- [ ] _____
  _____
  _____

- [ ] _____
  _____
  _____

- [ ] _____
  _____
  _____

- [ ] _____
  _____
  _____

- [ ] _____
  _____
  _____

- [ ] _____
  _____
  _____

- [ ] _____
  _____
  _____

- [ ] _____
  _____